Improving Human Rights

IMPROVING HUMAN RIGHTS

Michael Haas

PRAEGER

Westport, Connecticut
London

Library of Congress Cataloging-in-Publication Data

Haas, Michael.
    Improving human rights / Michael Haas.
      p. cm.
    Includes bibliographical references and index.
    ISBN 0–275–94352–6 (alk. paper)
    1. Human rights. I. Title.
  K3240.4.H33 1994
  341.4'81—dc20   94–16457

British Library Cataloguing in Publication Data is available.

Library of Congress Catalog Card Number: 94–16457
ISBN: 0–275–94352–6

First published in 1994

Praeger Publishers, 88 Post Road West, Westport, CT 06881
An imprint of Greenwood Publishing Group, Inc.

Printed in the United States of America

The paper used in this book complies with the
Permanent Paper Standard issued by the National
Information Standards Organization (Z39.48–1984).

10 9 8 7 6 5 4 3 2 1

CONTENTS

PREFACE

Human rights underpin the very concept of democracy yet often seem an abstraction until their violation comes close to home. When I grew up in Hollywood in the early 1950s, the impact of the blacklisting of motion picture artists was my first experience of how ambitious, unscrupulous leaders sought to sacrifice productive careers of filmmakers on the altar of political demagoguery. In the early 1960s, I saw a similar spectacle as courageous civil rights leaders, seeking to extend civil rights to black citizens, were abused by police. In the late 1960s, hysteria over protests against U.S. participation in the civil war in Vietnam increased to the point where a colleague of my department was unjustly fired for his political views and, then, after a year of campus unrest, was rehired. In the 1970s, as I sought to bring federal civil rights officials to Hawai'i to investigate complaints that I filed on behalf of ethnic minorities and women, I found my telephone wiretapped.

Internationally, possessions of my hotel room were searched without a warrant, and I was interrogated on a police fishing expedition for "consorting with Sinhalese" (going on a tour of batik art, courtesy of the Principal Information Officer of the Colombo Plan) under emergency rule in Sri Lanka in 1971. In Singapore during May 1987, as I began a summer on a Fulbright research grant, the government presented a case against a dozen Christian social workers, accusing them of being Marxists because they had been helping Filipina maids to counteract mistreatment by their employers. The twelve were held without formal charges on the basis of an anachronistic Internal Security Act designed to prevent treasonous conduct, yet they were accused only of forming organizations to exercise the right of free public expression. As the summer unfolded, the Singapore government paraded a series of phony rationalizations to justify continued detention and a denial of the writ of *habeas corpus*. Subjected to mental and physical torture, they were forced by the Singapore government, lest they be detained for the rest of their lives, to admit to being part of a Marxist conspiracy to overthrow the government, and they later disavowed their "confessions." At a public forum, I even heard the U.S. ambassador to Singapore pooh-pooh the significance of these violations of basic human rights.

How could it be that Singapore, one of the most affluent countries in the world, would be so threatened by a handful of clearly mousy yet pious Christians? The question remains unanswered today. Upon obtaining a copy of Charles Humana's *World Human Rights Guide* (1987) at a bookstore in Singapore, I vowed during midsummer 1987 to pursue the question, using a research design that would compare a large set of countries.

Accordingly, I applied for a grant from the U.S. Institute of Peace in 1990 to assemble a comparative body of data on human rights performance, and then to perform multivariate analyses in order to explain why some countries observe human rights better than others and what conditions are conducive to improvements in human rights. This book reports the results.

I want to take this opportunity to thank Janice Lu and Arvin Wu, two students who worked on the project. In addition, Jo Ann Takemoto and Rhoda Miller of the Spark M. Matsunaga Institute for Peace, University of Hawai'i, deserve warm thanks for administering my grant. I also want to acknowledge assistance from Ted Gurr and Mike Stohl. For the shortcomings of this volume I am, of course, solely responsible.

Improving Human Rights

Chapter 1

TYPOLOGIES

Imagine a person with fascinating ideas who is engaged in a lecture tour in a particular country. This thinker articulates the idea that legitimate authority accrues alone to those who show acts of mercy, such as providing comfort and relief to those who are less fortunate. Suppose the authorities in the country become frightened that this person, who has a small following of devoted adherents, might cause the populace to overthrow the regime. Accordingly, the police arrest the person, though without stating any specific charge. Further, let us assume that this individual is tortured during an interrogation because the authorities seek self-incriminating testimony regarding some sort of crime. The accused person, whom the civil authority later admits has committed no crime, is nevertheless condemned to death, while a person who has shown criminal defiance of the same civil authority is set free.

If these events occurred today, we would lament the fate of the thinker, who would be deemed a "prisoner of conscience," paying the ultimate price for sticking to firmly held beliefs. How, we would ask, could so many sordid violations of human rights occur?

THE RISE OF THE CONCEPT OF HUMAN RIGHTS

The perspicacious reader will note a certain similarity between the aforementioned hypothetical events and the fate of a certain Nazarene within a Roman colony some two thousand years ago. Indeed, the belief that Jesus suffered from a violation in fundamental civil rights is a central element in the historical understanding of Christian political theory (Durr 1981). That Jesus had compassion for the poor and chided the rich for selfishness is yet another strand in a Christianity that argues for the establishment of a just social order. The view that no person, whether famous or humble, should be subjected to arbitrary mistreatment by persons in authority is central to those who understand Christian doctrine as one of the first attempts in human history to establish the principle that individuals have civil, cultural, economic, political, and social rights that no state has authority to tear asunder.

Despite an auspicious beginning as a radical effort to confront and reject "might makes right" political doctrines, Christian beliefs were later invoked to legitimate violations of human rights. One example, the Spanish Inquisition, reminds us that contemporary individual rights grew in part as an effort to find a philosophical justification for tolerating religious differences.

While the origin of thinking about human rights may be traced to Sophocles and Cicero (Szabo 1982), Thomas Aquinas and Jean Gerson were the first to argue that human law is legitimate to the extent that it conforms to natural law, which in turn is derived from divine law through the exercise of human reason (Bigongiari 1953; Tuck 1979). Gerson wrote in the twelfth century before the signing of the Magna Carta, but few rulers were forced to limit their power in the way King John was confronted at Runnymede in 1215. Aquinas wrote soon after King John's pen made history, but the theory of rights was developed further in the seventeenth century, particularly by Hugo Grotius (1625), to mean that laws of governments could neither transgress natural law nor violate natural rights. In contrast with Thomas Hobbes's (1651) concept of the social contract under which humans surrendered their "state of nature" rights to governmental authority, John Locke (1688) believed that government was set up to protect natural rights. Locke's logic in turn inspired Thomas Jefferson to formulate reasons for thirteen of the British colonies in North America to declare themselves independent (Blitz 1982; Howard and Donnelly 1986b:3). Jefferson espoused a theory of inalienable rights endowed by God.

The English Bill of Rights of 1689, the Declaration of Independence of 1776, the Bill of Rights adopted shortly after the U.S. Constitution of 1787, and the Declaration of the Rights of Man of 1789 were proclaimed because of the increasing view that governments should allow individuals to determine their own destinies (Claude 1976). Constitutions sought to safeguard fundamental rights by stipulating limitations on the powers of government; to ensure that government did not exceed its powers, judicial organs were expected to develop uniform procedures. As these *civil rights* were codified into law, citizens were accorded certain basic rights in civil society; that is, individuals were free to operate outside the political realm. In the nineteenth century, as the concept of democracy gained popularity, *political rights* joined these civil rights as fundamental principles of how citizens choose to be governed. In the twentieth century, *economic and social rights*, which amount to claims by the people on government, have gained increasing formal expression throughout the world.

Two egregious practices established the momentum for the modern concern with human rights. The suppression of slavery was the first practice to evoke an international campaign, although the U.S. government did not follow the lead of Britain until the Civil War (Fairbanks 1982). The second practice was genocide. Although pogroms against the Jews in Imperial Russia and the massacre of Armenians by the Turkish state shocked world public opinion at the time, the wholesale incarceration and slaughter of millions of minorities by Nazi Germany meant that the international community could no longer continue as before to ignore what states do inside their borders.

Several international agreements, as advocated by Eleanor Roosevelt and others, have sought to affirm human rights principles. The Universal Declaration of Human Rights of 1948 was placed on a treaty basis in 1966 by the International Covenant on Civil and Political Rights (Appendix A) and the International Covenant on Economic, Social, and Cultural Rights (Appendix B). The International Convention on the Prevention and Punishment of the Crime of Genocide was also adopted in 1948. In 1950, a Convention on Freedom of Association and Protection of the Right to Organize was adopted. Involuntary servitude was the subject of the Abolition of Slavery Convention of 1957 and the Abolition of Forced Labor Convention of 1959. In 1965, the International Convention on the Elimination of All Forms of Racial Discrimination was signed. In 1974, Third World countries met at the United Nations (U.N.) in New York to draw up the parameters of the New International Economic Order; one document adopted at the time was the Charter of Economic Rights and Duties of States. The Final Act of the Conference on Security and Cooperation in Europe of 1975, known as the Helsinki Accords, sought to reaffirm and to promote human rights principles. The International Convention Against Torture and Other Cruel, Inhuman or Degrading Treatment or Punishment was adopted in 1984, and the International Convention on the Rights of the Child was signed in 1989. Today, the right to development and the right to live in a safe environment are gaining increased acceptance as additional human rights.

The concept of natural rights was attacked by both liberal Jeremy Bentham (1780) and conservative Edmund Burke (1789/1790) in the early nineteenth century (see Waldron 1987). Without social equality, Karl Marx (1844) believed that the French Declaration of the Rights of Man was a sham. The concept of human rights was unfashionable in Germany long before Adolf Hitler rose to power (Cranston 1983). The twentieth century has unfortunately provided the technological means for widespread suppression of liberties, and the covenants of 1966 have been ratified by only half of the members of the United Nations. Although one of the major ideological struggles of the twentieth century has been between democratic and undemocratic countries, support for authoritarian dictatorships by internally democratic countries has given rise to such phenomena as subfascism, under which human rights are violated by illegitimate dictatorial regimes that are kept in power by means of arms provided by democratic governments (Chomsky and Herman 1979; Duvall and Stohl 1988:247). Meanwhile, capitalist countries have argued that civil and political rights are basic, whereas socialist countries have stressed economic and social rights (Holleman 1987). Atheists Karl Marx and Friedrich Engels (1848) wanted to bring about a society that would accord with the well-known Christian principle "From each according to his ability, to each according to his need," whereas Christian authorities have been tolerant of the excesses of capitalism.

Initially, the United States refused to ratify the United Nations Declaration of Human Rights because southern senators could not accept any agreement that condemned the policy of racial segregation (Tolley 1987:3-4). Later, when the civil rights revolution resulted in legislation to outlaw discrimination and segregation, Congress mandated human rights as a screening criterion in provisions of the International Development and Food Assistance Act of 1975 and the International Security Assistance and Arms Export Control Act of 1976.

The presidency of Jimmy Carter is often claimed to be a turning point in regard to worldwide attention to human rights attainments (see Cohen 1979; Kirkpatrick 1982; Nanda 1981). Annual U.S. State Department reports on human rights around the world began, congressional hearings were held, and executive officials read speeches condemning human rights abuses in specific countries. Nevertheless, Carter was far less reluctant than Congress to use human rights violations as grounds for delaying or prohibiting foreign aid until countries in the Third World made human rights improvements (Forsythe 1991:133). Carter, for example, sent some aid to the Khmer Rouge government of Cambodia, but Congress soon prohibited such aid (Haas 1991:80). The European Community, in due course, joined the United States in applying human rights as a criterion for denying development aid to such countries as Burma, Ethiopia, Indonesia, Perú, Sudan, and Zaïre.

For Ronald Reagan's U.N. ambassador Jeane Kirkpatrick (1981), Carter's conception of human rights was so broad that few countries could pass muster; she urged that more emphasis be placed on individual rights than on cultural, economic, and social rights, since otherwise Communist countries could rationalize restrictions on human freedom as necessary to provide better socioeconomic conditions. Soon, Third World countries began to complain that Western countries were narrow-minded in regard to human rights, focusing on civil and political rights much more than cultural, economic, and social rights. Poorer countries even pointed to the fact that Reagan was eager to supply "freedom fighters" with the wherewithal to burn the crops of humble peasants in Nicaragua, and George Bush authorized action in his first term in office to install a government in Panamá in 1989 through military action that resulted in the loss of some four thousand lives.

By the time Bill Clinton took office as president in 1993, U.S. policy toward human rights was clouded by difficult choices in Bosnia, Cambodia, China, and elsewhere. Although the Cold War had ended, a new focus for foreign policy had not yet emerged, and the human rights situation around the world remained deplorable.

Writing in the mid-1980s, Charles Humana (1987:xix) noted that only one in five persons in the world was living in a country "protected by laws and constitutions." The U.N.'s World Conference on Human Rights, held at Vienna in midsummer 1993, recommended the establishment of a U.N. High Commissioner on Human Rights, and the U.N. Secretary-General soon began the search for a person to assume that post. Respect for human rights is increasingly the litmus test of civilized nations and thereby an important criterion to identify developing countries worthy of foreign economic assistance from developed countries.

Thus, human rights increasingly form the centerpiece of a new focus on international morality. But awareness of the extent of human rights violations is often limited to such major international events as the massacre of protesters in Beijing during 1989 who were rallying under the symbol of the Statue of Liberty. The flow of refugees from undemocratic countries, which often impose serious violations of human rights, is an even more painful reminder to developed countries that the cost of insisting that all governments should abide by basic principles of human rights is much less than the international burden of caring for refugees.

Accordingly, the world community needs to know how to promote an ounce of human rights efforts today so that it will not have to effect a pound of cure tomorrow. Where should efforts be undertaken first? Will an emphasis on stopping the practice of caning as a form of judicial punishment lead to improvements in other human rights? Or is the practice of corporal punishment a culturally idiosyncratic phenomenon, isolated from other types of human rights? Information is lacking on how to answer these questions. Without knowledge of this sort, efforts to improve human rights are likely to be unsystematic, triggered by press disclosures of the moment rather than part of a coherent strategy to advance human dignity.

TYPES OF HUMAN RIGHTS

Variance in worldwide human rights observance, thus, raises at least one fundamental empirical question: Is the concept of human rights unidimensional, or is the concept so broad that there are identifiable subsets of human rights? According to the Vienna conference of 1993, "All human rights are universal, indivisible, and interrelated." Alternatively, the existence of several international agreements on human rights suggests that there are separate categories of human rights.

Thomas Marshall (1964) presented one of the earliest conceptual frameworks for human rights, positing three categories. According to his formulation, *civil rights* involve freedom of speech and the right to security and justice; these appear in the Bill of Rights of the Constitution of the United States. *Political rights* are guarantees of the right to participate in the political process, notably by voting or running for office. *Economic and social rights* cover the guarantees of the welfare state, including the right to food, clothing, shelter, and medical care.

According to Cyrus Vance and Edmund Muskie, Carter's two Secretaries of State, there are three important categories of human rights, namely, the "right to be free of violations of the human person'' (including "torture, arbitrary arrest or imprisonment, summary execution, and denial of due process''), the "rights of fulfillment of economic needs'' ("food, shelter, education, and health care''), and "civil and political rights'' ("freedom of thought, expression, assembly, travel, and participation in politics'') (Muskie 1980:8; Vance 1977[1979]:310). Muskie and Vance, thus, provide a categorization of *judicial rights, socioeconomic rights*, and *civil-political rights*.

For Henry Shue (1980), the fundamental rights are for *liberty, security*, and *subsistence*. By "security," Shue refers to the obligation of the state to provide public order, that is, protection from crime. Strangely, few thinkers have stressed the need for a society without murder, rape, robbery, and other criminal acts as a basic human right.

John Boli-Bennett (1981) has four basic categories. These are *civil rights, judicial rights, political rights*, and *social/economic rights*.

The Norwegian yearbook on human rights has five sections (see Nowak and Swinehart 1989). The classification focuses on *political rights* (right to participate), *civil liberties* (life, liberty, integrity of the person), *administration of justice and freedom of movement, socioeconomic rights*, and what might be called *equal opportunity rights* (equality, nondiscrimination, rights of peoples and minorities).

Jack Donnelly and Rhoda Howard (1988) identify *survival rights* (the right to life, food, and health), *membership rights* (family rights, nondiscrimination, and legal equality), *protection rights* (*habeas corpus* and an independent judiciary), *empowerment rights* (right to an education, free press, freedom of association, and free elections), and *other rights* (mostly rights established under international law). Donnelly and Howard, unlike the other typologists, call for empirical research to put their categories to the test (248).

The Political Freedom Index of the United Nations Development Program (UNDP) is based on five categories, which in turn are based on several subcategories (UNDP 1992:31). By *equality of opportunity*, UNDP refers to absence of harassment or violence against particular groups, equal pay for equal work, equal employment opportunity, no exclusion of groups from political participation, and a legal system that enforces equality for all regardless of color, ethnicity, gender, race, or religion. Indicators of *freedom of expression* are freedom from mail inspection, media censorship and government control, wiretapping, and any other restrictions on free speech. *Personal security* rights refer to an absence of arbitrary arrest and detention, cruel treatment including torture, disappearances, and summary executions. Rights of *political participation* include elections at regular intervals, freedom of association, freedom of opposition parties, free and fair elections, and the opportunity for the public to participate in decision making at the local and national levels. Finally, UNDP stresses the *rule of law* as a fifth basic right; examples are speedy public trials with ample time to prepare a defense, legal counsel freely chosen by a defendant, independent judiciary, right to have a sentence appealed, and prosecution of state officials who abuse power or violate human rights.

Whereas the above proposed typologies consist of what we would call "mental factor analyses" that differ in the number of *a priori* factors derived, a quantitative factor analysis of actual human rights attainments might derive only one or two factors. Indeed, human rights may be interrelated empirically in at least five ways:

Unidimensionality. If a good record on civil and political rights predicts to a good record on due process rights and socioeconomic rights, then human rights might constitute a unidimensional phenomenon. According to Patricia Derian (1979:270), the first Assistant Secretary of State for Human Rights, regimes that deny civil and political rights are "almost certain" to deny their people basic human needs, so "Progress in insuring political rights cannot be divorced from progress in satisfying basic human needs." Improvement on any one right may set in place the momentum for better observance of other human rights (Hewitt 1977; Hoffmann 1983; Romulo 1993).

Multidimensionality. If progress on civil-political rights has no effect on either due process rights or on socioeconomic rights, the Vance/Muskie trichotomy may have empirical validity. We would know that efforts to improve human rights must focus on three or more separate problem areas.

Hierarchy. Some rights may unlock others; the attainment of some rights might have to wait until other, more basic rights are granted. The Supreme Court of the United States has often argued that voting rights are prior to all other rights. By focusing on freedom from torture and prisoners of conscience, Amnesty International and various scholars (Forsythe and Wiseberg 1979) appear to claim that they stress core rather than peripheral rights. In 1989, after the world community witnessed on television a massacre of dissidents near Tiananmen Square, the government in Beijing began to defend itself with the argument that the right of survival—the feeding of more than one billion persons—is more important than and prior to political rights (Vatikiotis and Delfs 1993). Although China's argument could be traced to the Jacobin desire to advance the welfare of the people by any means necessary (see Spalding 1988:175; Vincent 1986:107), the country's dissidents appeared to agree with the U.S. position that more political rights would open the door for opportunities to achieve greater prosperity (Awanohara, Vatikiotis, and Islam 1993; see Lizhi 1990).

Inverse relationship. Alternatively, an improvement in some rights might entail a decline in others. According to Samuel Huntington (1968), the attempt to increase democracy often conflicts with the goal of economic development, as the masses may demand a more equitable distribution of the benefits of increased prosperity, thereby disrupting the imperatives of capital accumulation by shrewd entrepreneurs. Political instability fomented by frustrated egalitarians, he claims, can slow economic progress.

Curvilinearity. A final possibility is that human rights improve under certain conditions up to an asymptote, then fluctuate randomly while at intermediate levels until a second threshold is reached, whereupon improvements occur in a linear manner again. In one study, for example, democracy was found to vary with socioeconomic development up to a threshold, but thereafter the two variables were unrelated (Neubauer 1967).

One practical implication of these five alternative dimensional possibilities is the realization that we cannot develop meaningful strategies for improving human rights in general until we know how specific human rights interrelate empirically. A second implication is that instead of holding all countries to the same high standards, we might better "aim ameliorative efforts at specific types of noncompliance, and recognize clusters which may be too intractable to justify attention at this time . . . enabl[ing] the efficient application of limited resources" (Banks 1985:158). It is therefore important to test dimensionality assumptions so that potentially more effective strategies for advancing human rights can be devised.

DATA ON HUMAN RIGHTS

Some scholars have sought to collect data on human rights. In many cases, they have measured specific variables. On several occasions, researchers have collapsed a set of variables into an index of human rights. Multivariable indices, however, may combine apples and oranges. Only a few studies have sought to determine whether specific variables are so highly interrelated statistically that a composite index is warranted.

Indicators and Indices

Qualitative efforts to compare countries on levels of human rights observance began nearly three decades ago (see Cain, Claude, and Jabine 1992). From 1958, the U.S. Social Security Administration has published regular qualitative assessments on the scope of social welfare programs around the world. Amnesty International has published annual reports from the 1960s but makes no effort to compare ratings across countries (Amnesty International 1987:2). A third source is the U.S. Department of State's annual *Country Reports on Human Rights Practices*, which attempt to provide comparability in judgments across more than 150 countries, excluding the United States. Initially, the *Country Reports* were divided into three categories, consistent with the Vance/Muskie threefold classification, but most information on economic and social rights was dropped from the reports during the Reagan era (see Innes 1992). In 1985, Norway commissioned private scholars to compile annual reports on the human rights record of countries around the world, an effort now joined by experts in several smaller Northern European countries (see Howard 1990).

Although statistical publications by the United Nations and World Bank have for decades contained various measures of economic and social attainments of countries around the world, the earliest systematic quantitative cross-national comparisons of civil and political human rights referred to a limited set of variables. Raymond Nixon (1960; 1965) rated 85 countries on press freedom, and Ralph Lowenstein (1967) repeated his effort. Arthur Banks and Robert Textor's *A Cross-Polity Survey* (1963) rated 115 countries on such 4-point scales as constitutionalism, freedom of the opposition, regime representatives, and press freedom. Banks (1971; 1979) later scaled countries over time on such variables as legislative competitiveness. The first edition of the *World Handbook of Political and Social Indicators* (Russett et al. 1964) explicitly sought to measure a wide variety of rights proclaimed in the Universal Declaration of Human Rights (v).

Efforts to measure "democracy" became a growth industry after 1955. Russell Fitzgibbon (1956) used a dozen or so judges to assess the extent of democracy for twenty Latin American countries for 1945, 1950, and 1955. His fifteen measures of "democracy," however, included not only cultural beliefs, educational levels, and standard of living, but also such familiar political characteristics as freedom of the political opposition and civilian control of the military. When the exercise was repeated for 1960 with forty judges, three measures were correlated with the other twelve, and all correlations came out high (Fitzgibbon and Johnson 1961). Equally lacking in precision, Seymour Martin Lipset's (1959) pioneering study, which found socioeconomic development highly correlated with democracy, gave a coding of 1 to a country that he considered "democratic" (a polity where there is an effective, legitimate political opposition) and a 0 to all other countries.

Next, Phillips Cutright (1963; Cutright and Wiley 1969) constructed a four-point index of democracy (initially called "political development" but later renamed "political representation") from the extent of legislative party competition and the degree to which chief executives are selected through contested elections; he also constructed an educational development index, of which two variables (percentage in higher education and literacy rate) are relevant to the International Covenant on Economic, Social, and Cultural Rights. In an effort to retest Cutright's hypotheses, Deane Neubauer (1967) constructed an index of democratic development from five variables (percentage of adults eligible to vote, extent to which legislative seats are proportionate to voter support, press ownership diversity, alternation of political parties in office, and average size of victorious political parties). Irma Adelman and Cynthia Taft Morris (1967) relied primarily on Banks and Textor (1963) in constructing an index of strength of democratic institutions from presence of competing parties, party system stability, and voter turnout; they also coded countries on such conceptual variables as press freedom, aggregation of interests by political parties, labor union strength, strength of nontraditional elites, civilian control of the military, and administrative efficiency. Arthur Smith (1969) pooled voter turnout percentages with nineteen scales from Banks and Textor (1963) to form an index of democracy. William Flanigan and Edwin Fogelman (1971) developed a democracy scale based on four considerations: popular election of the legislature, popular election of the chief executive, political competition, and lack of political suppression. In an effort to replicate Neubauer (1967), Robert Jackman (1975) constructed yet another index of democratic development from electoral competitiveness, election regularity, press freedom, and voter turnout. Phyllis

Frakt's (1977) index of democracy, constructed from Banks and Textor (1963), consisted of electoral competitiveness, interest articulation by associational groups, press freedom, and regime representativeness. Reviewing a dozen or so such measures, Kenneth Bollen (1980) developed an index of democracy based on four components: fairness of elections (freedom from bribery or coercion), freedom of the opposition, freedom of speech during an election, and freedom of the press. His sources were Banks and Textor (1963), Nixon (1960; 1965), and Charles Lewis Taylor and Michael Hudson (1972). Nancy Spalding's (1988) index of democratic institutions combined two variables—the number of political parties and government decentralization. Strangely, few of these writers distinguished between procedural democracy (observance of political rights) and substantive democracy (representativeness, or control of elites by nonelites), and a few forced the two elements into a single measure. Bollen and Burke Grandjean (1981), for example, factor analyzed both types of measures, found no chi-square difference between factors based on the two sets of variables, and concluded that the analytical difference was of no empirical consequence. Aware of the tendency to conflate concepts in many measures of democracy, Zehra Arat (1991) constructed a procedural index that combined four elements: participation (selection of a government head and an autonomous legislature by election), inclusiveness (percentage of population eligible to vote), competitiveness (freedom of opposition), and noncoerciveness (a ratio between number of domestic disturbances and extent of governmental sanctions to crack down on civil unrest). Arat found that her measure had high correlations with most alternative measures; the exception was Neubauer's scale.

Cutright (1965; 1967a; 1967b) also constructed two measures of social security attainments from U.S. Social Security Administration data on countries around the world—Social Insurance Program Experience (SIPE) and Social Insurance Program Completion (SIPC). SIPE summed data for the years since a country adopted five types of social security programs (family allowance plans, old-age and survivor pensions, sickness and/or maternity programs, unemployment insurance, and work-injury programs). Cutright's SIPC index counted the number of new welfare programs adopted from the 1920s to the 1960s.

Ted Gurr (1966), meanwhile, collected data on economic, political, and social discrimination against ethnic groups, and he identified separatist groups in a compendium involving a large sample of countries for 1960. His data were reprinted and updated for 1975 in a compendium of cross-national statistics (Gurr and Gurr 1983) and were updated more recently for the 1980s (Harff and Gurr 1988; Gurr 1993).

Ivo and Rosalind Feierabend (1971) constructed two composite measures. Their index of political coerciveness was based on the lack of protection of civil rights, ineffectiveness of the political opposition, and the lack of independent political institutions and procedures to check the chief executive. Their index of socioeconomic characteristics (called a frustration index) was based on eight measures: per capita figures for caloric intake, gross national product (GNP), newspapers, physicians, radios, and telephones per capita as well as percentages of the population who are literate and living in cities. In a second study, the authors constructed an index of the extent to which government policies toward minorities were discriminatory (Feierabend, Feierabend, and Nesvold 1969).

Some scholars prepared rankings based on single conceptual variables. Dankwart Rustow (1967) prepared a table listing the first year of continuous free elections for 31 countries around the world from 1788. Robert Dahl (1971) placed 114 countries onto a 31-point scale, measuring opportunity to oppose the government; his data were based on frequency of holding elections and percentages of citizens eligible to vote in 1969. R. J. Rummel provided a 3-point scale for freedom of group opposition across 82 countries in his *The Dimensions of Nations* (1972:275). The second edition of the *World Handbook of Political and Social Indicators* (Taylor and Hudson 1972:51-53) provided scales for electoral irregularity and irregular executive transfers of power. Christopher Hewitt (1977) measured democracy by counting the number of years in which countries have had elective chief executives, secret ballots, and universal suffrage, relying for the data on 3 sources (Seymour and Frary 1918; Mackie and Rose 1974; Rokkan and Meyriat 1969).

Raymond Gastil of Freedom House first issued a "Comparative Survey of Freedom" for 1972 (Gastil 1973). He considered two scales—political rights and civil liberties—to be analytically distinct from human rights (Gastil 1988: 4, 7). With ratings claimed to be based on seventeen types of civil rights and nineteen political rights, Gastil's survey classified more than one hundred countries along seven-point scales for both concepts, and then issued a composite rating of each country's "status of freedom." Subsequently, Gastil published his comparative ratings on an annual basis, and he added an index of economic freedom that placed market economies at the top and closed economies at the bottom (Gastil 1982:78–83; 1987/1988:74–75) and a "political terror scale" based on the extent of incarcerations for political opinions, use of brutality and torture, disappearances after police arrest, and political executions (Gastil 1980: 38–39).

By the mid-1970s Ernest Duff and John McCamant (1976) and Kenneth Johnson (1976; 1982) rated Latin American governments on such violations of human rights as harassment of political opposition, media censorship, and restrictions on political parties. Lars Schoultz (1981a; 1981b) derived a four-point scale on human rights in Latin America from ratings by thirty-eight regional experts. David Cingranelli and Thomas Pasquarello coded African (Pasquarello 1988) and Latin American countries (Cingranelli and Pasquarello 1985) for violations of personal integrity and civil-political liberties, using annual State Department compilations for the early 1980s. John Boli-Bennett (1981) coded provisions of constitutions in force from 1870 to 1970, and then pooled twenty measures of civil rights, seven judicial rights, four political rights, and eleven socioeconomic rights into a "citizen rights index."

Michael Stohl, David Carleton, and Steven Johnson (1984) content-analyzed

Amnesty International and State Department reports to derive a five-point "political terror scale" for twenty-three countries for 1986 and 1981. Later, Carleton and Stohl (1985) expanded their database to fifty-seven countries from 1978 to 1983, and Rick Travis (1989) extended the Carleton-Stohl compilation to 1984. Neil Mitchell and James McCormick (1988) used Amnesty International reports for 1984 to derive two five-point scales—for arbitrary imprisonment and systematic use of killings and torture of prisoners. From the mid-1980s, Ruth Leger Sivard's *World Military and Social Expenditures* (1986–) has provided a three-point scale on official violence against citizens and a four-point scale on limitations on the right to vote, though mostly for Third World countries.

The third edition of the *World Handbook of Political and Social Indicators* (Taylor and Jodice 1983: Volume 2) provided two new types of measures—political protest and state coercion. The former counted assassinations, demonstrations, protests, riots, and deaths from political violence. The latter compared countries on imposition and relaxation of government sanctions (states of emergency) and political executions.

The most ambitious undertaking by far is the *World Human Rights Guide*, a compilation by Charles Humana (1984; 1987; 1992), a former employee of Amnesty International. Basing his rating on Amnesty International reports and more than two dozen other sources, Humana identified many specific human rights. His first effort rated 111 countries along 40 4-point scales; in addition, he reported on 10 other aspects of human rights, using qualitative or quantitative measures, and he provided a composite rating expressed as a percentage. Humana's second guidebook expanded to include 121 countries, but with only 45 variables. His final effort covered 104 countries for 40 variables. Still seeking a magic number to scale countries, he employed a weighting system that gave more importance to 7 of his conceptual variables. Using scales devised by Gastil and Stohl, Alex Schmid and associates classified countries into three groups, and then applied a discriminant analysis to test Humana's weights; they found some similarities and some differences, leaving as much classificatory confusion as before (Gupta, Jongman, and Schmid 1993).

Similar efforts have been undertaken to construct measures of the attainment of social and economic rights. Douglas Hibbs (1973) developed a Social Welfare Index from calories and protein per capita, infant mortality, and physicians per capita. M. D. Morris (1979) of the Overseas Development Council constructed a Physical Quality of Life Index (PQLI) from three measures: infant mortality, life expectancy, and literacy. Harmon Ziegler (1988) labelled the percentage of government spending on education, medical services, and welfare as his Index of Social Progress.

Some organizations have joined the bandwagon. The Population Crisis Committee first issued *The International Human Suffering Index* in 1987, rating 130 countries on 10 measures (civil rights, clean drinking water, daily calorie supply, GNP per capita, infant immunization, life expectancy, political freedom, rate of inflation, secondary school enrollment, and telephones per capita). The index was reissued in 1992 for 141 countries.

In *Human Rights: Theory and Measurement* (1988), a collection of essays edited by David Cingranelli, several new databases were identified. Kathleen Pritchard (1988) constructed a composite measure of judicial independence from ratings of separation of powers (Banks and Textor 1963; Banks 1971), presence of judicial review (Blondel 1969), and type of and effect of judicial review (Kommers 1970). Cingranelli and Kevin Wright (1988) went through U.S. State Department *Country Reports* of 152 countries for 1981 to develop a scale of extensiveness of due process guarantees based on the presence of fair trials and the absence of several conditions—unreasonable search, arbitrary arrest or imprisonment, extrajudicial abductions, and torture. They also rated countries on consistency in application of due process if four of the five conditions were found in written constitutions and laws and were observed in customary judicial and police practices.

From 1990, UNDP has issued an annual *Human Development Report*, which provides data on a variety of socioeconomic indicators, including a Human Development Index originally based on attainments in life expectancy, literacy, purchasing power, and (from 1993) sex equality among 177 countries. In 1991, the U.N. body accepted Humana's summary percentages as its Political Freedom Index. When Third World countries objected, UNDP came up with its own composite measure based on five types of indicators (Barsh 1993), as noted above.

Clearly, the diversity among these compendia indicates general agreement that not all human rights are the same. There is disagreement on the number of categories required in a mutually exclusive, exhaustive delineation of types of human rights. Dissensus extends as well to the importance of specific rights in cross-national compilations of human rights performance.

The shortcomings of comparative data, meanwhile, have been noted by many scholars (Barsh 1993; Bollen 1986; Goldstein 1986; Lopez and Stohl 1992; McCamant 1981; McNitt 1988; Mitchell et al. 1986; Samuelson and Spirer 1992; Stohl et al. 1986; Weisberg and Scoble 1981). All have agreed on the need for more reliable data, but there are few clear signposts on how to proceed. Gastil has been fired by Freedom House, evidently for this reason.[1] Now that Humana is dead, no scholar may be able to continue his work. Certainly it might be a waste of effort to collect even more data at this point; attention to a few well-chosen measures of human rights would be more cost-effective for research purposes. But which ones? Since the dimensionality question remains a puzzle, there is no empirical basis for determining the human rights indicators on which major attention is now needed. Although most scholars view human rights as a multidimensional phenomenon, the identification of specific human rights clusters has not gone beyond literary theory. Whenever a "mental factor analysis" derives a classification scheme, the author implicitly is saying that a multivariate statistical procedure, if applied to data collected for the various human rights, would yield several precise clusters. The categorizers, in short, predict clustering in data on human rights but rarely test their own predictions.

Dimensional Analysis

Many efforts to measure human rights involve pooling separate indicators into composite measures. If the variables are highly intercorrelated, they probably form a single empirical dimension. If the variables have low or even negative correlations, they may contain several empirical dimensions, and such a composite index will be conceptually meaningless.

One method for dealing with the problem of determining the number of clusters of independent variation within several variables is to test for unidimensionality. Cutright (1965:540), for example, reported that the five measures in his SIPE index formed a perfect Guttman scale, a common test for unidimensionality (Guttman 1944). Adelman and Morris (1967) found that their indicators of democracy clustered on the same factor with other political human rights in a factor analysis involving eighty-two countries from 1948 to 1961. Before using his democracy index, Bollen (1980) ran intercorrelations among his variables; as noted above, when he later ran a factor analysis, he found only one distinct cluster of variables (Bollen and Grandjean 1981). Cingranelli and Pasquarello (1985) computed eigenvectors, the first step in factor analysis, for data coded from the U.S. Department of State's *Country Reports*, but rather than using the two separate factors thus extracted, they calculated a single measure from a personal integrity violations factor and a civil-political liberties factor. Bruce Moon and William Dixon (1985b), meanwhile, found intercorrelations within the three-variable PQLI to be at .93 or above.

Because dimensionalizing is a principal objective of multivariate clustering techniques, David Banks decided to pursue this quest in three studies. He first reported correlations at the +.90 level between the Gastil and Humana data (Banks 1985; see 1992). Next, he analyzed seventy-four countries from the 1982 Humana data (Banks 1986), finding six clusters of rights with one multivariate technique, three clusters with a second technique, and five clusters with yet another procedure. Although he then clumped the countries into several empirically distinct groups, he concluded that his statistical exercise was "uninformative" (157). A few years later, when I attempted to replicate Banks for 1982 and 1986, I found that most of Humana's variables clustered together on the first eigenvector in a factor analysis (Haas 1986; 1989). Possibly unaware of my efforts, Banks reported similar results in a later study (Banks 1992:382). Although he also analyzed the 1982 and 1986 data with alternative forms of multivariate analysis, he found more than three different groups of variables for each of the two years, again reporting "disappointing" results (Banks 1992: 389). Pasquarello (1988) found one factor from fifteen variables coded from the *Country Reports* for 1981.

When Pritchard (1988) factor-analyzed Boli-Bennett's (1981) data, she found three independent sources of variation corresponding to civil rights, political rights, and constitutional rights, though she also ignored the multidimensionality of the data in constructing a composite measure of the three dimensions. Similarly, when she intercorrelated Gastil's civil rights and political rights scales with the PQLI, she found "substantial" interrelationships and constructed a composite Human Rights Index from all three sources (Pritchard 1989). Cingranelli and Wright (1988), finding positive correlations between all their measures of due process rights, treated levels as one dimension and consistency with constitutional-legal provisions and judicial-police practices as a second dimension, however.

Thus, statistical comparisons of human rights observance have made two fundamental assumptions that might be false: (1) that certain forms of human rights may be collapsed together into composite indexes–in short, that one or more unidimensional clusters of human rights can be meaningfully summarized by cluster-specific statistical measures; and (2) that analytical typologies correspond with empirical reality—that is, that empirical clusters are isomorphic with analytical categories.

If civil, political, and other human rights are empirically distinct, the unidimensionality assumption is false; quantitatively, unidimensionality would be refuted if measures of civil, political, and other human rights formed many empirical clusters. If, instead, we derived several human rights clusters statistically, but the composition of each cluster differed from the typological predictions of various scholars, then the second assumption is incorrect. Accordingly, one aim of this book is to test both assumptions.

A RESEARCH AGENDA

One theory of knowledge is that truth is advanced not by a mere cumulation of definitive studies but instead through an ongoing process of placing previous empirical efforts into larger theoretical perspective (Kuhn 1962). Accordingly, an exhaustive analysis of comparative human rights attainments would appear to require the completion of several distinct tasks:

1. We need to specify theories about why human rights are protected in some countries rather than in others.
2. We need to identify reliable, valid indicators of human rights, based on these theoretical perspectives, for at least two time points.
3. We should dimensionalize our indicators to determine empirical subsets, if any.
4. We should regress predictor variables onto our dimensions.

These tasks provide the research agenda for this volume.

Accordingly, this study will begin by reviewing the theoretical literature to determine which concepts are most important for studying human rights. Data will then be assembled to measure attainments in civil, cultural, economic, political, and social rights. Next, multivariate clustering procedures will be employed to determined the underlying empirical structure of cross-national data on human rights. To cross-check alternative multivariate methods, we will use factor analysis and cluster analysis programs provided by the Statistical Analysis System Institute (1982:chapters 21, 22). The factor analysis will start with a principal components analysis, and then try an orthogonal varimax solution. Varclus, the clustering program, will next perform an oblique component analysis (Anderberg 1973; Harman 1976). The final statistical procedure will be stepwise multiple regression: Variables hypothesized to account for variations in human rights observance will be regressed onto variables that best represent the major empirical dimensions of human rights.

The purpose of these operations is to answer the following questions: (1) Which kinds of countries are most likely to violate human rights? (2) What exogenous variables, if any, most parsimoniously account for cross-national and cross-temporal variations in observance of basic human rights? (3) What are the most critical areas where pressure can be effectively applied in order to encourage countries to improve the protection of the human rights for those who live under their jurisdiction? In short, the analysis will focus both on why some countries have better human rights records than others and on why some countries improve more than others over time.

NOTE

1. I am indebted to Michael Stohl for this information. Stohl indicates that Humana admitted that his ratings were impressionistic rather than systematic.

Chapter 2

THEORIES

With measures of human rights, it is possible to scale countries from low to high levels of performance. To explain why countries differ, we need to explore visions of how political systems operate. Theories of explanation, often based as they are on ideological biases, need to be unpacked into specific hypotheses, which in turn should be tested with data.

THEORIES OF HUMAN RIGHTS OBSERVANCE

Regardless of the varieties of human rights, can we explain progress in human rights on the basis of exogenous variables, that is, by regressing variables other than human rights onto human rights performance data or improvement? Some *relativists* argue that human rights may be appropriate in Western societies, do not fit the circumstances or outlook of non-Western peoples, and hence cannot be advanced by applying foreign pressure (Johnson 1988; Lee 1987; Zvobgo 1979; see Donnelly 1989: part 3). Nevertheless, several alternative theories compete for acceptance. Some optimistic theories explain why human rights flourish, but others are more pessimistic, seeking instead to explain why human rights are denied.

Among the optimistic theories, *economism*, harking back to Adam Smith (1776), sees the advancement of economic rights as prior to all other rights, whether civil, political, or social (see Horowitz 1976). Economistic theorists, thus, assign priority to the level of economic prosperity.

Developmental theorists stress the need for economic growth as a precondition to human rights in addition to the level of current economic attainments. Many developmentalists claim that the trickle-down of capital accumulated as a country shifts from an agricultural to an industrial to a postindustrial society will bring ever-increasing democracy and prosperity (Kerr et al., 1964; Organski 1965). Thus, if developmentalism explains the rise of human rights, we would expect to find that increases in economic variables alone would predict human rights performance.

The theory of *liberal democracy* stresses the need for free elections, the free flow of information, a competitive economy, contending political parties, and a neutral legal-rational bureaucracy as components of a social order that will bring human rights for all (Dahl 1971; Myrdal 1957; Weber 1913, 1918). Liberal democrats, thus, believe that economistic theorists have left out the bureaucratic and information infrastructure of modern societies from their predictions.

The theory of *social democracy*, reflecting especially on the success of Scandinavian political systems, argues that masses must be committed to democracy, and elites must be willing to use their roles as democratic leaders by granting social welfare reforms in order to ensure political stability (Lenski 1966; Hewitt 1977). Hence, liberal democratic theory leaves out the components of the welfare state, which social democrats believe are crucial preconditions to the advancement of human rights.

Mobilization theorists believe that no rights are granted without a struggle, so well-organized groups can alone advance their own cause (Carmichael and Hamilton 1967; Tilly 1978). If this theory is correct, we would find that human rights are highest in countries with higher voter turnout as well as strong minority protest movements, trade unions, and women's organizations.

Turning to theories that are more pessimistic, *trade-off* theory postulates that civil and political rights are attained at the expense of economic and social rights, or vice versa (see Donnelly 1989: part 4). Thus, we would expect advances in civil-political rights to be associated empirically with declines in economic-social rights or the reverse.

Group conflict theorists believe that certain groups in heterogeneous societies seek to advance their own kind and thus restrict the rights of others (Harff 1986; Kuper 1981; Mazian 1990; Van Den Berghe 1981). According to this view, human rights fare better in homogeneous than in heterogeneous societies, which tend to have too much internal conflict.

If the groups in conflict are elites versus nonelites, regardless of ethnicity, then *power elite* theory is described. According to power elite theory, those on top seek to maintain power by erecting barriers to equal rights for nonelites. One version of power elite theory believes that rulers carefully weigh costs and benefits of repression (Duvall and Stohl 1988:253–264; Lindblom 1977). Another version believes that there is an ''iron law of oligarchy'' (Michels 1915; Mosca 1896; Pareto 1916). Still other power elite theorists note that the rhetoric of ''national security'' has served as a rationale for restricting human rights. The Cold War, for example, has been viewed as a ruse by ruling elites in both the Soviet Union and the United States to justify internal and external disinterest in democratization (Chomsky 1991; Mills 1956; Stohl 1986). Power elite theory cannot be tested definitively through correlations, but a clue may be found in situations where external or internal conflicts prompt leaders to restrict human rights.

For *Marxian* theorists, the various power elites trample on human rights in order to preserve their economic hegemony, which ultimately rests on exploitation at home or abroad (Arendt 1951; Frank 1967; Lenin 1917; Marx and Engels 1848; Milliband 1969; Poulantzas 1972). In short, power elite theory is concerned with preservation of political power, whereas those influenced by Karl Marx believe that the bourgeoisie's imperative of capital accumulation is why elites under capitalism do not want nonelites to enjoy basic human rights. To demonstrate the validity of Marxian theories of human rights denials, measures of economic dependency and inequality would be critical.

This brings us to three theories that believe economic fluctuations to be central in accounting for the absence of human rights. *Frustration-aggression* theorists believe that socioeconomic deprivation and discrimination constitute frustrations that can lead the masses to engage in violent protest, thereby inviting government repression and escalating violence and repression (Feierabend and Feierabend 1971; Gurr 1970; Lifton 1986; Rubenstein 1983; Staub 1989). For these theorists, economic downswings should precede human rights restrictions. *Mass society* theorists, in contrast, caution that no political system can cope with massive social dislocation accompanying extremely rapid economic growth; if human rights are granted too quickly, the result will be political turmoil, so shrewd governments will put human rights in the back seat as their countries undergo extremely rapid economic growth (Huntington 1968; Owen 1987; Strouse and Claude 1976). One variant of mass society theory stresses that totalitarian rule, by depriving citizens of the freedom to form a civil society, serves to build up pressures that cannot be expressed politically but are instead evident in high rates of death due to cancer, heart disease, and suicide (see Haas 1968; Kornhauser 1959). For *Freudian* theorists, any industrialization, whether gradual or rapid, means that individuals must repress spontaneity in order to have the discipline to perform repetitive tasks in factories and offices. Such repression creates a longing to express savagery, whether in the form of genocide or lesser violations of human rights (Charny 1982; Cohn 1967; 1970; 1977; Freud 1930; Marcuse 1955; see Fein 1993).

Some of the pessimistic theories are merely antonymic expressions of the optimistic theories. *Developmentalism*, for example, is the opposite of *frustration-aggression*, *mass society*, and *Freudian* theories. *Marxians* believe that the *economistic theorists* are mistakenly Panglossian, that increased economic and political "freedom" results in monopolistic practices rather than increases in human rights. *Power elite* theorists believe that *liberal democracy* and *social democracy* theorists are naïve. In principle, therefore, an empirical study should be able to determine which theory best explains why some countries have higher human rights attainments than others.

HYPOTHESES

Some scholars have unpacked the above theories into specific predictions that may be tested by correlational analysis. One theme is that socialist countries observe socioeconomic rights better than capitalist countries (see Hoffmann 1983:29; Kolakowski 1983; Poulantzas 1972). In addition to economic system as a predictor variable, other scholars have hypothesized that human rights are most consistently observed by countries that enjoy peace (Kant 1795), are politically stable (von Mises 1981:1,400), have peoples with profound religious convictions (Tracy 1983), have a large percentage of entrepreneurs (Claude 1976:42), have considerable competition among political elites (Claude 1976: 42), have a large percentage of politically active persons with lower incomes (Claude 1976:42), and have considerable trade (Alston 1982) or receive a lot of aid from other countries (Vincent 1986:134). Countries most likely to violate human rights have been predicted to be those with civil wars and ethnolinguistic minorities (Hoffmann 1983:27), with economic downturns (Rimlinger 1983), with economic underdevelopment (Weinstein 1983), with economic dependency (Greenberg 1982), with military or unrepresentative rule (Claude 1976:43; Conway 1982), or that cope with conditions of extreme civil unrest or international instability (Gurr 1986; 1988).

Consensus is absent regarding many hypothesized correlates of human rights. There is disagreement concerning whether restrictions on human rights facilitate economic development (Farer 1983; Huntington 1968:41, 52) or whether lower performance on human rights discourages economic development (Weinstein 1983). Alternatively, some view human rights as a luxury for rich countries (Vatikiotis and Delfs 1993), while others note that even rich countries can provide the capabilities to poor countries for state terror "far beyond their limited means" (Duvall and Stohl 1988:247; see Chomsky and Herman 1979). For some, economic freedom is an essential concomitant of human rights (Smith 1776[1937]:538); for others, capitalism is inherently a license for exploitation (Marx and Engels 1848). The view that U.S. power has promoted human rights (Huntington 1981:246–259) is contradicted by such recent examples as Nicaragua and Panamá (see also Chomsky and Herman 1979). Democracies provide a seedbed for human rights, according to most scholars (see Howard and Donnelly 1986a), but democracies also support foreign authoritarian states (Chomsky and Herman 1979), which Jeane Kirkpatrick (1979) once argued could become democratic more readily than totalitarian states.

CORRELATES

Empirical efforts to explain worldwide and temporal variations in human rights observance have been undertaken by several scholars. Results, as the following summary indicates, have wider areas of disagreement than agreement (see Table 2.1 in Appendix C). For purposes of convenience, the focus herein will be on correlates of five dependent variable clusters: democratic rights, regime coerciveness, general civil-political rights, physical quality of life, and the attainment of social security and welfare rights.

Political (Democratic) Rights

In one of the earliest quantitative studies, Seymour Martin Lipset (1959; see 1994) found across fifty-four countries for the early 1950s that democracies not only had higher income and electricity consumption per capita but also more newspapers, physicians, radios, and telephones per capita as well as higher percentages of the population literate, living and working in cities, and enrolled in institutions of primary, secondary, and higher education. "Free elections," that is, the presence of political rights, defined what he meant by "democracy."

Phillips Cutright (1963; 1965), following up Lipset's study, constructed a four-point index of democracy (initially called "political development" but later renamed "political representation") from the extent of legislative party competition and the degree to which chief executives are selected. Cutright discovered that almost two-thirds of the variance in "democratic development" across seventy-seven nations from 1940 to 1960 was due to communication development (literacy rate, per capita newspapers, newsprint, mail, telephones); economic development, educational development, and urbanization, though positively correlated, explained much less. Regime instability was inversely correlated with democracy. He also found that democratic development contributed to greater economic equality for fifty-two countries in the first decade after World War II (Cutright 1967a). Although Cutright thus refuted Lipset (1959), his study was called into question, too. Using Cutright's correlation matrix, Donald McCrone and Charles Cnuddle (1967) tried a path analysis, which found that the data best fit a linear model: Urbanization led to more educational development, which resulted in more communications development, which in turn strengthened democracy. McCrone and Cnuddle thereby showed that Cutright and Lipset missed important causal connections between their variables.

With a sample of 19 First World and 3 Third World democratic nations, presumably for the 1950s or early 1960s, Deane Neubauer (1967) also disputed Cutright, finding that democratic rights increased as countries became more affluent; after reaching a certain threshold, he discovered that additional socioeconomic progress was unrelated to further democratization. For Neubauer, educational development and urbanization were unrelated to democracy, but communications development was a solid predictor of democracy. Analyzing 44 countries from 1800 to 1960, William Flanigan and Edwin Fogelman (1971a; 1971b) noted that few democracies have emerged in recent years. They found a curvilinear relationship between democratization and both urbanization and increases in the percentage of the nonagricultural labor force, an inverse correlation with domestic violence, and a positive association with educational enrollments. Robert Jackman (1975), using similar indicators across 122 countries, derived the same curvilinearity as Neubauer. When Cutright responded to criticisms by cross-tabulating his index by high and low levels of economic development (per capita energy consumption) for 40 countries from 1927 to 1966, he reported that economic development and literacy best accounted for improvements in democracy among both affluent and poor countries (Cutright and Wiley 1969). Although other studies have supported the link between literacy and democracy (Feierabend, Feierabend, and Nesvold 1969a; McCrone and Cnuddle 1967; Nesvold 1969), Zehra Arat (1991), for 65 countries from 1948 to 1982, found that fluctuations up and down her democraticness scale were more likely among midrange developing countries than among the least or most developed countries. She also reported that democracy is unrelated to equality but tends to correlate with lower domestic violence. Several scholars indeed concur that democracies are stabler than nondemocracies (Banks 1972; Cutright 1965; Feierabend and Feierabend 1971b; Feierabend, Feierabend, and Nesvold 1969a; Hibbs 1973; Nesvold 1969).

According to Kenneth Bollen, most studies report no relationship between democracy and equality (Bollen and Grandjean 1981; Bollen and Jackman 1985; 1988). Richard Rubison and Dan Quinlan (1977), however, found that income equality was the best predictor of democracy for thirty-two countries in the mid-1960s, using both Jackman's index of democracy and a measure of governmental checks and balances from the compendium of Arthur Banks and Robert Textor (1963). Edward Muller (1988) reported that reduced equality endangered democracies, using Bollen's measure for fifty-five countries in the mid-1960s, and several other studies concur that equality promotes democracy (Jackman 1975; Stack 1978; Weede 1980; Ziegler 1988). Thus, the jury on the relationship between democratic political rights and equality is still out.

Based on a study of seventy-four less developed countries from 1950 to 1964, Irma Adelman and Cynthia Taft Morris (1967) reported that the best predictor of democracy was union strength, but the same measure washed out in a later study (Frakt 1977). Christopher Hewitt (1977), studying twenty-five industrial countries for 1965, found that as per capita GNP increased, so did both democracy and equality (measured by percentages of students in higher education from low income families and percentages of tax revenues spent on social security). Hewitt's data also showed that those living in democratic states did not uniformly fulfill their economic and social needs; leftist parties must provide the leadership. Peter Lange and Geoffrey Garrett (1985; 1987) extended this analysis, finding that countries with strong leftist parties and vigorous trade unions were most likely to experience long-term economic growth, but Jackman (1987) noted that their sample of fifteen countries for 1960–1980 was too heavily weighted toward certain Western European countries to have much global significance, and the correlation washed out when he increased the sample (see also Hicks 1988). Harmon Ziegler (1988) then found that *laissez faire* capitalism was consistently related to democracy, contradicting Hewitt, Lange, and Garrett.

Bollen also tested the notion that economies that began to prosper many decades ago would be more democratic than more recent boom economies. Although he reported no evidence to support the timing-of-development hypothesis, he found that current levels and rates of change in per capita energy consumption were the best predictors of democracy (Bollen 1979; 1980; 1983). Phyllis Frakt (1977) and Muller (1988) also found a linkage between economic development and democracy, but Arat (1991) cautioned that too rapid economic growth undermines democracy, and yet another study (Feierabend, Feierabend, and Nesvold 1969a) found the relationship to be curvilinear. Bollen echoed Flanigan and Fogelman (1971a; 1971b), noting that few Third World countries have become democracies (Bollen 1983; Bollen and Jackman 1985).

In any case, there is no dispute that democracies tend to have lower levels of domestic violence, a higher per capita national income, a higher rate of literacy and communications development (newspapers, radios, televisions), many physicians per capita, and larger percentages of Protestants. There is dissensus or incomplete evidence on the remaining correlates.

Regime Coerciveness

Several studies have focused on the use of coercion and repression through mass arrests, torture, and other forms of governmental terror. Regime coerciveness, in a study by Ivo Feierabend, Rosalind Feierabend, and Betty Nesvold (1969b), was unrelated to regime stability. Later, they found an overall negative correlation with moderate levels of political stability, but they found that totalitarian regimes are so repressive that they are able to maintain political stability, so they reported a curvilinear relationship (Feierabend and Feierabend 1971b; Markus and Nesvold 1972). Regime coerciveness also correlated negatively with per capita income, but some moderately affluent countries (Argentina, Morocco, and South Africa in their data) were also politically coercive (Feierabend, Feierabend, and Bororiak 1967). When they intercorrelated an index of external aggression with regime coerciveness, the relationship was positive but weak. In other studies, the authors found that policies of discrimination toward separatist ethnic minorities correlated with the levels of international conflict, political violence, regime coerciveness, and socioeconomic deprivation (Feierabend, Feierabend, and Nesvold 1969b:13–17). Douglas Hibbs (1973) also found a positive relationship between governmental violence and internal conflict and instability and a negative correlation with voter turnout across 108 countries for 1960. Later studies have tended to agree that domestic violence provokes regime repression (London and Robinson 1989; Muller and Seligson 1987; Moaddel 1994), but a recent study reported that indicators of the two phenomena were uncorrelated (Walton and Ragin 1990). A flurry of studies has demonstrated that there is no relationship between the propensity to engage in external violence and the extent of democratic rights (Chan 1984; Maoz and Abdolali 1989; Maoz and Russett 1993; Morgan and Campbell 1991; see Banks 1972).

In an extensive study of measures of state terrorism across 102 countries with a per capita GNP under $3,000 in the early 1980s, Miles Wolpin (1986) found many relationships with exogenous variables. For example, Latin America had the highest representation of both violent and minimal state repression, while other parts of the world had higher levels of institutional repression and intermediate levels of severity of state terror; but both variables correlated with the duration of a country's independence, so the correlation might be spurious. "Open door" capitalism was also associated with both extremes, whereas state capitalism or socialism entailed more institutional repression. Violent repression was unrelated to the percentage of trade unionists among wage and salary earners as well as governments with high percentages of military spending in the total government budget, but positively related to regimes kept in power by military rule. Foreign military threats were associated with institutional repression more than with either violent or minimal repression; countries with larger percentages of their armed forces trained in the Soviet Union had larger percentages of their populations serving in the armed forces, and such countries tended to meet dissent with violence. When the Soviet Union dispatched troops to a country, Wolpin found the associated condition to be institutional yet nonviolent repression. When a country with military rule sent a large portion of its army to train in the United States, the likelihood of subsequent violent repression was considerable, whereas civilian regimes that allowed their armies to train in the United States engaged in minimal repression. If U.S. troops intervened heavily in a country, the repression was more apt to be violent; if U.S. allies did so, the repression was usually minimal. Military regimes engaged in more institutional repression when they received weapons from either superpower; civilian regimes that imported such arms displayed considerable violent repression. Civilian regimes were more likely to engage in violent repression than military regimes when their economies had heavy foreign investment. As civilian regimes increased in industrial production, there was more likelihood of violent repression; all three forms of repression were used by military regimes at all levels of national wealth. National income per capita predicted lower levels of repression, but growth rates were unrelated. Longer life expectancy and higher levels of postsecondary school enrollment were correlated with minimal repression. Civilian regimes with higher infant mortality used more violent repression; military regimes with higher infant mortality had more institutional repression. As literacy increased in civilian regimes, repression was less likely; increased literacy in military regimes was associated with either minimal or violent repression. Where minorities were treated poorly, repression was violent regardless of regime type. Islamic countries had more violent repression than other countries, but there was no correlation between repression and the relative size of the Christian population. As this summary of Wolpin's study indicates, military (versus civilian) rule is a crucial variable (see Adelman and Morris 1967), and his threefold categorization of degrees of repression served to identify some curvilinear relationships.

Wolpin's findings regarding economic growth and ethnic diversity were supported in a recent study by Mansoor Moaddel (1994), who used multivariate procedures to analyze about sixty-five countries in the 1970s. Moaddel's finding that economic dependency is higher in repressive regimes, however, contradicted two earlier studies (Cingranelli and Pasquarello 1985; Cingranelli and Wright 1988). Regarding regime instability, Moaddel's data supported the Feierabend studies and Hibbs.

In a study of 132 countries for 1984, Neil Mitchell and James McCormick (1988) found that arbitrary imprisonment associated with mass arrests and the systematic use of killings or torture of prisoners were found among countries with lower levels of per capita income. Countries that traded a lot tended to violate these judicial human rights, but per capita trade volume was unrelated. Countries with high amounts of investment had lower levels of observance, though the correlation was not high and disappeared when controlled for population size. Former British colonies better observed these human rights, but the relationship washed out when the two researchers controlled for GNP. They found no relationship between years of political independence and human rights. Authoritarian regimes most tended to use torture, and totalitarian regimes had more political prisoners, but Mitchell and McCormick noted that democratic regimes were much less likely to use torture or to engage in mass arrests of political dissidents.

A few studies have sought to determine whether U.S. foreign aid has served to encourage better human rights or instead, as suggested by Wolpin, has been used by the recipient nation to suppress its people. Among twenty-three Latin American countries in the mid-1970s, Lars Schoultz (1981a; 1981b) found that U.S. military aid during Gerald Ford's administration went disproportionately to countries that expert judges determined to be more repressive regimes, but the correlates reversed in the era of Jimmy Carter. Schoultz's findings were contradicted in a twenty-nation study by David Carleton and Michael Stohl (1985) for the years 1976 and 1981. Using data coded from Amnesty International (1962–), Freedom House's annual index of political freedom (Gastil 1978–), and the annual human rights report of the U.S. State Department (1977–), they reported that aid was uncorrelated with human rights. Steven Poe and Rangsima Sirirangsi (1992), after constructing a Human Rights Abuse Scale by coding information on sixty-six countries from similar sources from 1981 to 1986, found that higher amounts of U.S. economic and military aid in both the Carter and Reagan years went to countries with fewer human rights violations.

Terry Boswell and William J. Dixon (1990) studied economic dependence as a wellspring for regime coerciveness, running regressions on seventy-two countries for the early 1980s. They found that Western arms imports were indeed related to repression, but there was no correlation with periphery or semi-periphery status despite the excellent human rights records of some core countries in the world economy. Other findings disputed previous research: They found that domestic violence has a curvilinear relationship with repression, economic equality is unrelated, former British colonies and Protestant countries have no special advantage in regard to human rights records, and per capita national income is inversely related to repression.

The consensus, therefore, is that serious violations of civil and judicial rights occur in countries with ethnic diversity, considerable per capita foreign investment, and higher levels of military spending. Countries at war also tend to be coercive domestically. Otherwise, the studies paint a cloudy picture.

Civil and Political Rights

According to John Boli-Bennett's (1981) analysis of 142 constitutions, citizen rights have historically increased along with the power of government, measured in terms of the increasing obligations imposed by governments on the people (to serve in the military, etc.) as well as by the percentage of national income derived by the state from taxes. Boli-Bennett also found that the constitutions of Catholic countries listed more rights than those of Protestant countries.

In the same vein, Frakt (1977), seeking to determine why some countries adopt labor reforms contained within agreements drawn up by the International Labor Organization, examined seventy-eight countries from 1960 to 1966. For less developed countries, her measure of democracy best accounted for labor reforms. For developed countries, trade union strength was the best predictor. For both types of countries, the second best predictor was economic development (per capita energy consumption).

In a pioneering analysis, James Strouse and Richard Claude (1976) ran bivariate correlations with Raymond Gastil's ratings for 122 countries in the early 1970s. They found that countries with higher ratings tended to have higher levels of per capita economic development and wealth, more rapid economic growth, higher rates of literacy and communication facilities, and more regime stability and urbanization, but they found no relationship with per capita economic growth and absolute levels of national wealth (see Conway 1982).

Michael Timberlake and Kirk R. Williams (1984) reported that Gastil's ratings for seventy-two countries in the early 1980s were higher in countries with more economic development and per capita foreign investment. There was a curvilinear relationship with domestic violence.

In the next major study, Han Park (1987) used a sample of over 100 countries around 1980. He reported that civil-political rights were highest in countries with larger percentages of Christians, more income equality and urbanization, higher percentages of the national budget spent on welfare and lower military spending, and lower percentages of Moslems, but he found education ministry spending percentages to be uncorrelated.

Other studies have supported both of these pathbreaking research efforts. Ziegler (1988:207) found that GNP per capita explained about one-third of the variance in Gastil's political freedom index and in his own Index of Social Progress; a competitive party system, Gastil's economic freedom index, and voter turnout percentages were much less significant predictors. Milton Friedman

(1988), similarly, reported that Gastil's data showed that civil liberties and political rights are best observed where there is high per capita GNP and low infant mortality. Nonetheless, the absolute level of national wealth, which Strouse and Claude found to be unimportant statistically, emerged as the primary predictor in a study of thirteen demographic and economic factors that were intercorrelated with clusters derived from a multivariate analysis of David Banks (1985).

Dissensus arose regarding the connection between civil-political rights and propensity to engage in war. Data presented by Michael Haas (1965) and R. J. Rummel (1983) showed that democracies make fewer wars, but Jack Vincent (1986) and Erich Weede (1984) found no such correlation. In any case, there is a consensus that civil and political rights are lower in countries under military rule (see Adelman and Morris 1967; Conway 1982).

A further unresolved controversy revolves around the role of U.S. aid. Some scholars find that U.S. economic aid tends to go to countries that most respect civil and political rights (Cingranelli and Pasquarello 1985; Poe 1991). Looking only at Africa, Thomas Pasquarello (1988) noted a negative correlation. Two other studies, however, found no correlation between levels of U.S. economic aid and Gastil scale scores (Stohl, Carelton, and Johnson 1984; Travis 1989). With respect to military aid, two studies found a negative correlation (Pasquarello 1988; Poe 1991), two reported no correlation (Cingranelli and Pasquarello 1985; Stohl, Carleton, and Johnson 1984), but one research project found that U.S. military aid was higher to countries that most respected civil and political rights (Travis 1989).

Finally, Dipak Gupta, Albert Jongman, and Alex Schmid (1994) ran correlations based on a threefold classification of levels of human rights observance, using data from the latest two compilations of Charles Humana. They found that military governments were more repressive than democracies, and per capita GNP correlated with better human rights. Comparing countries over time, using Humana's second and third volumes, they found that human rights abuses increased for all forms of government at all levels of economic prosperity. They concluded that the end of the Cold War may have unleashed more human rights abuses by governments onto the peoples of the world.

In sum, observance of civil and political rights appears to go together with higher economic development, equality, literacy, nonmilitary rule, and per capita income. Many disagreements are due to different procedures and samples, leaving the overall picture somewhat blurred.

Quality of Life

The International Covenant on Economic, Social, and Cultural Rights assures all people of the right to basic human needs, such as a healthy life and the right to receive an education. The Physical Quality of Life Index is a simple way of measuring attainments of these basic guarantees, though some scholars have used more complex measurements.

The earliest large-sale effort to find correlates of levels of economic and social attainments was undertaken by Robert Jackman (1975), who performed multivariate analyses on 60 countries for 1960. He reported that the quality of life is higher in countries with slower population growth, lower domestic violence, and slower per capita economic growth. He found curvilinearity in regressions on measures of economic development, regime stability, unionization, and years since the first establishment of democratic institutions. Unrelated were ethnic diversity, government spending, progressivity of taxation, trade dependency, and voting for left-wing political parties. Jackman's research confirmed earlier studies on the connection between regime stability and socioeconomic attainments (Feierabend and Feierabend 1971a; 1971b; Nesvold 1969).

Most economists have sought to explain economic growth entirely on the basis of the formation of economic capital. Following an earlier study that provided quantitative evidence that as much as 45 percent in GNP growth in the United States was due to advances in educational attainments (Denison 1974: 128), Norman L. Hicks (1979) compared 69 countries from 1960 to 1973, concurring that human capital formation accounted for about half the variance in per capita growth rates; education and health improvements explained equal amounts of variance. Bruce Moon and William Dixon then sought to determine why basic human needs are satisfied in some countries more than in others, using the PQLI. In one study, Dixon (1984) reported that high economic growth and welfare expenditures best accounted for PQLI improvements across 74 less developed countries from 1960 to 1980, whereas measures of economic dependency (monocrop exports and trade partner concentration) washed out. Thus, his data contradicted Jackman's finding about the negative effect of economic growth on economic and social rights. Analyzing 116 countries for the early 1960s, Moon and Dixon (1985a; 1985b) found that the best predictor by far was per capita GNP; measures of democracy (from Bollen 1980) and leftist government leanings (from Blondel 1969) were moderate predictors. Robert Rosh (1988:193), however, disputed their methodology. Using PQLI measures across 68 Third World countries for 1970, 1975, and 1980, Rosh reported that the variable with the most impressive explanatory power was the form of government: Democracies provided a better physical quality of life than nondemocracies (Rosh 1988:199–200). In addition, he discovered that countries with commodities concentrated on one main export and with higher levels of military spending had a lower PQLI. Arms imports, however, were unrelated to indicators of quality of life.

Park (1987) also shed light on economic and social rights observance. He found positive correlations with the percentage of Christians, economic equality, ethnic diversity, urbanization, and government spending on welfare, and an inverse relationship with percentage of Moslems. Contradicting Rosh, he reported a negative correlation with military spending. He found no correlation with levels of government spending on education.

Nancy Spalding (1988), regressing various measures on the PQLI for 1979 across 141 Third World countries, however, found the quality of life to be inversely related to the percentage of government budgets devoted to education. She discovered that economic variables (especially per capita GNP and percentage of nonagricultural workers) had more impact than political variables, but democratic institutions appeared to play a role in bringing about a higher quality of life for the masses. Per capita GNP was more likely linked to spending on education than to spending on health, whereas increases in the percentage of nonagricultural workers impacted government spending on health more than on education. Spalding speculated that as economic conditions perk up, the need for better training of workers increases while health conditions improve, so regimes tend to fund education ministries more than health ministries.

Looking at 133 countries for the early 1970s, Kathleen Pritchard (1988; 1989) sought to replicate Moon and Dixon (1986b). Although the latter found that civil-political and economic-social human rights negatively correlated with the size of a government's budget per capita, Pritchard found a positive relationship. She also found positive correlations with the extent of judicial independence and the comprehensiveness of constitutional guarantees of human rights (based on Boli-Bennett's data). For Pritchard, per capita GNP was also positively associated with human rights attainments, but the correlations were more moderate than Moon and Dixon. Using path analysis, she found that the best model was additive: Budgetary resources best predicted how well countries observed human rights; judicial independence added to the statistical explanation, and extent of constitutional guarantees explained some but a lesser amount of variance in human rights performance.

The consensus is that the quality of life is more satisfactory for countries with higher per capita national incomes, literacy rates, and welfare budgets. Not enough research has been undertaken to extend this short list of findings, however.

Welfare Rights

Concerning social security programs, Cutright (1965), studying seventy-six countries from 1934 to 1960, found that his measures of extensiveness of welfare benefits best correlated with his political representatives index, controlling for per capita energy consumption. Other correlates were economic development, literacy, regime stability, and urbanization. His data for fifty-two countries in the 1950s also showed that high voter turnout correlated with the portion of a country's GNP going to social security programs, though the percentage of nonagricultural workers was a better predictor for less developed countries (Cutright 1976b). Gains in literacy also had a strong effect on social security coverage increases, based on a sample of forty countries from 1927 to 1966 (Cutright 1965; Cutright and Wiley 1969).

Jackman (1975) used Cutright's index of welfare benefits, Hibbs's Social Welfare Index, and an indicator of income equality (Schutz 1951) across sixty countries for 1960, discovering that all three measures were higher in countries with more economic development, though they reached an asymptote and did not advance much among the most developed countries (Jackman 1975:chapter 3). Such variables as labor union strength, governmental and military spending, support for left-wing parties, tax progressivity, and trade dependence had no effect on Jackman's three social welfare measures; the relationships vanished when he controlled for level of economic development (chapters 6–7). Negative correlations with welfare benefits applied to domestic instability and violence, economic growth per capita, and population growth. Jackman concluded that the golden age of the "post-industrial society" was not likely to emerge, as predicted by Clark Kerr and associates (1964). In a later study, Jackman (1989) found that the economic growth rate, uncorrected for population size, was un-related to welfare benefits (see Hicks 1988).

Richard Rubison (1976) reported a positive relationship between Cutright's index of welfare benefits and the cost of social security programs, on the one hand, and economic development, government spending, and income inequality, on the other, for 47 countries from 1961 to 1968. He also found a negative relationship for economic dependence.

Mostly due to the paucity of studies, there are only two consistent findings relating to welfare benefits. Urbanization is positively related to welfare benefits, but economic growth is unrelated.

SUMMARY

There is some consensus in findings. About twenty variables have consistent patterns across two or more types of human rights for many variables (Table 2.1 in Appendix C). Countries with better records tend to import fewer weapons, have higher percentages of Catholics, are economically developed, have higher national income and per capita government spending, attain higher literacy rates, have civilian control of the military, have lower percentages of Moslems, are core countries in the world-system, have higher rates of physicians per capita and lower population growth, have many radios and televisions per capita, have considerable urbanization, allocate larger portions of the government budget for welfare spending, and have a long history of democratic rule. Otherwise, find-ings provide a confusion that needs to be resolved. Accordingly, the next chapter identifies a body of reliable, valid indicators of human rights and predictors of human rights observance.

Chapter 3

VARIABLES

My task in this chapter is to analyze the texts of basic documents on human rights in order to determine whether there are comparable, reliable, and valid indicators of each human right across a cross-national sample of countries for 1982/1983 and 1985/1986, which correspond to the years of Charles Humana's first two compilations (1984; 1987).[1] Civil and political rights will be discussed first. Afterward, I will delineate indicators of economic and social rights and exogenous variables hypothesized to explain why some countries observe human rights better than others do.

CIVIL AND POLITICAL RIGHTS

The International Covenant on Civil and Political Rights has a Preamble and fifty-three articles, with an Optional Protocol consisting of fourteen articles (Appendix A). Below I enumerate fifty relevant measures of civil and political rights (see Table 3.1 in Appendix C).

Article 1. All peoples have (a) the political right of self-determination, (b) the economic right to dispose of natural wealth, and (c) the economic right to have trade based on mutual benefit. From these principles we can derive several variables. To measure the exercise of self-determination, a country should be self-governing. If we were measuring sovereignty alone, independent countries would score 1, colonies 0. Since little data exist for the few remaining colonies, such as French Polynesia, Hong Kong, Macau, New Caledonia, and Tokelau Islands, a more useful operationalization is the years of independence that a country has experienced:

Variable A1. Years independent since 1800.[2]

Work on minorities by Ted Gurr and associates (Gurr and Gurr 1983; Gurr 1993) provides the best data source on peoples lacking self-determination:

Variable A2. Percentage of a country's population composed of ethnonationalists/separatists.
Variable A3. Number of separatist movements.

Humana is concerned about whether the state can take away personal property capriciously:

Variable A4. Freedom from arbitrary seizure of personal property (1986 only).

The right to have trade based on mutual benefit is partly an economic right and partly a civil-political right. Raymond Gastil (1978–) classifies most countries on a nine-point scale from a high of capitalist inclusiveness through mixed capitalism/socialism to socialist noninclusiveness, focusing on legal restrictions:

Variable A5. Economic freedom.

Economic indicators of trade based on mutual benefit are found in the discussion that follows on Article 1 of the International Covenant on Economic, Social, and Cultural Rights.

Articles 2-3. States are to respect provisions listed in the covenant without distinction of any kind. Discrimination based on race, color, sex, language, religion, political or other opinion, national or social origin, property, or birth status is proscribed. Governments are to establish remedies in cases where they are subjected to discrimination; administrative, judicial or legislative, or other bodies are to hear complaints and to provide these remedies. Humana is particularly concerned with gender equality. In his first volume, all countries are coded for the degree of equality in rights between men and women; although he does not indicate which rights he has in mind, his primary interest is in civil and political rights, so one might assume that this is his meaning. His second volume is more specific:

Variable A6. Political and legal equality for women.

Discrimination on ethnic grounds is listed below (variables A45, A51, A53).

Article 4. A government may suspend certain obligations under the covenant in time of national emergency, but with two qualifications: (a) Such suspension cannot affect rights stated in Articles 6-8 (regarding slavery and punishment for crimes), 11 (no criminalization of civil offenses), 15 (*ex post facto* legislation), 16 (right to recognition in court), and 18 (freedom of speech and religion); and (b) the U.N. Secretary-General must be notified of the provisions suspended, the reasons for such action, and the date when the suspension of rights is terminated. I derive a presence/absence rating by perusing the U.S. Department of State's *Country Reports*:

Variable A7. Emergency constitutional suspensions that breach basic rights.[3]

Article 5. Governments vary in how well they guarantee basic rights. The purpose of this article is to assure countries with higher standards than the covenant that they should not feel obligated to lower or reduce their standards in order to satisfy the various requirements.

Article 6. Although the covenant states that everyone has the inherent right to life, no provision prohibits the death penalty. Instead, this article limits capital punishment to apply in the following circumstances: (a) only for the most serious crimes, (b) only on adults, (c) never on pregnant women, (d) only after a fair trial by a competent court, and (e) only when those sentenced to death have the right to seek and receive amnesty, commutation of sentence, or pardon. "Most serious crimes" is undefined, but it would surely exclude executions on political grounds, which are noted in annual reports of Amnesty International and the *Country Reports*:

Variable A8. Number of political executions.
Variable A9. Number of reported extrajudicial killings or "disappearances."

Since the death penalty is itself increasingly regarded as inhumane, I add another variable from Humana:

Variable A10. Freedom from capital punishment by the state.

Article 7. Regarding other forms of punishment, the covenant goes on to prohibit torture and cruel, inhuman, or degrading treatment or punishment. Humana covers this provision with the following:

Variable A11. Freedom from court sentences of corporal punishment.
Variable A12. Freedom from torture or coercion by the state.

Humana's first volume compares countries on the severity of sentences for various crimes (bigamy, illegal abortion, possession of illegal drugs, rape, trade in pornography), but there is little variance across countries, and this feature is not included in his second or third volumes. Although the Universal Declaration of Human Rights proscribes revoking a person's citizenship, no such provision appears in the International Covenant on Civil and Political Rights. Nevertheless, I infer that the scope of Article 7 includes this right, as measured by Humana:

Variable A13. Freedom from deprivation of nationality.

Finally, the article notes that medical or scientific experimentation should occur only with free consent, but no cross-national judgments are available to compare countries on this provision.

Article 8. This article prohibits slavery, involuntary servitude, forced or compulsory labor, and the slave trade. There are some escape clauses: (a) Courts may require hard labor as a punishment for a crime; (b) governments may require alternative national service for conscientious objectors to military service; and (c) governments may require work that forms part of normal or emergency civic obligations. Humana is concerned about child labor and conscripted labor:

> **Variable A14. Absence of serfdom, slavery, and child labor.**
> **Variable A15. Absence of compulsory work permits and conscripted labor.**

Clearly, the obligation for military service without an alternative form of national service would violate this article. In Humana's first volume, the following right appears:

> **Variable A16. Freedom from compulsory military service (1982 only).**

Article 9. Some due process rights come next: (a) No person can be arrested or detained without cause. (b) At the time of an arrest, a person should be informed of the reasons for such action. An accused person should be (c) informed of specific charges when brought promptly before a judicial authority, (d) entitled to a trial in a reasonable time, and (e) accorded the right to be released on bail. (f) The article recognizes the right to file a writ of *habeas corpus* in order to ask a court to decide on the lawfulness of detention. (g) Those wrongfully arrested or detained have a right to compensation. (h) Deprivations of liberty can occur only on lawful grounds and through legal procedures. Humana has only one relevant conceptual variable:

> **Variable A17. Freedom from indefinite detention without charge.**

The right to have a prompt arraignment is subsumed under the right to a speedy trial, which appears below (variable A24).

Article 10. As soon as a person is detained lawfully, certain rights apply: (a) Accused persons are to be segregated from and treated differently from convicted persons; (b) accused adults are to be separated from accused juvenile persons, and the latter are to have their cases handled speedily; (c) within the penitentiary system, juveniles should be separated from adults and treated in accordance with their age and legal status, and (d) the aim of all treatment of prisoners must be reformation and social rehabilitation. No information on these rights has been compiled for countries around the world.

Article 11. Inability to fulfill a contractual obligation cannot be a basis for imprisonment. Cross-national comparisons are unavailable for this provision.

Article 12. Next, freedom of movement is guaranteed. (a) Within a country, the right includes freedom to choose one's residence. (b) All persons inside a state also have the right to leave the country. Humana lists the following:

Variable A18. Freedom to travel in own country.
Variable A19. Freedom to travel outside own country.

Both variables are qualitative, presumably dealing with bureaucratic impediments of various sorts. Humana also has a quantitative measure:

Variable A20. Number of countries forbidden for external travel.

Article 13. Aliens lawfully inside a state may be expelled only in accordance with legal due process, except in the case of compelling national security considerations. Due process must include (a) stating grounds for expulsion and (b) having legal representation before the competent authority. Although the *Country Reports* are concerned with the treatment of refugees, these persons do not fall within the scope of this article, which is otherwise unmeasured thus far.

Article 14. One of the lengthiest, this article enumerates procedures for ensuring equal justice in proceedings before courts and tribunals. Some provisions repeat guarantees in Article 9. Others appear for the first time:

(a) fair and public hearing before a competent, independent, impartial tribunal established by law;

(b) presumption of innocence in a criminal case;

(c) right of the defendant to choose approved legal counsel;

(d) free legal representation if unable to defray legal expenses;

(e) adequate time and facilities to prepare a defense, including communication with counsel;

(f) trial without undue delays;

(g) defendant present during trial;

(h) right to cross-examine witnesses testifying against defendant;

(i) right to subpoena witnesses supporting defendant;

(j) free services of an interpreter for a defendant who is unable to speak or understand the language of the court;

(k) right of a defendant not to be compelled to testify;

(l) procedures modified to take account of age and desirability of rehabilitation of accused juveniles; and

(m) no double jeopardy once acquitted or convicted.

Some provisions have qualifications:

(n) Courts can close trials to the public if publicity would outrage public morals, jeopardize public order or national security, compromise the privacy of the parties, or would prejudice the interests of justice.

(o) Outcomes of trials can be kept from the public when matrimonial disputes, guardianship of children, or the interests of juvenile persons are involved.

(p) If the defendant fails to disclose a fact that results in a miscarriage of justice, no compensation is warranted; otherwise, compensation to a person wrongfully incarcerated shall be in accordance with the law.

Humana rates countries on some but not all of these guarantees:

Variable A21. Right to civilian, public trials.
Variable A22. Independent courts.
Variable A23. Right to be considered innocent until proved guilty.
Variable A24. Right to a speedy arraignment (1982 only) and trial (1986 only).

Although the following is included in Humana's second volume, I instead devise a scale from the *Country Reports* so that ratings in 1982 and 1986 will be comparable:

Variable A25. Right to free legal aid when necessary and counsel of own choice.[4]

Other specific aspects of judicial proceedings, such as double jeopardy, have not been analyzed comparatively.

Article 15. Laws change over time. Two additional protections are (a) immunity from prosecution for acts that were legal when they were committed, even if later they constitute crimes, and (b) the lighter penalty when new laws change the nature of the penalty for a crime. The first guarantee, often known as a prohibition on *ex post facto* legislation, can be waived if the offense is generally considered a crime throughout the community of nations. Unfortunately, these provisions have not been analyzed comparatively.

Article 16. Everyone has the right to be considered a person before the law. Although children have some rights, as specified in Article 24, they lack full standing as parties to bring lawsuits in many countries. A relevant cross-national compilation does not exist thus far.

Article 17. The right to privacy is specified as noninterference with family, home, and correspondence. Those whose privacy is invaded are to claim protection of the law against such attacks and interference. Humana compares countries on the following privacy rights:

Variable A26. Freedom from police searches of home without a warrant.
Variable A27. Freedom from mail censorship.
Variable A28. Right to practice homosexuality between consenting adults.

For 1986, Humana specifically incorporates wiretapping along with mail censorship into his judgments.

Article 18. Freedom of conscience, the next category of rights, includes (a) the freedom to adopt a religion or belief and (b) the freedom to practice that religion or to express those beliefs. Limitations, which can only be prescribed by law, may be imposed to protect public safety, public order, public health, or morals, or the rights and freedoms of others. A second escape clause, evidently contradicting Article 16, hints that parents and legal guardians may prevail over the wishes of children and the state in providing religious and moral education. Overall, Amnesty International counts the number of prisoners of conscience:

Variable A29. Number of political prisoners.

Humana is also very interested in these freedoms:

Variable A30. Right to practice any religion.
Variable A31. Freedom from compulsory religion or state ideology in schools.

Article 19. A broad guarantee of freedom of speech comes next. The coverage includes (a) right to express opinions; (b) right to seek, receive, and impart information and ideas; and (c) freedom of expression in art or through any other media. However, governments can limit this right, either to respect the rights and reputations of others or to protect national security, public order, public health, or morals. Humana provides the following:

Variable A32. Freedom to teach ideas and receive information.
Variable A33. Freedom from political press censorship.
Variable A34. Independent book publishing.
Variable A35. Independent radio and television networks.

Humana has two additional relevant judgments for 1986 but not 1982. I therefore code for both years, using Arthur Banks's *Political Handbook of the World* (1975–) to rate the independence of newspapers, and *Country Reports* for judgments on the extent of government cooperation with organizations that monitor human rights:

Variable A36. Independent newspapers.[5]
Variable A37. Freedom to monitor human rights violations.[6]

Humana does, however, provide the following in his first two volumes:

Variable A38. Freedom from deliberate state policies to control artistic works.

Article 20. Some forms of communication are prohibited: (a) propaganda for war; and (b) advocacy of national, racial, or religious hatred that incites discrimination, hostility, or violence. This is yet another aspect of human rights that awaits more careful comparative study.

Article 21-22. The right of peaceful assembly is guaranteed except for situations that would jeopardize national security, public safety, public order, public health, morals, and protection of the rights and freedoms of others, as specified by law. Freedom to associate with others is covered, too. In addition to the familiar exceptions (national security, public safety, public order, public health, morals, protection of others), laws can place further restrictions on armed forces and police. The right to form and join trade unions is explicitly mentioned. Humana codes the following relevant to the observance of both articles:

Variable A39. Freedom to peacefully assemble and associate.
Variable A40. Freedom to form and join independent trade unions.
Variable A41. No compulsory membership in state organizations or parties (1986 only).

Article 23. Protection of the family is the centerpiece of this article, which recognizes (a) the right of adult men and women to marry, (b) free and full consent of both spouses in entering into marriage, (c) equal rights of spouses in getting married, (d) equal rights of spouses in dissolving marriages, and (e) protection of children after divorce. Humana is interested in two of these rights:

Variable A42. Right to interracial, interreligious, or civil marriage.
Variable A43. Equality of sexes in marriage (1986 only) and for divorce proceedings (both 1982 and 1986).

Article 24. Children also have rights: (a) protection as a minor by the family, society, and the state; (b) to be registered immediately after birth; (c) to have a name; and (d) to acquire a nationality. None of these rights is mentioned by Humana, though he does note that nationality cannot be revoked (variable A13).

Article 25. Political rights are found next, in particular: (a) to vote by secret ballot, (b) to have frequent and regular elections, (c) to run for office and be elected, and (d) to have access to public service. Restrictions to these procedural aspects of democracy, if any, should not be unreasonable. Humana incorporates some of these considerations in one conceptual variable in his second volume, whereas Michael Coppedge and Wolfgang Reinecke (1988) devise a comparable measure of ''polyarchy,'' a concept developed from Robert Dahl (1971), that can be used for 1982:

Variable A44. Polyarchy (1982 only); multiparty, secret, universal elections (1986 only).

Ruth Leger Sivard's *World Military and Social Expenditures* (1975–) focuses on voting rights:

Variable A45. Limitations on the right to vote.

The frequency and regularity of elections can be measured by the following:

Variable A46. Years since latest general election.

Humana looks at the voting process. For 1986, but not 1982, he codes the right to multiparty elections by secret and universal ballot, which appears to be subsumed by another variable used for both years:

Variable A47. Right to peaceful political opposition.

Gurr and associates, concerned with minorities, code exclusion from officehold-ing, other forms of discrimination in officeseeking, and inequality in access of minorities to government jobs, voting, and in the right to group representation and in legal protections:

Variable A48. Severity of minority political discrimination.

I use the *Country Reports* to rate the extent of female advancement into male-dominated bastions of political power:

Variable A49. Importance of females in politics.

Article 26. This article restates Article 2(1) regarding equality before the law for all categories of persons.

Article 27. Having restated nondiscrimination as a principle, the covenant goes on to make more explicit guarantees for ethnic, religious, or linguistic minorities: (a) right to enjoy their own culture, (b) right to profess and practice their own religion, and (c) right to use their own mother tongue. Humana codes countries on one of these rights:

Variable A50. Right to publish and educate in minority languages.

Articles 28-53. These articles set up the U.N. Commission on Human Rights and provide ratification procedures.

The fifty variables delineated above are not the only ones that could be used in a comparative analysis of attainments relevant to the International Covenant on Civil and Political Rights. Humana, for example, codes countries on whether they observed the right to purchase alcohol for 1982, but he abandons this effort in his second volume. Rather than generating more variables for every possible right at this time, my aim is to reduce the complexity by finding dimensions in existing data. A similar procedure is followed in specifying variables relevant to the International Covenant on Economic, Social, and Cultural Rights.

ECONOMIC AND SOCIAL RIGHTS

Although Manouchehr Ganji's *The Realization of Economic, Social and Cul-tural Rights: Problems, Policies, Progress* (1975) provides many useful sug-gestions for quantitative measures, few systematic efforts have considered that comparisons of national economic and social characteristics can serve in the analysis of differential attainment of human rights. I proceed in this section to specify variables from each article of the International Covenant on Economic, Social, and Cultural Rights (Appendix B).

Of the twenty articles in the covenant, a few duplicate those in the Interna-tional Covenant on Civil and Political Rights. Some rights are easily operation-alizable, but others provide formidable challenges for measurement. Most relevant data, unless otherwise noted below, are found in statistical compilations of the International Monetary Fund (IMF), the United Nations and its various specialized agencies, and the World Bank (Table 3.2 in Appendix C).

Article 1. All peoples have (a) the political right of self-determination, (b) the economic right to dispose of natural wealth, and (c) the economic right to have trade based on mutual benefit. Since the language is the same as Article 1 of the International Covenant on Civil and Political Rights, I focus here on provisions (b) and (c). Regarding the right to dispose of wealth, Gastil classifies most countries on a scale of economic inclusiveness. Accordingly we use the same indicator here as variable A5:

Variable B1. Economic freedom.

Economic freedom is supposed to encourage entrepreneurship and commercial activity. One measure of economic innovation, compiled by U.N. agencies, is as follows:

Variable B2. Trademarks applied for per capita.

To indicate the extent of trade based on mutual benefit, we can compute a measure of terms of trade (dividing the unit value of exports by the unit value of imports) and a measure of purchasing power of exports (dividing the unit value of exports by the dollar value of imports). U.N. figures are in index numbers for each country, thus unfortunately not comparable across countries; however, increases and decreases over time are available and comparable:

Variable B3. Improvement in terms of trade.
Variable B4. Improvement in purchasing power of exports.

Articles 2-3. There shall be no discrimination in economic and social rights (as specified in later articles) on the basis of sex, language, religion, national origin, property ownership status, and birth status. "Discrimination" is an undefined term but is usually understood to mean unequal treatment; thus, no laws should give preference to one category of humans over others. The concept of "inequality" implies that females and males should be accorded the right to the same substantive rights, as listed in later articles. Considerable work is needed to measure attainment of these guarantees in specific terms. A few scholars have attempted comparative assessments. Gurr and associates provide the following measures of discrimination against minorities:

Variable B5. Percentage of population suffering economic discrimination.
Variable B6. Severity of minority economic discrimination.

Humana has four-point scales for ethnic and gender inequality, though only for 1986:

Variable B7. No social and economic discrimination against minorities (1986 only).

Variable B8. No social and economic discrimination against women (1986 only).

Articles 4-5. These contain procedural language. They do not confer specific rights.

Article 6. All have the right to work at freely chosen employment. Two types of measures are possible. Humana surveys the extent of labor freedom (already identified as variables A14 and A15):

Variable B9. Absence of serfdom, slavery, and child labor.

Variable B10. Absence of compulsory work permits and labor conscription.

U.N. figures are readily available on the extent to which a government promotes a policy of full employment:

Variable B11. Unemployment rate.

Article 7. This article contains a long list of provisions regarding conditions of work: (a) fair wages, (b) equal pay and conditions of work for both sexes, (c) wages that provide a decent living, (d) safe and healthy working conditions, (e) equal opportunity for promotions, and (f) opportunities for rest and leisure through paid holidays and limitations on hours of work. The following are relevant U.N. data on cross-national attainments:

Variable B12. Average nonagricultural weekly wage rates.

Variable B13. Consumer spending per capita.

Variable B14. Percentage of workers injured on the job.

Variable B15. Percentage of workers losing work due to on-the-job injuries.

Variable B16. Percentage of workers injured fatally on the job.

Variable B17. Average hours of work per week in nonagricultural activities.

The U.S. Department of Commerce (1981; 1986) provides a list of commercial holidays:

Variable B18. Number of commercial holidays.

Article 8. The rights of trade unions and their members are delineated as follows: (a) right to form unions, (b) right to join unions, (c) right of unions to federate, (d) right of unions to function freely, and (e) the right to strike. The freedom to form and to join unions is also a civil-political right (variable A40).

Variable B19. Freedom to form and join independent trade unions.

The exercise of that right can be measured with data on union membership and activities, as recorded in U.S. Department of State publications:

Variable B20. Percentage of workers organized into unions.
Variable B21. Right of unions to federate.
Variable B22. Freedom of unions to operate.

In addition, the freedom of unions can be measured by quantifying strike activity from U.N. sources:

Variable B23. Ratio of strikes to persons employed.
Variable B24. Ratio of strikers to persons employed.
Variable B25. Ratio of work-days lost to number of strikes.

Article 9. There is a right to social security benefits. From the U.S. Social Security Administration, which keeps track of five types of social security programs by all countries in the world, I draw up scales on the extensiveness of these programs:

Variable B26. Extensiveness of family allowance plans.
Variable B27. Extensiveness of old-age and survivor pensions.
Variable B28. Extensiveness of sickness and/or maternity programs.
Variable B29. Extensiveness of unemployment insurance.
Variable B30. Extensiveness of work-injury programs.

Amounts allocated to these funds have been computed by the IMF (1977–) and Sivard (1975–).

Variable B31. Percentage of central government budget for social security and welfare.

Article 10. Up to this point the covenant specifies mostly economic rights. Social rights come next. The first set relates to families: (a) the right of dependent children to protection, (b) the right of dependent children to an education, (c) marriage by consent, (d) paid leave for childbirth, and (e) limitations on child labor. U.N. figures on deathrates index the first subcategory (protection of dependent children).

Variable B32. Deathrate of males aged 1-4.
Variable B33. Ratio of deathrate of females to males aged 1-4.

Sivard has data on immunization:

Variable B34. Percentage of infants immunized against diphtheria, tetanus, and whooping cough.

Education of dependent children is measured in Article 13, which delineates the right to education. Data on marriage by consent are unavailable, except in terms of restrictions based on ethnicity or religion (also variable A42):

Variable B35. Right to interracial, interreligious, or civil marriage.

Data on paid leave for childbirth are unavailable. Child labor is analyzed in Article 6.

Article 11. Governments are to ensure that their citizens enjoy an adequate standard of living. Specifically, sufficient food, clothing, and housing should be provided, and the state should pledge to eradicate hunger through domestic government policies as well as international aid. With respect to food supply, the following U.N. data seem most useful:

Variable B36. Caloric intake per capita.
Variable B37. Protein intake per capita.

Regarding clothing, which is often manufactured for export, statistics on consumption are unavailable. Textile and footwear production figures are in U.N. sources:

Variable B38. Cotton woven fabric production per capita.
Variable B39. Nonrubber footwear production per capita.

Sivard and U.N. sources provide useful data on the quality of and investments in housing:

Variable B40. Percentage of housing units with safe water.
Variable B41. Percentage of housing units with flush toilets.
Variable B42. Percentage of gross domestic product invested in housing.
Variable B43. Percentage of central government budget for housing.

Efforts to eradicate hunger can be measured with the following IMF data:

Variable B44. Percentage of central government budget for agriculture.

Among less developed countries (LDCs), agriculture tends to top the list of sectors receiving development aid. Foreign economic aid figures, though not broken down by sector, are available from the World Bank:

Variable B45. Overseas development aid received/gross domestic product.

Article 12. Health rights appear at this point. All countries pledge (a) to reduce stillbirths; (b) to reduce infant mortality; (c) to improve environmental and industrial health; (d) to prevent, treat, and control endemic, epidemic, and occupational diseases; and (e) to make medical services available to all. For stillbirths, the U.N. has the following:

Variable B46. Late fetal deathrate.

Sivard provides data on item (b):

Variable B47. Infant mortality rate.

U.N. sources break infant mortality down into separate rates for females and males. They also measure rates of death due to endemic and epidemic diseases:

Variable B48. Ratio of female to male infant mortality.
Variable B49. Deathrate due to infectious-parasitic diseases (males).

Other relevant data are presented by Sivard:

Variable B50. Percentage of government budget for health.
Variable B51. Persons per physicians.
Variable B52. Persons per hospital beds.
Variable B53. Percentage of childbirths attended.
Variable B54. Life expectancy at birth.

Another variable is from the World Bank:

Variable B55. Percentage of population with access to health care.

Article 13. The covenant affirms educational rights at this point. All persons are entitled to an education that will enable them to participate in a free society, with course content that promotes tolerance and awareness of the role of the United Nations. Governments also promise to offer the following: (a) free primary education, (b) free secondary education, (c) technical and vocational education, (d) higher education, (e) adequate student financial aid for postsecondary education, (f) improved working conditions for teachers, and (g) privately run educational opportunities. U.N. and World Bank reports have data on specific levels of educational attainment:

Variable B56. Years of compulsory education.
Variable B57. Percentage of school-age children in primary school.
Variable B58. Percentage of school-age females in primary school.
Variable B59. Percentage of school-age children enrolled in secondary school.
Variable B60. Percentage of education budget for vocational schools.
Variable B61. Percentage of tertiary students in science and engineering.
Variable B62. Percentage of adults enrolled in colleges.
Variable B63. Percentage of females enrolled in colleges.
Variable B64. Percentage of central government education budget for scholarships.
Variable B65. Percentage of central government education budget for teachers' salaries.

Sivard has some relevant data as well:

Variable B66. School-age population per teacher.
Variable B67. Percentage of population literate.
Variable B68. Percentage of females literate.
Variable B69. Percentage of central government budget for education.

No data source, however, reports on private educational opportunities.

Article 14. Countries that have not met the above standards are required to design a plan to do so within a few years. I measure success on this provision by comparing the 1982 with the 1986 data in chapter 5.

Article 15. Cultural rights are enumerated next. The following are recognized: (a) right to participate in cultural life; (b) right to enjoy the benefits of science; (c) copyrights and patent rights; (d) governmental conservation, development, and diffusion of culture and science; (e) freedom for creative and scientific activity; and (f) participation in efforts at international scientific and cultural cooperation. U.N. sources are rich on variables that measure participation in and diffusion of cultural life:

Variable B70. Fixed cinema seats per capita.
Variable B71. Cinema attendance per capita.
Variable B72. Museum attendance per capita.
Variable B73. Ratio of volumes in national libraries to gross national product.
Variable B74. Percentage of population registered as public library users.
Variable B75. Books published per capita.
Variable B76. Percentage of textbooks among all books published.
Variable B77. Ratio of textbooks published to students enrolled in schools and colleges.
Variable B78. Ratio of books translated to books published.
Variable B79. Books translated per capita.
Variable B80. Long films produced per capita.
Variable B81. Films imported per capita.
Variable B82. Ratio of films imported to long films produced.

The U.N. records data on scientific activity by counting industrial designs and patents:

Variable B83. Industrial designs applied for per capita.
Variable B84. Patents applied for per capita.

Humana believes that access to abortion and contraceptives fall within the scope of the right to enjoy the benefits of science:

Variable B85. Right to early abortion (1982 only).
Variable B86. Right to contraceptives.

U.N. sources obtain the following indicators of how the benefits of science are extended in each country:

Variable B87. Percentage of GNP on research and development (R & D).
Variable B88. Percentage of central government spending on R & D.

Humana provides a four-point scale on the degree of artistic freedom (same as variable A38):

Variable B89. Freedom from state policy to control artistic works.

Article 16. Each state must report annually on its human rights record to the U.N. Commission on Human Rights. Some states do so, but mostly to report new ratifications of human rights conventions and passage of new laws. Despite the effort of the U.N. Center for Human Rights and the United Nations Institute for Training and Research to prepare the *Manual on Human Rights Reporting Under Six Major International Human Rights Instruments* (1991), this responsibility has not yet been taken seriously.

Articles 17-19. These provisions specify procedures. They are not intended to be measured.

Article 20. Developed countries are obligated to provide technical assistance to other countries. The U.N. and World Bank provide data on students received from other countries, which is a major source of technical assistance, as well as on aggregate flows of economic aid:

Variable B90. Percentage of college students from abroad.
Variable B91. External economic aid sent/GDP.

Articles 21-31. These contain procedural provisions of various sorts.

The purpose of this part of the chapter has been to match cross-national statistical indicators with guarantees stated in the International Covenant on Economic, Social, and Cultural Rights. Not all provisions are operationalized or operationalizable. A common problem with the ninety-one indicators delineated above is that there is no specification of a minimum threshold of acceptability in the covenant.

PREDICTOR VARIABLES

The third set of variables to be operationalized herein is outside the realm of human rights. I delineate here variables that are hypothesized to predict why some countries observe human rights better than others do (Table 3.3 in Appendix C). Based on theories developed thus far to explain human rights observance cross-nationally, I have identified five categories of predictor variables: economic, political, conflict, Cold War, and cultural.

Economic Development and Equality

Several measures can be used to test whether human rights improve as countries become more economically developed. Affluence and rates of growth measure overall economic development. Sivard's compilations have data for the following:

Variable C1. Per capita GNP.

U.N. sources compute changes from year to year:

Variable C2. GNP per capita growth rate.

Structurally, economic development means the replacement of human labor by machinery and shifts in production from rural to urban locations. The U.N. and World Bank supply the following:

Variable C3. Percentage of workforce employed in agriculture.
Variable C4. Energy consumption per capita.

Sivard has relevant demographic data:

Variable C5. Percentage of population living in cities.

Increased communications are associated with development, so I include the following from U.N. sources:

Variable C6. Newspaper circulation per capita.
Variable C7. Radios per capita.
Variable C8. Telephones per capita.
Variable C9. Television sets per capita.

Some countries are more dependent on others for investment and trade. Measures of dependence on the world economy, available from the U.N. and World Bank sources, are as follows:

Variable C10. Investment received/gross domestic product.
Variable C11. Dollar value of exports and imports/GNP.
Variable C12. Percentage of trade with largest export partner.
Variable C13. Percentage of trade with largest import partner.
Variable C14. Food import dependency (1986 only).

Economic development does not always proceed equitably. One measure of equity is presented in the third edition of the *World Handbook of Political and Social Indicators* (Taylor and Jodice 1983) and by the U.N.:

Variable C15. Income inequality (percentage of income going to top 10 percent of population).

Earlier, equity in education and health attainments was stressed as social rights. *Percentages* of government spending devoted to these purposes were used to measure commitment to social rights. From the standpoint of developmental equity, the critical measure is how much is spent *per capita* for these purposes. Again, I use data from Sivard and the IMF (1977–):

Variable C16. Central government budget expenditures on education per capita.
Variable C17. Central government budget expenditures on health per capita.
Variable C18. Central government budget expenditures on welfare per capita.

Tax policies can be inequitable, too. The IMF has figures on the extent to which individuals and corporations contribute to government revenues:

Variable C19. Percentage of direct taxes collected.

One of the cruelest taxes is inflation, which can be determined from changes in the consumer price index, as provided by U.N. sources:

Variable C20. Rate of inflation.

Substantive Political Development

The term "political development" was used before anyone thought to supply a definition (Riggs 1984). The implied meaning was a tendency to diffuse political power from one dominant center to a variety of independent political institutions that can act effectively on behalf of diverse interests of the people. In the section on civil and political rights, such variables as freedom of political opposition and independence of the judiciary were proposed as measures of *procedural democracy.* "Political development," instead, can mean increases in *substantive democracy.* Procedural democracies offer free and fair elections, whereas in substantive democracies eligible adults actually vote, parliament represents all the interests of the people, the executive branch carries out the popular mandate, the bureaucracy is capable of implementing the will of the people, and the political system is legitimate and stable.

Even when elections are free and fair, voters may be so apathetic that the outcome represents the will of a minority of eligible voters. Using data from *Keesing's Contemporary Archives* (1931), one important indicator of substantive political development is readily available:

Variable C21. Votes cast/adults registered to vote.

The election results should not exclude or marginalize important interests. To oppose the majority effectively, the opposition should have enough seats to ensure that there is a healthy debate on issues of the day. For measures of legislative competitiveness, Banks's *Political Handbook of the World* has the following:

Variable C22. Number of political parties in parliament.
Variable C23. Percentage of seats held by largest political party or ruling coalition.

Developed polities can do more for their people. One measure of the willingness of the people to support effective government, from the IMF, focuses on budgets:

Variable C24. Government revenues/GNP.

Political development also entails peaceful transfers of power and increasingly stable rule. Sivard has data on coups:

Variable C25. Coups from 1960/years independent.

Unstable governments encourage the military to take control. A basic principle of political development is the need for civilian control of the military. Accordingly, the following measures from Sivard indicate the role of the military in politics:

Variable C26. Military-dominated government.
Variable C27. Years of military rule from 1960/years independent.

Domestic and International Turmoil

During times of civil unrest and international wars, governments must take unusual measures to cope with the outbreak or threat of violence. Several variables can assist in determining whether these conditions have an important impact on human rights performance.

Sivard has data on violence initiated by governments:

Variable C28. Official violence against citizens.
Variable C29. Years at civil war from 1960/years independent.
Variable C30. Deathrate due to domestic violence.
Variable C31. Years in international war from 1960/years independent.
Variable C32. Deathrate due to foreign conflict.
Variable C33. Percentage of population in the armed forces.
Variable C34. Military budget/GNP.
Variable C35. Arms imports/GNP.
Variable C36. Arms imports/military budget.

Gurr and associates provide the following measures of active pursuit of ethnic grievances:

Variable C37. Extent of minority political grievances (1986 only).
Variable C38. Extent of minority economic grievances (1986 only).
Variable C39. Extent of minority social grievances (1986 only).

Since terrorism can affect how a political system operates, an appropriate variable, collected by the U.S. Department of State (1983–), is as follows:

Variable C40. Number of terrorist incidents (1986 only).

The IMF has data on the cost of policing countries from the mid-1980s:

Variable C41. Percentage of budget for internal security (1986 only).

Cold War

Rivalry between the Soviet Union and the United States meant competition for spheres of influence up to the end of the 1980s. As the two superpowers penetrated weaker countries, selling weapons to opposite sides in many cases, there appears to have been considerable impact on human rights. Accordingly, the following indicators from Sivard are relevant:

Variable C42. Net arms exporting country (yes/no).
Variable C43. Western arms imports/all arms imports.

The U.S. Agency for International Development (U.S. Department of State 1945–) records aid data:

Variable C44. U.S. civilian aid/GNP.
Variable C45. U.S. military aid/GNP.

Returning to Sivard:

Variable C46. Percentage of troops abroad.
Variable C47. Foreign troops/domestic troops in country.
Variable C48. Western bloc troops in country/total troops in country (net).

Cultural Variables

The prevailing ethos of a country can be an important element in shaping attitudes toward human rights. Demography, ideology, and social tensions should be taken into account.

Several ethnographic variables can be derived from *Europa World Year Book* (Europa Publications 1926–):

Variable C49. Former British colony.
Variable C50. Percentage of Protestant population.
Variable C51. Percentage of Roman Catholic population.
Variable C52. Percentage of Moslem population.

A geographer in the Soviet Union (USSR 1964) has developed the following:

Variable C53. Index of ethnolinguistic heterogeneity.

Ideologically, some countries are more leftist, centrist, or rightist. Using data from Banks's *Political Handbook of the World*, the number of parliamentarians of various political parties can be percentaged. Counting Communists, socialists, and labor parties as the "left," one measure is as follows:

Variable C54. Percentage of leftists in parliament.

When stress afflicts a country, the result shows up in health problems. Three causes of death, obtained from U.N. sources, are particularly indicative of stress.

Variable C55. Cancer deathrate (males).
Variable C56. Heart disease deathrate (males).
Variable C57. Suicide deathrate (males).

CONCLUSION

In this chapter fifty variables are identified as measures of civil and political rights, ninety-one variables are generated to index economic and social rights, and fifty-seven variables are operationalized as predictor variables exogenous to human rights. The next step is to intercorrelate the variables across the eighty-eight countries in Humana's compilations for which he makes discrete judgments.[7] Afterward, as presented in chapters 4 and 5, the empirical objective is to determine whether human rights ratings (a) cluster together on just one empirical dimension or (b) comprise several empirically distinct clusters of rights. In chapter 6 regressions of predictor variables are run on selected measures of human rights attainments.

NOTES

1. I do not include data for Humana's third volume because quantitative data on social, economic, and cultural rights have not yet been published for the year covered by his latest set of judgments.

2. Sources for all variables are identified in Tables 3.1–3.3. Supplementary sources, for just one or two figures for a given measure, have also been used. In addition to references cited, I use Euromonitor (1962– ; 1975/1976–) statistical compilations for a few variables and the *Statistical Yearbook of the Republic of China* (China, Republic of 1982; 1986).

3. I have devised several scales from the *Country Reports* for this study. Each scale

generally has five positions, from 1 (low) to 5 (high).

4. In three cases, Humana has no codings for a conceptual variable in his first volume, and the human rights attribute first appears in his second volume. In regard to the three variables where my codings replace those of Humana, I compute a correlation between my codings and his as a measure of reliability. For this variable, the reliability measure is only .33. The remaining reliability coefficients, noted below, are higher but are below .85, thus casting doubt either on Humana or on my own efforts.

5. The reliability coefficient was .77.

6. The reliability coefficient was .84.

7. The countries are as follows: Algeria, Argentina, Australia, Austria, Bangladesh, Belgium, Benin, Bolivia, Botswana, Brazil, Bulgaria, Cameroon, Canada, Chile, China (People's Republic of), China (Republic of), Colombia, Costa Rica, Cuba, Czechoslovakia, Denmark, Dominican Republic, Ecuador, Egypt, Ethiopia, Finland, France, Germany (Democratic Republic), Germany (Federal Republic), Ghana, Greece, Hungary, India, Indonesia, Iraq, Ireland, Israel, Italy, Jamaica, Japan, Kenya, Korea (Democratic People's Republic), Korea (Republic of), Kuwait, Liberia, Libya, Malaysia, México, Morocco, Mozambique, Netherlands, New Zealand, Nigeria, Norway, Pakistan, Panamá, Papua New Guinea, Paraguay, Perú, Philippines, Poland, Portugal, Romania, Saudi Arabia, Sénégal, Sierra Leone, Singapore, South Africa, Spain, Sri Lanka, Sweden, Switzerland, Syria, Tanzania, Thailand, Trinidad and Tobago, Tunisia, Turkey, Union of Soviet Socialist Republics, United Kingdom, United States of America, Uruguay, Venezuela, Vietnam, Yugoslavia, Zaïre, Zambia, and Zimbabwe.

Chapter 4

DIMENSIONS

In this chapter, I seek to discover empirical dimensions of human rights through multivariate analyses of the variables described in chapter 3.[1] I begin with an analysis of civil and political rights (the A variables); next I examine economic, social, and cultural rights (the B variables); and I then pool the two data sets together (A + B variables). If proposed categories of human rights have empirical validity, this procedure will succeed in reducing the many variables of human rights into a smaller set of dimensions.

Two multivariate techniques are used: factor analysis and one of the many cluster analysis procedures.[2] These techniques are particularly well suited to this task, since perhaps the classic application of factor analysis is to determine whether there is a single dimension of intelligence or whether instead there are separate types of intelligence (quantitative, spatial, verbal, etc.) (see Gould 1980). Factor analysis and cluster analysis of human rights data hold a similar promise, as most product-moment intercorrelations among the human rights variables are positive. Factor analysis looks for unrelated, independent sources of variation, finds the most important factor first, and then extracts lesser factors, thus assisting efforts to test typologies of mutually exclusive sets of factors. The cluster analysis procedure used herein places all variables initially into one cluster, then splits the data into two clusters, and thence into further clusters on the basis of the proportion of variance explained. One advantage of cluster analysis is the ability to determine which rights are empirically prior to others. Whereas factor analysis may explain nearly all the variance in a set of variables, cluster analysis can fall considerably short.

CIVIL AND POLITICAL RIGHTS

One prominent factor dwarfed all other factors extracted from the 1982 and 1986 data. The second factor explained much less of the variance, and the remaining factors had roughly equal but descending importance. About thirty of the fifty variables had correlations (loadings) over ±.40 with the initial factor. The number of factors with eigenvalues over 1.0 for 1982 was nine; for 1986, there were eight factors; in the cluster analysis, seven clusters with eigenvalues over 1.0 were obtained for 1982, six for 1986 (see Tables 4.1 and 4.2, and Figures 4.1 and 4.2 in Appendix C).

Factor Analysis (A Variables)

The first factor, which may be called a general *civil and political rights* factor, accounted for one-seventh of the variance for the 1982 data and about one-sixth of the variance for 1986 (Table 4.1). Looking into variables with highest loadings, *judicial rights* enumerated in Article 14 of the International Covenant on Civil and Political Rights (and the Sixth Amendment to the U.S. constitution) and *privacy rights* in Article 17 (Fourth Amendment) were the most prominent for 1982 (Table 4.1). For 1986 data, the same variables were among the most important on factor 1 (Table 4.2), but even higher loadings were obtained for *freedom of expression rights* (Article 19 and First Amendment). Variables most strongly associated with this factor for both years were innocence until proven guilty, right to civilian and public trials, independence of the judiciary, freedom from mail censorship, and police searches only with a warrant. Also strongly related were some *voting rights*—the right to peaceful political opposition and free and fair elections (Article 25). With somewhat lesser associations for 1982 were variables indicating *freedom of association rights*—freedom to peacefully assemble and freedom to form and join independent trade unions (Articles 21 and 22 and First Amendment rights). These two freedom of association variables had the highest loadings on factor 1 for 1986. Other sets of variables uniquely associated with factor 1 were *prisoner's rights* (variables 10-13 and 17) and *freedom of movement rights* (variables 18-20).

Freedom of expression rights (Article 19 and First Amendment rights) defined factor 2 for 1982. Variables with highest associations from Article 19 were nongovernmental ownership of the press and artistic freedom. *Freedom of conscience rights* (Article 18), such as freedom of religion and absence of a state ideology in schools, had moderate associations with factor 2 for 1982; for 1986, these variables appeared separately on factor 3.

Women's rights variables came together on factor 6 for 1982 and factor 2 for 1986. Although women's rights might appear to be of lesser statistical importance than rights identified on factor 1 in the discussion above, this inference would be a *non sequitur*. Instead, the factor analysis merely discovered independent sources of variation from variables that rarely contrasted rights on the basis of gender. Had the data included such additional variables as economic freedom for women, freedom of women to travel inside and outside a country, fair trials for women, freedom of females from mail censorship and police searches, rights of Lesbians, and so forth, the number of rights dealing with women would have been so numerous that they might have defined factor 1. The factor analyses, thus, say only that *women's rights* are distinct from other rights.

Most of the remaining factors brought together pairs of interrelated variables. One factor isolated political terror variables, namely, "disappearances" and political executions, thus defining *freedom from government terrorism rights*. Another factor was defined by the number and percentage of separatist groups; this was a *minority rights* factor. The remaining factors had little dimensional significance.

Cluster Analysis (A Variables)

Initial cluster analyses of the same variables found similar but more ambiguous patterns. Accordingly, the maximum eigenvalue was set at .01 (instead of the usual 1.00) so that the entire set of variables would be decomposed into clusters of one or two variables; this procedure served to account for 100 percent of the variance. The resulting trees constructed from the results reveal fascinating patterns (Figures 4.1 and 4.2). In referring to the diagrams, I refer to the smallest clusters as "subclusters" and the largest two clusters as "superclusters."

The largest supercluster for 1982 had three components: (1) *freedom of association rights* and *freedom of expression rights,* (2) *judicial rights* and *prisoner's rights,* and (3) *minority rights* and *women's rights* (Figure 4.1a). The second supercluster in Figure 4.1 had less analytical clarity, as there were variables representing *freedom of conscience rights, freedom of expression rights, minority rights,* and *voting rights.*

For 1986, the first supercluster had five distinct sets of subclusters (Figure 4.2). *Freedom of association rights* were intertwined with *freedom of expression rights. Judicial rights* were juxtaposed with variables indicating *privacy rights. Freedom of conscience rights* formed a third set of variables. *Economic freedom rights* and *minority rights* arose separately. Variables measuring *women's rights* dominated the second supercluster in Figure 4.2, which also collected *freedom from government terrorism rights.*

Cluster analysis sometimes permits inferences about which rights come first. For 1982, the data suggest that *freedom of association rights* and *freedom of expression rights* are interconnected, and *judicial rights* develop separately. *Freedom from government terrorism rights* are then assured where all three sets of rights exist. *Women's rights* follow. *Freedom of conscience rights* emerge independently; thereafter, *minority rights* are fully respected.

Looking at hierarchies among the clusters for 1986, *judicial rights* and *privacy rights* develop only after countries observe *prisoner's rights. Freedom of association rights, freedom of expression rights*, and *voting rights* go hand in hand. Evidently, *freedom of conscience rights* are guaranteed at a somewhat later stage. Societies independently respect *economic freedom rights* and *minority rights. Women's rights* are respected much later, but only in societies with *freedom from government terrorism*.

Implications

The data from both the cluster analysis and the factor analysis suggest many inferences about interrelationships between various types of human rights, but the main purpose here is to assess dimensionality. Overwhelmingly, each civil and political right had a positive relationship with every other civil and political right. The only exception, which was observed for 1986 but not 1982, was a negative loading for a variable tucked away on the last factor, which in turn had little dimensional significance.

Clearly, the empirical findings conflict with some *a priori* typologies. Thomas Marshall (1964), for example, suggested a disjunction between civil rights and political rights. Instead, variables selected for Article 25 (free elections, right to vote, peaceful opposition) were strongly embedded within the first factors of the two factor analyses. The same variables were found on the *freedom of expression rights* subcluster with the larger *civil and political rights* clusters for both 1982 and 1986.

Edmund Muskie (1980) and Cyrus Vance (1977), who differed from Marshall in expecting *civil and political rights* to comprise a single dimension, are thus vindicated. The two former secretaries of state were also correct in identifying *judicial rights* as a separate dimension; arbitrary detention, denial of due process, and torture comprised a distinct set of variables. Muskie and Vance thought that numbers of summary executions would be a part of the *judicial rights* cluster, but this variable formed part of another cluster along with numbers of "disappearances."

Jack Donnelly and Rhoda Howard (1988), who encouraged an empirical test of their typology, were supported by the data as well. What they call "protection rights" is similar to *judicial rights*, as found in both the cluster analysis and the factor analysis. Their "empowerment rights" is nearly equivalent to the cluster of *freedom of expression rights*. One category needs some refinement, however. They classify family rights, legal equality, and nondiscrimination as "membership rights," but the data suggest that the variance across specific groups differs; societies do not recognize *gay and Lesbian rights, minority rights,* and *women's rights* in one fell swoop.

United Nations Development Program's (UNDP) latest fivefold Political Freedom Index scheme largely survived the empirical test (UNDP 1993). Indeed, I borrow the term *freedom of expression rights* from UNDP. Instead of UNDP's "rule of law" rights, I prefer *judicial rights*, referring to the same variables.

What UNDP calls "personal security" is herein called *freedom from government terrorism rights*. Although UNDP thought that political rights were separable, I found that they were embedded within a general *civil and political rights* cluster. Whereas UNDP identified equality of opportunity as an independent concept, the data showed that *gay and Lesbian rights, minority rights,* and *women's rights* are not attained at the same time but require separate struggles to achieve recognition across the countries of the world.

Regarding empirical efforts to dimensionalize civil and political rights, I differ from several scholars in finding no independent cluster of *political rights* (Adelman and Morris 1967; Bollen and Grandjean 1981; Pritchard 1988). Similar to David Cingranelli and Thomas Pasquarello (1985), I discovered separate factors for *civil and political rights* and for *freedom from government terrorism rights*. Raymond Gastil's (1980:21) "political terror scale," which sums up the concerns of Amnesty International, correctly predicted the clustering of disappearances after police arrest and political executions, but the other two variables in his scale (incarceration for political opinions and police brutality/torture) were found elsewhere in the multivariate analysis presented herein. Similarly, my study questions other *a priori* scales of human rights developed by various scholars over the years (Carleton and Stohl 1985; Duff and McCamant 1976; Johnson 1976; 1982; Mitchell and McCormick 1988; Stohl, Carleton, and Johnson 1984; Travis 1989). Charles Lewis Taylor and David Jodice (1983), nevertheless, correctly grouped states of emergency and political executions as related measures of "state coercion."

The data throw cold water on Gastil's economistic assumption of the primacy of economic freedom for attaining such other human rights as political freedoms. Charles Humana's summary scores for the human rights records of various countries thus appears to combine apples and oranges.

My data also fail to validate the various efforts to separate measures of political rights from other human rights (Adelman and Morris 1967; Arat 1991; Bollen 1980; Cutright 1963; Flanigan and Fogelman 1971; Frakt 1977; Neubauer 1967). One index of "democratic development," based on four variables, did not emerge as a coherent cluster or factor (Jackman 1975); instead, the two variables indexing procedural democracy were scattered about the multivariate analysis herein, whereas the remaining two variables measured substantive democracy and thus were included in my study only as predictor variables. Nevertheless, my results tend to support the centrality of a variable often thought to be a single indicator of democracy, namely, freedom of the political opposition (Lipset 1959).

In short, the rights delineated in the International Covenant on Civil and Political Rights are multidimensional. There is a direct, not an indirect, relationship between these rights; countries that have higher levels on some of these rights are more likely to observe other human rights.

In addition, the data show that there is a hierarchy among civil and political rights. *Freedom of association, freedom of expression,* and *judicial rights* are clearly the most basic, but they are granted initially to heterosexual males of the dominant ethnic group. *Freedom of conscience* and *absence of governmental terror* come next. Ultimately, civil and political rights are extended to all, regardless of ethnicity, gender, and sexual orientation. Although civil rights are generally established in the framework of democratic systems, the data do not show precisely where *voting rights* fit into the process. The facile view that voting rights are prior to all other rights, hence, lacks clear empirical support.

Interestingly, both the *a priori* "citizens rights index" of John Boli-Bennett (1981), based as it is on thirty-one civil, judicial, and political rights, and the "due process rights" scale of Cingranelli and Kevin Wright (1988) are closer to the mark than indices used by other scholars. However, Boli-Bennett also includes eleven socioeconomic rights in his scale. Similarly, the Population Crisis Committee's Human Suffering Index (1987; 1992) combines civil rights with economic and social attainments. Whether my broad *political and civil rights* factor is mirrored statistically by a general economic and social rights factor is the next quantitative exercise to be reported in this chapter.

ECONOMIC AND SOCIAL RIGHTS

The typologies presented earlier assume only one distinct dimension of economic and social rights. Accordingly, a second set of multivariate analyses was run on the ninety-one variables derived from the International Covenant of Economic, Social, and Cultural Rights. The number of factors extracted with eigenvalues over 1.0 for 1982 was twenty-two; for 1986, there were twenty-three factors (Tables 4.3 and 4.4). In the corresponding cluster analyses, there were nineteen clusters with eigenvalues over 1.0 for 1982 and twenty clusters for 1986, accounting respectively for 64.9 and 62.3 percent of the variance (Figures 4.3 and 4.4).

Factor Analysis (B Variables)

One dominant factor emerged (Table 4.3). The first factor for both 1982 and 1986 data accounted for about one-fourth of the total variance in all variables. The second factor, which extracted about one-sixteenth of the variance, was followed by a train of factors that accounted for decreasing amounts of variance.

Variables representing Articles 11-13 dominated the first factor for both 1982 and 1986, especially long life expectancy, low infant mortality, and percentage literate. Since these rights are concerned with standard of living, health, and education, the inference permitted is that *quality of life rights* are the most basic economic and social rights. Some fifty of the ninety-one variables had loadings exceeding ±.40 on this factor.

The second factor for both 1982 and 1986 pulled together measures of *economic rights*. Although Gastil's measure of entrepreneurial freedom had a reasonably high loading, variables with stronger associations indexed *worker's rights* from Article 8, including absence of compulsory work and freedom for trade unions as well as the freedom of artists to work without interference from the state. Anomalies (low cinema attendance and low R & D spending) appeared for 1986 data only.

Minority rights variables defined factor 5 for 1982 and factor 8 for 1986. There was no distinctive gender inequality factor despite many measures of the differences between males and females. The factor analysis otherwise failed to delineate other broad classes of factors.

Some of the rest of the factors presented correlations more than dimensions. For example, variables measuring industrial accidents, though found on factor 1, had moderate loadings on factor 3 for 1982; but, since cotton and footwear production were more important on the factor, one might infer that inhuman sweatshops exist in countries with significant clothing industries. Cotton and footwear production also had high loadings on factor 5 for 1986 along with industrial accidents. Improved terms of trade and purchasing power of exports, two variables constructed from the concept of *fair trade* in Article 1, topped factor 3 in the data for 1986; the frequent filing of industrial designs and patents had moderate loadings on the factor, suggesting an explanation for the improved trade performance. Nonetheless, these trade and industrial creativity variables were not found together for 1982, as three of the four were absorbed into the first factor. For 1982, factor 6 had a +.82 loading for number of commercial holidays, −.43 for number of years of compulsory education, and −.54 for the percentage of the education budget for scholarships, perhaps suggesting a continuum for countries that stress the pursuit of entertainment versus the pursuit of knowledge. Higher teacher's salaries had the highest loading on factor 17 for 1982, along with a moderate positive loading for the percent share of a country's budget for education and a moderate negative loading for the percentage of that budget spent on scholarships; this odd factor did not reappear for 1986.

In some cases, the factors brought together small and specific sets of indicators. For example, variables indicating the exercise of the *right to strike* joined together in both years (factor 10 for 1982, factor 18 for 1986). Factor 9 for both years had a few high loadings for textbooks per student and the percentage of books translated. The percentage of textbooks among all books published clustered with high usage of public libraries for 1982, but no such factor emerged for 1986. Film imports defined factor 4 for both 1982 and 1986, but variables with moderate loadings on the factor also included the percentage of the government budget spent on housing (for 1982) and the percentage of college students coming from external countries (for 1986). Cinema seats and attendance defined factor 20 for 1982 but failed to come together for 1986.

For brevity, there is little need to display loadings for all factors. Only the first eight are reported in Table 4.3.

Cluster Analysis (B Variables)

Cluster analyses presented a more complex picture. The data formed three, not just two, superclusters (Figures 4.3 and 4.4). In view of the large number of variables for each article in the International Covenant on Economic, Social, and Cultural Rights, there was no reason to decompose the variables into clusters of just one or two variables, so results are presented below in generic terms.

The largest superclusters for both years pointed toward *quality of life* as the central concept in both Figures 4.3 and 4.4. Educational attainments, a healthy population, medical infrastructure, and a high standard of living were at their cores, with the *right to strike* and *cultural rights* (cultural preservation and innovation) on the margins. Both superclusters painted pictures of an affluent, competitive, and creative society. An anomaly in the cluster for 1986 was a high unemployment rate.

The second superclusters for 1982 and 1986 had *worker's rights* at their cores. *Minority rights* were nearby. *Cultural rights* (especially imported films) were in the margins. These variables suggest a cosmopolitan, liberal society.

The third superclusters for 1982 and 1986 differed. For 1982 (Figure 4.3), *worker's rights* were one set of variables, whereas *cultural rights* related to books and *educational rights* were in the second set of subclusters. For 1986 (Figure 4.4), *welfare rights* and *worker's rights* were at the core. Cluster analysis performs a binary decomposition of variables, so it is necessary to report that the third superclusters emerged from the first rather than the second superclusters.

Implications

The analysis of indicators of economic, social, and cultural rights leads to some clear conclusions. A unitary set of *economic and social rights*, as predicted by many observers (Boli-Bennett 1981; Donnelly and Howard 1988; Marshall 1964; Muskie 1980; Nowak and Swinehart 1989; Shue 1980; Vance 1977), is more consistent with the data than a multiplicity of empirically distinct rights, as suggested by the International Covenant on Economic, Social, and Cultural Rights.

Regarding UNDP's earliest Human Development Index (1990), an effort to construct overall dimensions of economic and social rights, the data showed that the index gave far too much weight to sex equality as an integral component. In contrast, Phillips Cutright (1965; 1967a, 1967b) was on the right track in studying *welfare rights* as an important smaller dimension. The findings show that Douglas Hibbs's (1973) four-variable Social Welfare Index, M. D. Morris's (1979) three-variable Physical Quality of Life Index, and Harmon Ziegler's (1988) Index of Social Progress selected indicators that were indeed at the top of the general *quality of life rights* factors and clusters. However, since these variables are so highly interconnected, the data showed that the three composite measures are equivalent as well as redundant.

A few inverse relationships were evident in the factor analyses. They tended to wash out in the cluster analyses, however.

Some hierarchy was evident. Minorities and the working class are treated well in terms of economic and social rights only if the general quality of life is also high in the middle class mainstream within a particular country. As quality of life indicators increase across the sample of countries, the status of women improves in terms of economic and social rights.

COMBINING CIVIL-POLITICAL WITH ECONOMIC-SOCIAL RIGHTS

Most scholars assume that political and civil rights are analytically distinguishable from social and economic rights. Are the two kinds of human rights empirically distinct as well? In order to test this hypothesis, all fifty variables representing political and civil rights were factor analyzed and clustered with all ninety-one economic and social rights (Table 4.5; Figures 4.5 and 4.6). The factor analysis for 1982 generated thirty factors; for 1986, there were thirty-two factors. The corresponding cluster analysis for 1982 had twenty-five clusters and twenty-three clusters for 1986, accounting respectively for 62.5 and 61.8 percent of the variance.

Factor Analysis (A+B Variables)

Results vindicated the hypothesis that *political and civil rights* are distinct from *economic and social rights* (Table 4.5). The factor analyses for 1982 and 1986 extracted two enormous factors, which each explained about one-fourth of the variance across all A and B variables. The percentage of variance extracted by the third factor for both years was less than 4 percent, and each successive factor accounted for fractionally lower amounts of variance.[3]

For 1982, there was very little overlap; that is, most B variables (fifty-three of the ninety-one indicators) had high loadings on the first factor, and A variables (thirty-two of the fifty indicators) dominated the second factor. There was some crossover, nevertheless. All variables coded as both A and B indicators gravitated toward the *civil and political rights* factor. Political and legal equality for women (variable A6) had a moderate loading on the *economic and social rights* factor, and measures of worker's rights (variables B12, B21, B22, and B29), industrial creativity (variables B83 and B84), and the percentage of adults in college (B62) had moderate loadings on the *civil and political rights* factor.

The factor analysis of the 1986 data produced similar results. *Civil and political rights* dominated the first factor; thirty-seven of the fifty A variables had loadings of ±.40. *Economic and social rights* defined the second factor; forty-nine of the ninety-one B variables had loadings of ±.40. Some variables crossed over from A to B, as with the 1982 data. The *civil and political rights* factor had moderate loadings for per capita trademarks (B2), worker's rights (B19, B21, B22, B29, and B89), housing investment (B42), health budget (B50), and the percentage of adults enrolled in colleges (B62). *Economic and social rights* were again linked to *women's rights* (A6, A43) and *gay and Lesbian rights* (A28).

Factors beyond the first two were familiar, having emerged from the separate analyses of the A and B variables. Accordingly, there is no need to discuss them further.

Cluster Analysis (A+B Variables)

The cluster analysis searched for hierarchical connections within the data. Amid twenty-five clusters for 1982 (Figure 4.5) and twenty-three clusters for 1986 with eigenvalues over 1.0 (Figure 4.6), there were three superclusters. As the factor analysis suggested, a *civil and political rights* supercluster had mostly A variables, but the largest supercluster decomposed into two sets of *economic and social rights* (B variables).

Many variables were grouped together at the core of the *civil and political rights* (second) superclusters for both years. For 1982, two large subclusters dominated the picture in the second supercluster of Figure 4.5. The first subcluster had variables representing six types of rights: *freedom of association rights, freedom of expression rights, judicial rights, prisoner's rights, privacy rights,* and *voting rights*. The second prominent subcluster had *freedom of conscience rights, worker's rights, voting rights,* and more variables relating to *freedom of expression rights*. Two later sets of subclusters joining the core had a mix of A and B variables. The first such set of clusters contained a few *cultural rights* (especially imported films), *minority rights,* and *welfare rights* (health budget, housing investment). The final set of subclusters to join the *civil and political rights* supercluster consisted of *freedom from government terrorism rights* and two more *cultural rights* (cinema attendance, textbook publishing).

For 1986, *cultural rights*, relating to films, and *minority rights* were at the core of the second supercluster (Figure 4.6). The first set of subclusters to join the core pulled together *freedom of association rights, freedom of expression rights, freedom of movement rights, judicial rights, prisoner's rights, privacy rights,* and *voting rights*. The second set to join the core attracted *freedom of expression rights* and *worker's rights*.

With respect to B variables, the first supercluster for 1982 (Figure 4.5), had quality of life at the core, in particular educational and health attainments, a high standard of living, some welfare rights (old-age insurance, unemployment insurance), and certain *cultural rights* (books published, patents, R & D spending). For 1986 (Figure 4.6), civil-political *women's rights*, violations of *worker's rights*, and college education attainments formed the core of the first super-cluster.

The second superclusters of B variables were the reverse images of the first superclusters. Civil-political *women's rights, minority rights,* and *union rights* appeared at the core along with some *cultural rights* (books translated, books published, cinema seats) for 1982 data. *Minority rights, union rights,* and similar *cultural rights* were central to the 1986 data.

Implications

The effort to merge variables derived from the International Covenant on Civil and Political Rights and the International Covenant on Economic, Social, and Cultural Rights failed. Political and civil rights were largely distinct from economic and social rights, despite Westerners' arguments that the former unlock the latter and contrary to despotic leaders' contentions that poor societies must become more affluent before they can grant civil and political freedoms. Nevertheless, there was some crossover: Worker's rights, in particular, proved to be as much a matter of civil and political rights as of economic and social rights, whereas women's rights proved to have more relevance to economic and social rights. A few cultural rights had more affinity to civil and political rights than to economic and social rights.

In terms of hierarchical relationships, most civil and political rights appear to go together. Minority rights, gay and Lesbian rights, women's rights, and worker's rights are observed only in countries where the heterosexual male middle class mainstream enjoys basic rights protections. Raising the general quality of life in terms of education and health evidently comes before advances in other economic and social rights, especially for minorities, women, and the working class.

CONCLUSION

The empirical analysis has vindicated the distinction between political and civil rights, on the one hand, and economic and social rights, on the other hand. Many *a priori* categorizations of human rights are inconsistent with the data. Instead, freedom of association, freedom of expression, and judicial rights go hand in hand, whence government terror becomes unthinkable. Attaining a high quality of life in terms of education and health is more basic than other economic and social rights. Middle class heterosexual males of the dominant ethnic group, who comprise the so-called mainstream in many countries, gain human rights before constitutional guarantees are extended to females, ethnic minorities, workers, and sexual minorities.

In sum, efforts to find a single number in order to rank countries on the extent of human rights observance are clearly misguided. There are many varieties of human rights, mainstream and nonmainstream. Thus, the principal research task herein is redefined as ascertaining conditions favorable to all varieties of human rights.

ADDENDUM: PREDICTOR VARIABLES

In chapter 6, I will seek to explain the key variables for each empirical dimension delineated above in terms of fifty-seven predictor variables, which are chosen to measure economic development and equality, political development, domestic and international turmoil, the Cold War, and various cultural characteristics of the eighty-eight countries under analysis. Since this fivefold delineation of predictor variables presupposes that the data constitute five empirical dimensions, consistency in research methods demands a further multivariate analysis of the C variables. Accordingly, a factor analysis was run on the hypothesized independent variables. A brief summary of the results appears below.[4]

Factor Analysis (C Variables)

The factor analyses for 1982 and 1986 C variables derived more than the five predicted dimensions, although the first factor accounted for considerably more of the variance. For 1982, there were thirteen factors (Table 4.6); for 1986, sixteen factors (Table 4.7). The first factors for both years extracted about one-ninth of the variance, but the second factors accounted for less than 4 percent of the variance, and each factor thereafter dropped off incrementally in explanatory power.

Most of the first twenty variables, classified in chapter 3 as economic development and equality, dominated factor 1 for both years; ethnic homogeneity (C53), lack of civil war (C29), and cancer and heart disease deathrates (C55-C56) had moderate loadings. Trade dependency variables (C12-C13) were on separate factors for both years. Measures of political development and domestic and international turmoil were found respectively on factors 8 and 2 for 1982 but were scattered on various factors for 1986. Gurr's (1993) measures of grievances defined factor 4 for 1986. Cold War variables were dispersed on various factors; for example, U.S. civilian and military aid (C44-C45) were on factor 9 for 1982 and on factor 6 for 1986. Cultural variables found their way to factors 2, 5, and 10 for 1986. Two generalizations from the cultural variables were consistent across both years: Former British colonies tended to be Protestant, and deathrates from cancer, heart disease, and suicide went together.

In general, the predictor variables were more diverse than expected. Whether they explain human rights attainments remains to be seen in chapter 6.

NOTES

1. All variables were screened for normality, using the Shapiro-Wilk (1965) test. Except for scaled variables (those wherein rankings were made), all variables that had a

coefficient of normality below .85 were transformed logarithmically to pull in the tails of the distribution. In a few cases, however, even logarithmic transformations did not succeed in normalizing a variable.

2. More technically, the factor analysis used a principal components analysis with 1.0 as the estimated initial intercorrelation of each variable with itself; factors with eigenvalues over 1.0 were rotated orthogonally (varimax procedure), using the algorithm developed by the Statistical Analysis System Institute (1982: chapter 21). After trying three alternative forms of cluster analysis, the clustering procedure used herein is based on an oblique component analysis related to multiple group factor analysis (Anderberg 1973; Harman 1976), as programmed by the Statistical Analysis System Institute under the acronym Varclus (SAS Institute 1982:chapter 32). Varclus begins with a principal components analysis, as in factor analysis, but after splitting data initially into two clusters, the program recalculates principal components in order to determine whether the next eigenvalue exceeds a certain amount; if so, the program proceeds to split variables from an existing cluster to form a new cluster until the remaining variance is such that no further cluster can be identified with an eigenvalue over 1.0. As a result of the recalculation interactions, there are generally fewer clusters than factors.

3. Although a cutoff at an eigenvalue of 1.0 is customary in factor analysis, the scree test is sometimes used instead. According to the scree test, a precipitant drop in eigenvalues marks the end of meaningful factors. Thus, the scree test would identify only two factors in the analysis of A and B variables combined.

4. A cluster analysis was unnecessary, since hierarchical relationships were not being tested.

Chapter 5

CHANGES

From 1982 to 1986 there were a few changes in the family of nations. The world emerged from recession. Argentina and the Philippines shed authoritarian for democratic rule, thanks to "people's power" activism. As indicated in human rights judgments by Charles Humana, Moslem fundamentalism was on the rise. Otherwise, changes were more subtle. Although one study argues that civil and political rights declined in the 1980s (Gupta, Jongman, and Schmid 1994), our task is to determine whether these changes fall into a coherent pattern.

Analysis of human rights data across eighty-eight countries, as determined in chapter 4, enabled us to conclude that civil and political rights develop independently from economic and social rights. What about the changes? Do human rights improve or decline in predictable patterns for all countries? The purpose of this chapter is to ascertain dimensions from changes in human rights, based on differences in each country sampled between 1982 and 1986.

METHOD

As in chapter 4, multivariate statistical procedures are used herein. Arithmetic differences in value between 1982 and 1986 were calculated, and both factor analyses and cluster analyses were run on the change data.[1] Not all variables are available for both years, so the data set is somewhat smaller.

CIVIL AND POLITICAL RIGHTS

Some forty-five variables measuring civil and political rights changed from 1982 to 1986. These are analyzed below.

Factor Analysis (A Variables)

A total of sixteen factors were extracted with eigenvalues over 1.0 (Table 5.1; all tables and figures appear in Appendix C). The first factor extracted less than 5 percent of the variance, the second factor accounted for about 3 percent of the variance, and variances for the remaining factors tapered gradually downward.

The main theme of the first factor was improved *judicial rights*. Countries that made incremental advances in the right to civilian, public trials were also easing indefinite detention and restrictions on in-country travel, while granting more presumption of innocence, speedier court proceedings, and limiting the ability of law enforcement authorities to undertake searches or to censor mail.

Prisoner's rights appeared on factor 2, especially limits on capital punishment and a reduction in torture methods by the police. Improvements in these two rights were also associated with a reduction in the number of countries forbidden for external travel.

Both factors 1 and 2 had moderate loadings for a *political right* (freedom to peacefully assemble) and a *freedom of expression right* (freedom to teach and receive information). Evidently, improvements in the administration of justice did not occur in isolation from advances in some of the most basic civil and political rights.

Restrictions on the *right to travel* appeared prominently on factor 3. Two *women's rights* variables (right to marry and equal rights in marriage) also had moderate loadings.

Reduced assertion of *self-determination rights* dominated factor 4, that is, declines in the percentage of ethnonationalists and number of separatist movements. Also moderately associated with this factor was an increase in independent book publishing.

Freedom from government terrorism rights came together on factor 5. Appropriately, there was a strong association with a reduction in the practice of stripping citizens of their nationality. More subtly, countries abandoning state terror also granted more independence to radio and television stations.

Most of the remaining factors had moderate or high loadings for only one or two variables. They are of little help in delineating analytically coherent dimensions.

Cluster Analysis (A Variables)

There were ten clusters with eigenvalues over 1.0, explaining only 46.9 percent of the variance (Figure 5.1 in Appendix C). The cluster tree consisted of two superclusters; the first contained about twice as many variables as the second. The core of the first supercluster had a complex structure. *Judicial rights* were prominent on one subcluster. *Freedom of expression rights* dominated another subcluster, which was closely joined by a subcluster containing several *prisoner's rights* and *judicial rights*. All these subclusters merged together, and then *political rights* defined the final subcluster. Procedural rights, thus, improved together.

A mixture of rights was at the core of the second supercluster. *Freedom of conscience rights* and *freedom from government terrorism rights* merged with the core subcluster first, and then *self-determination rights* joined the supercluster. The second supercluster, thus, combined more substantive rights for nonmainstream groups.

Implications

The factor analysis demonstrates that decreased or increased fairness in the administration of justice was the most basic type of change in civil and political rights from 1982 to 1986. *Judicial rights* and *prisoner's rights*, in other words, were the most likely to fluctuate. *Minority rights* and *women's rights* were less important in the factor analysis, though this is an artifact of the database; had more variables measured these rights, they might have appeared on factor 1.

The cluster analysis reaffirmed this judgment. The rights of citizens in general were portrayed on the first supercluster, with abandonment of arbitrary state power as the central theme. Improved civil and political rights for nonmainstream groups (gays and Lesbians, minorities, women, workers) gravitated toward the second supercluster.

ECONOMIC AND SOCIAL RIGHTS

Eighty-four variables measuring economic and social rights displayed changes from 1982 to 1986. Patterns were rather difficult to discern.

Factor Analysis (B Variables)

Whereas factor analyses of economic and social rights extracted an enormous first factor for 1982 and 1986, improvements in these rights were quite idiosyncratic. Some thirty-one factors emerged from eighty-four variables with eigenvalues over 1.0 (Table 5.2). The largest factor accounted for just 4.0 percent of the variance, the next largest extracted 3.3 percent, and the remaining factors trailed off explaining fractionally smaller percentages of the variance.

Only five variables had loadings above ±.40 on factor 1. All referred to increased *cultural rights*, including the right of access to books, films, and museums. The highest loadings on factor 2 indicated increasingly *lucrative exports*; moderately associated with the factor was a decrease in the rate of stillbirths and an increase in deathrate due to infectious-parasitic diseases. Factor 3 was defined by increased *primary school attendance*. The highest loadings on factor 4 were increased consumer spending per capita, increased female literacy, increased government spending on R & D, and decreased filing of patents per capita. Increased caloric and protein intake dominated factor 5, which thus shows that the *right to food* did not improve along with the right to clothing or shelter. Improved *social rights* and *health rights* of various sorts defined factor 6. Increased college attendance variables were at the top of factor 7, which may be called a *right to higher education* factor. Factor 8 brought together increased years of compulsory education and higher percentages of imported films, thus combining *educational rights* with *cultural rights*. The remaining factors pertained to just one or two variables and are not explicated further.

Cluster Analysis (B Variables)

Twenty-eight clusters formed, explaining 57.1 percent of the variance (Figure 5.2). The first supercluster had thirty-one variables, the second thirty-four variables, and a third supercluster of eighteen variables split off from the first.

Advancements in *educational rights* were at the core of the first supercluster. Some *worker's rights* and *health rights* were also prominent.

Cultural rights defined the second supercluster, though negative and positive trends were present. One subcluster, for example, combined increases in *educational rights* with decreased spending on R & D. Another second set of clusters paired increased attainment of *cultural rights* (access to books, films, and museums) with decreased *self-determination rights*.

The third supercluster brought together advances in *social rights, standard of living rights, health rights,* and *cultural rights.* The *right to strike* was decreasingly exercised along with improvements in work-injury welfare benefits, but these variables were at the periphery of the third supercluster.

Implications

From 1982 to 1986, overall changes in economic and social rights did not occur in a clearly dimensionalizable manner. Most of the time, an increase in one social and economic variable could be predicted neither from knowledge about trends overall nor from trends of related variables. Mainstream and non-mainstream groups, however, marched to quite different drums.

CIVIL, POLITICAL, ECONOMIC, AND SOCIAL RIGHTS

To determine interrelationships across both sets of data, civil and political rights were pooled with economic and social rights. The result, a matrix of 121 intercorrelated variables, was also subjected to factor analysis and cluster analysis.

Factor Analysis (A + B Variables)

The sixteen factors derived from changes in political and civil rights plus the thirty-one factors from improvements in economic and social rights would appear to add up to forty-seven factors. In the factor analysis of all these variables, forty-two factors with eigenvalues over 1.0 were extracted instead (Table 5.3). The first factor accounted for only 8 percent of the variance, the second factor 4 percent of the variance, and the remaining factors trailed off gradually.

The first factor snared sixteen *civil and political rights* variables with six *social and economic rights* above the level ±.40. Improvements in *civil and political rights* joined hands with increased film viewing but decreased teachers' salary allotments from national education budgets.

The second factor contained moderate to high loadings for five variables measuring various *economic and social rights*. No civil and political rights had loadings above ±.40 on this factor. Associated variables pertained to *cultural rights*.

Minority rights were found on factor 3, but later factors were not readily interpretable. Advances in *women's rights* were not found together on any of the forty-two factors.

Cluster Analysis (A + B Variables)

The cluster analysis (Figure 5.3) whittled the variables down to thirty-six clusters, which explained only 54.6 percent of the variance. Two large superclusters formed with about the same number of variables. Within each supercluster there was a cluster so sizeable that four superclusters are presented herein.

The first supercluster incorporated most of the *civil and political rights*, with *freedom of movement rights, judicial rights*, and *freedom of expression rights* at the core (Figure 5.3a). Some *economic and social rights* were also at the core— decreased stillbirths and a reduced percentage of textbooks among all books published. Civil-political *minority rights* and *women's rights* were found on the first supercluster, but not at the core.

The third supercluster, which emerged from the first, was divided into two parts (Figure 5.3b). One set of subclusters featured *prisoner's rights, political rights*, and a smattering of *economic and social rights*. The other set had more *economic and social rights*, but only two had a common theme—increased primary school enrollment, that is, variables indicating *educational rights*.

The second supercluster was dominated by *economic and social rights* (Figure 5.3c). Two sets of subclusters were at the core of the second supercluster, with *cultural rights* and *health rights* more prominent than other types of rights. Among the civil-political rights on this supercluster were increased *minority rights* and *women's rights*.

The fourth supercluster, which broke away from the second supercluster, was divided into two parts. One part gave prominence to some increased *cultural rights*, the second to decreased *worker's rights*.

Implications

In general, a chasm existed between advances in civil and political rights, on the one hand, and economic and social rights, on the other hand. In the factor analysis, increased civil and political rights were associated with increased intellectual freedom. The cluster analyses had more ambiguous results. Improvements in minority rights and women's rights were at the core of none of the superclusters, and were not found on the first factors in the factor analyses, indicating that they were next in line for redress after the mainstream cashed in on human rights advances.

CONCLUSION

The purpose of this chapter was to determine whether improvements in human rights over time might yield dimensions similar to comparisons of countries in particular years. The results suggest that the specific provisions within the International Covenant on Civil and Political Rights and the International Covenant on Economic, Social, and Cultural Rights do not identify empirically separate dimensions. Instead, improvement patterns are similar for civil and political rights as well as for economic and social rights, but the two types of rights change at different rates. In addition, improvements for mainstream and nonmainstream groups also proceed at a different pace for both civil-political rights and economic-social rights. In general, thus, the longitudinal analyses are similar to the cross-sectional analyses.

NOTE

1. As in chapter 4, all variables were tested for normality. Except for ranked data, variables lacking normality were transformed logarithmically. Where a log transformation did not produce sufficient normality, an alternative procedure was to reduce the numeric value of the tail of a distribution so that it was closer to the second largest or smallest value for that variable.

Chapter 6

RELATIONSHIPS

In the two previous chapters, a large number of indicators of human rights was reduced through multivariate analysis to a smaller set of empirical dimensions. We know now that civil and political rights are empirically distinct from economic and social rights, both of which have various subdimensions. Now is the time to determine which non-human-rights variables, if any, best explain relative attainments and improvements in human rights.

An important task is to determine whether any of the theories of human rights are consistent with the data. To review, *economism* expects that high levels of industrialization and economic conditions will alone predict higher human rights performance and improvements over time. *Developmentalism* adds the need for economic growth as a precondition to granting human rights. *Liberal democracy theory* goes beyond developmentalism, positing the free flow of information, competitive political parties, and a neutral bureaucracy as preconditions to progress in human rights. *Social democracy theory* argues that human rights do not really advance until a liberal democracy becomes a welfare state. *Mobilization theory* predicts that organized groups must protest injustices so that governments will be forced to grant human rights. *Group conflict theory* blames social diversity for shortfalls in human rights. *Power elite theory* views repression of human rights as a tool by which elites maintain power over nonelites, as in societies with little civilian control of the military due to external conflict. *Marxian theory* sees the denial of human rights as a function of the inherent socioeconomic inequality of capitalism, both inside countries and within the capitalist world economy. *Frustration-aggression theory* links short-term economic downswings with human rights repression. *Freudian theory* believes that the imperatives of industrialization create a longing to undertake savage violations of human rights. *Mass society theory* points to extremely rapid economic growth as the wellspring for political turmoil that prompts governments to suppress human rights. *Relativists*, however, expect that patterns for Western societies will not apply to non-Western societies, and thus predict that regressions with less developed countries (LDCs) will differ radically from regressions with a sample of developed countries. *Trade-off theory*, which expects improvements in civil-political rights to result in reductions in economic-social rights and vice versa, is inconsistent with the evidence presented in chapter 5.

Most of these theories can be tested by regressing C variables onto A and B variables. In order to find relationships between predictor variables and the two sets of human rights, this chapter will undertake several empirical exercises. First, the C variables will be factor analyzed along with the A and B rights variables in order to determine whether any close relationships exist. Second, predictor variables will be regressed onto each empirical dimension of human rights. The multivariate procedure is stepwise regression, which identifies a variable that best explains a dependent variable first, and then proceeds to find the second best predictor variable, and so forth until all possible variance has been explained.[1]

The factor analyses and regressions will begin separately with data for 1982 and 1986, followed by analyses of the change data. Regressions will first be run with the full sample of eighty-eight countries. Parallel regressions will be run on the sixty-seven less developed countries, that is, the full sample minus Australia, Canada, Japan, New Zealand, the United States, and the countries of Western Europe outside the former Iron Curtain. With these two sets of regressions, it will be possible to determine whether the same predictor variables explain results for both samples. Alternatively, LDCs may exhibit different patterns from developed countries.

PREDICTING CIVIL AND POLITICAL RIGHTS

Factor Analysis

In a factor analysis of A and C variables, some twenty-two factors emerged for the 1982 data and twenty-three factors for the 1986 data. The first two factors together extracted about 36 percent of the variance; thereafter, there was a sharp drop. The first factors for both 1982 and 1986 represented a broad spectrum of *civil and political rights* (Tables 6.1 and 6.2; all tables and figures appear in Appendix C). In each case, two predictor variables had reasonably high loadings: Respect for civil and political rights was higher when the size of the parliamentary majority was smaller and the parliament had more political parties. There was also a consistent if moderate loading for lower military budgets in countries with higher levels of civil and political rights. The second factor captured *economic development* variables. The only human rights variable with a prominent association was freedom from serfdom, slavery, and forced labor, though gay and Lesbian rights had a moderate loading on this factor for 1986.

Factor 3 for 1986, which highlighted *women's civil-political rights*, also had moderate loadings for voting restrictions, leftists in parliament, and deathrates due to cancer, heart disease, and suicide. Factor 7 for 1982 linked domestic violence deathrate with "disappearances" and political executions; for 1986, the latter two had high loadings on factor 8 along with war propensity. There were no other convergences.

In case there was a time-lag effect, the next exercise was to determine predictor variables that best explained improvements in civil and political rights from 1982 to 1986. To answer this question, a factor analysis was run with C variables for 1982 along with A variables for 1986 (Table 6.3). Among the resulting twenty-two factors, the first reproduced the broad *civil and political rights* factor, and *economic development* defined the second factor; together, they extracted 37 percent of the variance, but later factors were of much less consequence. Many political parties and small majorities in 1982 were prominent on the *civil and political rights* factor in 1986; per capita spending on welfare had a moderate loading. As before, the *economic development* factor had a rather high loading for freedom from serfdom; equality of the sexes in divorce and marriage and gay and Lesbian rights had moderate loadings. Factor 5 brought together percentage of Moslems with limitations on marriage and voting rights. Factor 7 linked separatism with ethnolinguistic heterogeneity and trade dependency. The other factors were uninformative.

Next, C variables for 1982 were regressed onto changes in A variables from 1982 to 1986 (Table 6.4). Among the resulting twenty-eight factors, the first was *economic growth*. The only associated civil-political right was increased sex equality in marriage from 1982 to 1986. *Improved civil and political rights* clustered on the second factor, but no C variable had a loading above ±.40 on the factor. The first two factors together accounted for 20 percent of the variance, but there was a sharp drop in explained variance thereafter. Factor 3, defined by variables indicating a *remilitarized society*, had moderate loadings for decreased restrictions on voting and on marriage. *Increased foreign conflict* was associated with decreased conscripted labor and decreased freedom of external travel on factor 4 and with decreased gay and Lesbian rights on factor 10. The percentage of GNP extracted as taxes in 1982 was prominent on factor 5 along with increased "disappearances" and decreased revocations of nationality, thus suggesting an *increased government terrorism* dimension. According to factor 6, countries that stopped indoctrinating schoolchildren with a state ideology or religion by 1986 had a lot of trade dependency. Increased ethnolinguistic homogeneity had a moderate loading on factor 8 along with measures of separatism.

The final factor analysis involved changes in both A and C variables from 1982 to 1986 (Table 6.5). Among thirty factors with eigenvalues over 1.0, the first two together accounted for 16 percent of the variance, and later factors were much less important statistically. *Economic growth* variables dominated the first factor, which was associated with improved human rights in regard to marriage. *Improved civil and political rights*, which defined factor 2, had only two C variables with moderate loadings: decreased percentage of direct taxes and decreased voter turnout. Factor 3, which was defined by *remilitarization*, had moderate loadings for decreased rights of broadcasters and trade unionists. Factor 4, which indicated *increased government terrorism*, had a high loading for increased domestic violence deaths and a moderate loading for increased voter turnout. Factor 6 had high loadings for increased taxation, decreased revocations of nationality, and reduced "disappearances." Factor 7 brought together increased percentage of workers in agriculture with increased monitoring by human rights organizations. Factor 8 linked *increased foreign conflict* with the return of the death penalty.

Liberal democratic theory explains most of these results. A competitive party system is far more important than any other element in accounting for rights of mainstream groups. Developmentalism, however, best applies to nonmainstream civil and political rights. Power elite theory seems to account for temporary crackdowns in mainstream rights, due either to domestic or foreign conflict.

Regression Analysis

Although an omnibus *civil and political rights* factor emerged in chapter 4 when indicators of all types of human rights were in one pool, distinct subtypes emerged when multivariate analyses were performed on the A variables alone. In the regressions, accordingly, each subdimension of *civil and political rights* is represented below by a variable that best indicates each factor. Variable A9 ("disappearances"), for example, was repeatedly at the top of *freedom from government terrorism* clusters and factors and thus can be used as a representative indicator. *Freedom of movement rights* were best operationalized by the number of countries allowed for external travel (A20). The right to teach ideas and receive information (A32), one of the *freedom of expression rights*, had a very high loading throughout the multivariate analyses. Limitations on the right to vote (A45) emerged as one of the best indicators of *political rights*. Freedom from mail censorship (A27) was the most prominent type of *privacy right*. Among *judicial rights*, the most central tended to be the right to civilian and public trials (A21). Freedom from indefinite détention (A17) was the most representative of *prisoner's rights*. The importance of women in politics (A49) best indexed *women's rights*. The percentage of separatists (A2) is chosen as an indicator of lack of *minority rights*. *Gay and Lesbian rights* (A28) had only one variable and played a modest role in the multivariate analyses. In sum, ten types of *civil and political rights* are to be explained.

For each variable, ten regressions are run. Half use the full sample, and the other five are based on the LDC sample. The first two regressions pool A and C variables for 1982 and 1986, and the rest parallel the various combinations of A and C variables undertaken in the factor analyses.

Freedom from Government Terrorism. About 33 percent of the variance in "disappearances" for 1982 was consistently explained by the ratio of arms import purchases to GNP, and another 11 percent was explained by the number of deaths due to domestic violence (Table 6.6, a, b). For 1986, the only consistent predictor was government violence against citizens, which accounted for 11 to 21 percent of the variance (Table 6.6, c, d). The percentage of military troops abroad was the best predictor for LDCs, explaining 18 percent of the variance in "disappearances" for 1986. Regressing 1982 C variables onto "disappearances" for 1986, the best and most consistent predictor was the percentage of years at civil war since 1960, which accounted for about 15 percent of the variance (Table 6.6, e, f). "Disappearances" decreased from 1982 to 1986 in countries that had low tax revenues and low arms imports as a percentage of GNP in 1982; the two variables explained about 40 percent of the variance, but tax revenues contributed twice as much (Table 6.6, g, h). About half the variance in decreased "disappearances" from 1982 to 1986 was explained by changes in three C variables that made nearly equal contributions: decreased deaths due to domestic violence, decreased taxes as a percentage of GNP, and decreased workers employed in agriculture (Table 6.6, i, j). Decreased arms imports as a percentage of GNP added 7 percent to the regressions. In short, government terrorism was associated with a general atmosphere of militarization and domestic violence, perhaps suggesting a rational actor version of power elite theory wherein leaders weigh costs and benefits of repressive acts in order to retain power. A campaign to reduce "disappearances" must appeal to the need of rulers for greater stability, though not at the cost of even more repression.

Freedom of Movement. The percentage of years under military rule since 1960 was the best and only consistent predictor for 1982, explaining about 20 percent of the variance in the number of countries forbidden for external travel (Table 6.7, a, b). For 1986, the percentage of seats held in parliament by the majority party accounted for about 25 percent of the variance for the total sample but less than half as much for the LDC sample; the best predictor for the LDC sample, heart disease deathrate, explained 16 percent of the variance (Table 6.7, c, d). Regressing 1982 C variables onto the number of countries forbidden for external travel in 1986, the only consistent predictor, accounting for 6 to 7 percent of the variance for the two samples, was a high rate of foreign investment (Table 6.7, e, f). The best predictor for the full sample was the size of the majority party, while heart disease deathrates best predicted later restrictions on foreign travel for LDCs; the two accounted for from 21 to 26 percent of the variance. Regressing 1982 C variables onto reductions in foreign travel restrictions from 1982 to 1986, the only consistent predictor was radios per capita; for the total sample, this variable explained only 5 percent of the variance, though for LDCs radio acquisition was the best predictor, accounting for 13 percent of the variance (Table 6.7, g, h). Explaining 16 percent of the variance, lower heart disease deathrates in 1982 best predicted decreased restrictions on foreign travel for the full sample. Finally, reductions in official violence against citizens and reduced direct tax revenues per capita each explained nearly 10 percent of the variance in increased freedom of external travel (Table 6.7, i, j). Consistent with the theory of liberal democracy, decreased restrictions on external travel occurred along with a loosening of elite control as evidenced by small legislative majorities, reduced direct taxes as opposed to indirect taxes, decreased government violence, and increased radios per capita. The connection with heart disease deathrate appears to be that societies with oppressive governments produce stress for their citizens, consistent with mass society theory.

Freedom of Expression. Consistently, the smaller the size of the majority party or legislative coalition, the more freedom to teach ideas and receive information. For 1982 and 1986, the explained variance was more than 30 percent (Table 6.8, a, b, c, d). The smaller the majority in 1982, the greater the freedom of expression in 1986; the variance explained for the full sample was 40 percent, but 24 percent for LDCs (Table 6.8, e, f). The best predictor of increased intellectual freedom among 1982 C variables was government violence, which accounted for about 10 percent of the variance in both samples (Table 6.8, g, h). Lifting of military rule explained 10 percent of the variance in increased intellectual freedom (Table 6.8, i, j). In short, liberal democracy and power elite theories best account for the results: As societies shed military rule and adopt competitive party systems, prospects for intellectual freedom improve.

Political Rights. Military rule accounted for about 10 percent of the variance in voting restrictions for 1982, whereas government violence against citizens explained 22 to 36 percent of the variance for 1986 (Table 6.9, a, b, c, d). Low newspaper circulation in 1982 explained 17 to 31 percent of the variance in voting restrictions in 1986, and fewer parliamentary parties added 9 percent more to the explanation (Table 6.9, e, f). The situation was similar in regard to improvements in voting rights. About one-tenth of the variance in increased voting rights was explained by a lower percentage of years with coups as of 1982 (Table 6.9, g, h). Lack of government violence against citizens in 1982 was a slightly better predictor for the full sample, as was a lower extent of trade export dependency; the two variables each accounted for about 10 percent of the variance. Changes in C variables provided no consistent predictor of increased voting rights. Countries shedding military juntas in the full sample best managed to extend voting rights, whereas increased telephones and television sets per capita had the same effect for LDCs (Table 6.9, i, j). The three variables explained from 7 to 14 percent of the variance. Thus, liberal democracy theory, as the opposite of power elite theory, appears to explain why societies broaden political rights.

Privacy Rights. The smaller the size of the majority party, the more freedom from mail censorship and wiretapping. For 1982 and 1986, smallness of the majority accounted for more than 30 percent of the variance in mail privacy (Table 6.10, a, b, c, d). The size of the majority in 1982 explained 40 percent of 1986 mail privacy for the full sample, but only 13 percent for LDCs (Table 6.10, e, f). Lower percentages of military spending added 11 percent to the variance in mail privacy for the full sample and 31 percent for LDCs. Decreased mail censorship was a different story. Among C variables for 1982, smaller arms imports in military budgets and number of parliamentary parties for LDCs accounted for 6 percent of the variance in increased mail privacy (Table 6.10, g, h). Countries abandoning civil war from 1982 to 1986 showed the most dramatic increase in mail privacy; about 18 percent of the variance was explained thereby (Table 6.10, i, j). Consistent with power elite theory, mail censorship appears to be an expedient for a one-party regime coping with civil or foreign war to stay in power. When the threat passes, parliamentary liberal democracy and mail privacy can resume.

Judicial Rights. For 1982 and 1986, the smaller the majority party, the fairer a country's trials. The variance explained in full samples for both years was about one-third; for LDCs, the percentage was only one-sixth (Table 6.11, a, b, c, d). Number of nongovernmental terrorist incidents added 6 percent to both samples for 1986. Low military budgets in 1982 consistently predicted fairer trials in 1986, but the variance explained was only 6 percent for the full sample and 16 percent for LDCs (Table 6.11, e, f). Smaller majority parties was the best predictor in the full sample, accounting for one-third of the variance; for LDCs, skimpy majorities added 8 percent to the regression prediction. Increases in fairness of trials were explained by different sets of variables. Using C variables for 1982, countries experiencing fewer coups, low percentages of arms imports in military budgets, yet frequent civil wars had freer judiciaries by 1986; the three variables equally accounted for about 8 percent of the variance (Table 6.11, g, h). Countries ending civil wars between 1982 and 1986 showed the most increase in fair trials over the same time period; nearly one-fourth of the variance was explained thereby (Table 6.11, i, j). Two other variables added a total of about 15 percent to the explained variance in increased judicial rights: increased trade as a percentage of GNP and increased years at war. Consistent with liberal democracy theory, fair trials are best guaranteed in societies with a free flow of trade, where opposition parties and even nongovernmental terrorism can thrive. To increase judicial rights requires a dismantling of military power elites, but this can best occur when civil wars (a likely cause of nongovernmental terrorism) stop.

Prisoner's Rights. Once again, the tinier the parliamentary majority, the more civil and political rights—in this case, the more freedom from indefinite detention (A17). For 1982, small majority size accounted for nearly 40 percent of the variance in the full sample, though half that for the LDCs (Table 6.12, a, b). For 1986, the variance explained by majority size was about 15 percent, though the best predictor was less government violence against citizens, which accounted for just over 40 percent of the variance in lawful detention for the full sample, and half as much for the LDC sample (Table 6.12, c, d). Regressions of 1982 C variables onto the practice of indefinite detention for 1986 yielded no consistent predictor. For the full sample, television sets per capita accounted for about one-third of the variance, and smallness of the ruling majority for nearly one-seventh of the variance in freedom from indefinite detention (Table

6.12, e). The best predictor for the LDC sample was the smallness of the military budget, but only one-eighth of the variance was explained by this variable (Table 6.12, f). Regressions involving improvements in freedom from indefinite detention from 1982 to 1986 bagged little variance. One C variable was a consistent predictor: Countries with lower arms imports as a percentage of GNP in 1986 tended to ease off the practice of indefinite detention, though only 5 to 6 percent of the variance was explained by this variable (Table 6.12, g, h). Finally, increased years at war from 1982 to 1986 explained 13 percent of the variance in decreased use of indefinite detention over the same time interval (Table 6.12, i, j). Evidently the practice of indefinite detention is a tool used by power elites; when the military no longer needs to cling to power, indefinite detention can be discarded. Consistent with liberal democratic theory, parliamentary democracy appears to be crucial in protecting the rights of prisoners. The linkage between increased wars and reduced indefinite detention suggests that the rise of foreign adversaries prompts elites to be more selective in defining internal enemies, consistent with power elite theory.

Minority Rights. Ethnolinguistic heterogeneity explained about half the variance in the percentage of separatists for 1982 (Table 6.13, a, b). For 1986, which included Ted Gurr's various measures of minority grievances, the extent of political grievances and percentage of leftist parties in parliament each accounted for about 15 percent of the variance, but heterogeneity washed out (Table 6.13, c, d). Using 1982 C variables to account for the percentage of separatists in 1986, the best predictors were the deathrate due to foreign conflict and ethnolinguistic heterogeneity, which each explained about 10 percent of the variance (Table 6.13, e, f). Regressions were then run on improved attainments from 1982 to 1986. Results showed that separatism declined most among countries that were ethnolinguistically homogeneous; the variance explained was about 30 percent (Table 6.13, g, h). Finally, changes in C variables were regressed onto decreased separatism from 1982 to 1986, and about 25 percent of the variance was accounted for by two variables: increased telephones per capita and decreased workers in agriculture (Table 6.13, i, j). The former variable was more than twice as important as the former. In short, minority rights appear least respected in poor countries with heterogeneous populations, consistent with group conflict theory. Liberal democratic theory appears partially vindicated, for a developed information infrastructure is associated with lower minority discontent. Mobilization theory is inadequate since the extent of grievances is associated with fewer rather than more minority rights.

Women's Rights. The best predictors of the role of women in politics for 1982 were smaller shares of a government's budget devoted to the military sector and higher levels of social welfare spending (Table 6.14, a, b). Together, the two variables explained about 25 percent of the variance, although the former was twice as important as the latter. For 1986, lack of government violence and higher levels of U.S. civilian aid out of GNP were the most consistent top predictors; the former accounted for approximately 20 percent of the variance, the latter about 6 percent (Table 6.14, c, d). Regressing 1982 C variables onto 1986 A variables did not provide a consistent picture. Lower percentages of military rule since 1960 explained 14 percent of the variance in the full sample, and GNP from U.S. civilian aid topped predictors for LDCs at 13 percent (Table 6.14, e, f). Among C variables for 1982, improvements in the status of women in politics from 1982 to 1986 yielded two consistent predictors: the share of U.S. military aid out of GNP and a smaller majority party in parliament (Table 6.14, g, h). In both cases, the explained variance was 11 percent. Finally, increases of the workforce in agriculture topped predictors of improvements in the status of women in politics from 1982 to 1986, accounting for about 12 percent of the variance; increased deathrate due to heart disease and increased taxes out of GNP each explained about 8 percent of the variance in the increased role of women in politics (Table 6.14, i, j). These results indicate some support for social democratic theory, insofar as weaker military elites, a favorable investment climate, and a stronger welfare state evidently pave the way for more rights for women. The role of U.S. aid suggests that violations of women's rights weighed heavily in denying foreign assistance in the 1980s. The linkage between women's rights and higher percentages of agricultural workers, however, is anomalous.

Rights of Gays and Lesbians. Per capita television sets accounted for 25 to 31 percent of the variance in increased gay/Lesbian rights in the full sample of countries in 1982 and 1986, and smallness of the majority party added 5 percent for 1982 and 15 percent for 1986 (Table 6.15, a, c). Among LDCs, the size of the Catholic population explained 14 percent of the variance in 1982 and 21 percent in 1986 (Table 6.15, b, d). For 1986, high deathrates due to heart disease added from 6 to 10 percent to the variance in gay/Lesbian rights (Table 6.15, c, d). Using 1982 data to explain 1986 gay/Lesbian rights provided similar results, though per capita welfare spending topped the full sample, explaining 33 percent of the variance, and Catholicism was again the top predictor for sample of LDCs, accounting for 21 percent (Table 6.15, e, f). No predictor variable for 1982 explained 5 or more percent of the variance in increased gay/Lesbian rights for the full sample, but for LDCs some 10 percent of variance in gay and Lesbian rights was explained by both a smaller tax bite and lower levels of arms exports (Table 6.15, g, h). Reduced military spending from 1982 to 1986 explained 6 to 7 percent of advances in rights for gays and Lesbians over the same years for both samples (Tables 6.15, i, j). Decreased foreign conflict deaths added 7 percent to the explanation for the full sample, whereas a withdrawal of troops from abroad added 14 percent to the equation for LDCs. Liberal democratic theory best accounts for these findings, as the data suggest that a transformation from a militarized to a civilian government with a wider information infrastructure serves as a seedbed for more rights for gays and Lesbians.

The LDC sample did not always agree with the full sample. Looking at the differences, a pattern emerges. LDCs that were most likely to have higher levels of civil and political rights also had lower military budgets and greater signs of improvement in information infrastructure (telephones and televisions). U.S. civilian aid tended to predict better civil and political rights for LDCs, unlike the full sample.

Implications

Consistent with liberal democratic theory, where economies become more developed, information is more readily available, multiparty political systems arise, and civil and political rights are increasingly observed. Power elites coping with domestic unrest tend to clamp down on civil and political rights in order to maintain power, but they can be undermined by increased social communications, which lead to stronger liberal democracy. Thus, power elite theory is the other side of the liberal democratic coin.

Minority rights and gay and Lesbian rights improve more quickly when a more prosperous liberal democracy is perfected. Women's rights are more fully observed after a welfare state is in place.

The findings suggest that restrictions on rights are linked to the archetypal decision, made some millennia ago by power-seeking men, to assert the primacy of violence as the final arbiter of political authority (Eisler 1987). When the military pretends to be indispensable in society, civil and political rights are restricted. As the military recedes in importance, civil and political rights blossom.

PREDICTING ECONOMIC AND SOCIAL RIGHTS

Factor Analysis

The next exercise was to factor analyze B and C variables together, providing a database of some 140 variables. Economic development variables, not unexpectedly, were found on the same dimensions as attainments on economic and social rights.

For 1982, thirty-four factors were extracted with eigenvalues over 1.0 (Table 6.16). The first factor explained about 30 percent of the variance, the second factor accounted for only 8 percent of the variance, the third factor extracted about 5 percent of the variance, and the remaining factors dropped off incrementally in explanatory power. The first factor attracted most of the B variables, especially those that appeared to define the dimension as a *qualify of life* factor. Thirteen C variables, all measuring economic development, also had high loadings. The second factor identified a *worker's rights* dimension; the only related C variables were more political parties in parliament, a lower percentage of seats held by left-wing parties, and a lower percentage of seats held by the largest political party or ruling coalition. The third factor profiled patterns of *life expectancy*: Countries with high rates of death due to cancer, heart disease, and suicide had excellent child survival rates, though this may be simply a demographic tautology. In the remaining factors, the only finding of interest was the linkage between trade partner dependency and industrial accidents.

There were two more factors for 1986 than for 1982. Once again, about 30 percent of the variance was explained by the first factor; factor 2 accounted for nearly 9 percent, factor 3 for about 7 percent, factor 4 for 5 percent, and the remaining factors trailed off in explanatory power (Table 6.17). The first factor again brought together *quality of life* variables along with economic development measures, though with moderate loadings for the latter, as well as absence of government violence against citizens and ethnolinguistic homogeneity. The second factor once more tapped variance in measures of *worker's rights* and of centrist parliamentary democracy, but there were some new associated variables: extent of economic freedom, low foreign investment as a percentage of GDP, and low percentages of military spending. Factor 3 was a clone of the third factor for 1982, indicating *life expectancy*. Factor 4 juxtaposed minority grievances with *social and economic discrimination against minorities*. Factor 5 brought together measures of *militarization*, but no variables relevant to economic and social rights emerged. Factor 6 linked trade dependency with *economic growth*. After that, the results were useless for testing theories of human rights.

Combining 1982 C with 1986 B variables, thirty-six factors were extracted (Table 6.18). The first factor explained 35 percent of the variance, the second factor only 9 percent, the third 5 percent, the fourth 4 percent, and the rest dropped off gradually. The first factor had higher loadings for both *quality of life* and economic development variables. *Worker's rights* dominated factor 2 along with number of parties in parliament and smallness of the parliamentary majority. Factor 3 had no crossover between B and C variables. *Women's rights* and military spending had the highest loading on factor 4 along with a high positive loading for percentage of Catholics and a high negative loading for percentage of Moslems. Factor 5 resembled the *economic growth* factor of Table 6.17 without trade dependency. No other factors provided clues to possible relationships between B and C variables.

Improvements in economic and social rights from 1982 to 1986 had a similar pattern when factor analyzed with C variables for 1982 (Table 6.19). The first factor accounted for about one-seventh of the variance, the second and third factors plunged considerably in explanatory power, and the remaining thirty-nine factors were of little consequence. *Economic development* variables dominated factor 1; associated B variables were decreased consumer spending per capita and increased patents per capita. The second factor extracted a dimension of *militarization* from C variables alone. Factor 3 combined increased *propensity to strike* in the 1980s with centrist parliamentary democracy though low voter turnout in the early 1980s. Factor 4 linked economic growth with improved purchasing power of exports and improved terms of trade. Otherwise, the factor analysis provided little additional information.

The factor analysis of changes in both B and C variables yielded forty-one factors (Table 6.20). The first factor explained 11 percent of the variance. Factor 2 plunged to 4 percent, and other factors tapered off gradually. *Economic growth* variables dominated factor 1. There were no crossover variables for factor 2, which consisted of *increased enjoyment of cultural rights*. Results for later factors were murky.

These results suggest some validity to the developmentalist theory of human rights. As countries develop economically, the general quality of life improves. More freedom for workers, however, awaits liberal democracy.

Regression Analysis

Although the factor analysis of indicators of economic and social rights in chapter 4 extracted one dominant factor, regressions onto B variables involve the most prominent variable from the factor analyses for each article in the International Covenant on Economic, Social, and Cultural Rights, just in case there are subtle differences. For Article 1, which focuses on broad *economic rights*, the extent of economic freedom (B1) and improvements in terms of trade (B3) tap somewhat different aspects. For Article 2, the percentage of the population suffering from economic discrimination (B5) measures *minority rights*. No *women's rights* factor emerged, so to satisfy the requirements of Article 3 a variable is picked more or less at random: percentage of school-age females in primary school (B58). After Articles 4 and 5, which are procedural, Article 6 sets forth *worker's rights*, which are examined through the variable absence of compulsory work permits and labor conscription (B10). For *just conditions of work*, as enumerated in Article 7, consumer spending per capita (B13) and the percentage of workers injured fatally on the job (B16) measure quite distinct aspects. *Trade union rights*, enumerated in Article 8, are represented by the right of unions to federate (B21). *Welfare rights*, covered in Article 8, are best indexed by the extensiveness of family allowance welfare benefits (B26). *Children's rights* are stated in Article 9; the percentage of infants immunized against diphtheria, tetanus, and whooping cough (B34) proved to be the most representative in the factor analyses. The percentage of housing units with safe water (B40) topped the variables measuring decent *standard of living* in Article 11. Life expectancy (B54) is central to *health rights* in Article 12. The *educational rights* of Article 13 are best captured by the percentage of school-age children enrolled in secondary school (B59). Article 14 asks countries to make *improvements in economic and social rights*, which of course are measured by calculating changes from 1982 to 1986. For *cultural rights* mentioned in Article 15, the percentage of the population registered as users of public libraries (B74) and freedom from state policies to control artistic works (B89) measure subdimensions of the data. After Articles 17 through 19 state procedural aspects of the covenant, Article 20 insists that developed countries provide technical assistance to LDCs. Accordingly, the percentage of GDP devoted to foreign aid (B91) measures *international assistance obligations.*

Economic Rights: Economic Freedom. From 33 to 52 percent of the variance in Raymond Gastil's scale of economic freedom was explained by the percentage of nonleftist parties, and about 10 percent by lower percentages of arms imports out of GNP for both 1982 and 1986 (Table 6.21, a, b, c, d). Regressing 1982 C variables onto economic freedom in 1986 yielded an almost identical result (Table 6.21, e, f). Only one C variable for 1982 consistently predicted improvements in economic freedom from 1982 to 1986: Countries with lower inflation rates were able to release government controls of the market, though only about 10 percent of the variance was explained thereby (Table 6.21, g, h). The final set of regressions sought to predict changes in economic freedom from changes in C variables (Table 6.21, i, j). Increased urbanization did so for the full sample, whereas increased voter turnout and tax revenues topped the predictor variables for LDCs; each variable, however, explained only 5 percent of increased economic freedom. The results suggest that politics is as important as economics in differentiating between the economic freedom of countries, thus supporting liberal democracy theory more than developmentalism.

Economic Rights: Improved Terms of Trade. The best predictor of favorable terms of trade for 1982 was GNP per capita, which accounted for about one-fifth of the variance (Table 6.22, a, b). The percentage of Moslems in a country contributed another 12 percent to the explained variance, indicating that oil-exporting countries were cashing in on their comparative advantage in the early 1980s. For 1986, growth rates explained 17 percent of the variance in improved terms of trade (Table 6.22, c, d). Among C variables for 1982 regressed onto terms of trade in 1986, per capita GNP growth rates were consistent predictors, accounting for about one-sixth of the variance; television sets per capita consistently added from 5 to 9 percent to the explained variance (Table 6.22, e, f). Regressing 1982 C variables onto improved terms of trade for 1982–1986, telephones per capita was the best predictor for both samples (Table 6.22, g, h), accounting for approximately one-fifth of the variance. Increased trade from 1982 to 1986 as a percentage of GNP was the best predictor of increased terms of trade over the same years, accounting for nearly 30 percent of the variance; decreased energy consumption per capita added 5 to 10 percent more to the explained variance (Table 6.22, i, j). The developmentalist theory of human rights seems vindicated in most respects. Countries that most improved terms of trade probably had lower per capita GNPs in 1982 because these countries had fundamental economic strength but were in a temporary economic slump.

Worker's Rights. Lack of compulsory work permits and labor conscription was best explained by the percentage of nonleftist political parties for 1982 and 1986 (Table 6.23, a, b, c, d). The explained variance ranged from 20 to 44 percent. For 1986, four other variables consistently made additional contributions: lower military spending as a percentage of GNP (12 to 13 percent), higher percentages of trade out of GNP (8 to 9 percent), higher rates of inflation (5 to

10 percent), and lower percentages of years at civil war since 1960 (5 to 6 percent). The percentage of nonleftist parties in 1982 was the only consistent predictor of levels of labor freedom in 1986, explaining 26 to 38 percent of the variance (Table 6.23, e, f). Three C variables for 1982 consistently explained reduced labor conscription from 1982 to 1986 (Table 6.23, g, h): Decreased percentage of Moslems accounted for about 15 percent of the variance, increased income equality added another 10 or so percent, and increased U.S. military aid as a percentage of GNP contributed 6 percent more of the explained variance. Regressing increases in C variables onto decreased compulsory work permits netted two consistent predictors: Increased foreign conflict deathrate explained nearly one-fifth of the variance, and increased newspaper circulation per capita added 8 percent to the explained variance (Table 6.23, i, j). Liberal democratic theory and power elite theory appear to be consistent with the evidence, since one-party leftist and military regimes are the worst offenders of workers' rights. Because U.S. military aid and foreign conflict explain some of the variance, one interpretation may be that Washington is more likely to aid countries at war that have reasonably satisfactory human rights.

Decent Working Conditions: Consumer Spending Per Capita. For 1982, energy consumption per capita explained 30 percent of the variance in consumer spending per capita for the full sample, and the percentage of government budgets for social security and welfare accounted for 38 percent of LDC consumer spending (Table 6.24, a, b). There was more consistency in 1986, since the smaller the percentage of workers employed in agriculture, the higher the consumer spending; the explained variance was from 34 to 40 percent (Table 6.24, c, d). C variables for 1982 yielded no consistent predictor of 1986 consumer spending; radios per capita explained 36 percent of the variance for the full sample, whereas government spending on social security and welfare accounted for 44 percent of the variance for LDCs (Table 6.24, e, f). Per capita GNP in 1982 explained 30 percent of the variance in increased consumer spending for the full sample and 9 percent for LDCs; the best predictor for less developed countries, accounting for 24 percent of the variance, was a small army relative to the size of a country's population (Table 6.24, g, h). Decreased per capita education expenditures accounted for about one-third of the variance in increased consumer spending for the full sample, whereas decreased per capita GNP explained about the same percentage of variance among LDCs (Table 6.24, i, j). The results suggest some validity for social democracy theory for LDCs, but for more affluent countries consumer spending appears to decline because of an economistic propensity to plough profits into savings.

Decent Working Conditions: Percentage of Fatal Industrial Accidents. For 1982, the only consistent predictor of the percentage of workers dying from industrial accidents was cancer deathrates, which explained only 7 to 8 percent of the variance; foreign investment rates explained 10 percent of the variance in industrial deaths for the full sample, and telephones per capita topped the predictors for LDCs with 15 percent of explained variance (Table 6.25, a, b).

Voter turnout was the best predictor for 1986, accounting for from 12 to 18 percent of the variance (Table 6.25, c, d). Investment rates again had some importance for the full sample, and low coup propensity for LDCs, though each accounted for only 5 percent of the variance. Among C variables for 1982, higher voter turnout was the best predictor of fatal industrial accident deathrates in 1986 for the full sample, and cancer deathrates for LDCs, but these two variables explained only about 10 percent of the variance (Table 6.25, e, f). No clear pattern emerged when 1982 C variables were regressed onto increases in industrial accident deathrates (Table 6.25, g, h). Regressing changes in C variables onto increased fatal industrial accident percentages, the results showed that 11 percent of the variance for the full sample was explained by an increase in the size of the majority party, whereas for LDCs increased income equality, decreased numbers of political parties in parliament, and increased cancer deathrates were the only variables accounting for more than 5 percent of the variance (Table 6.25, i, j). These findings appear to state that rapid democratic and economic progress means more fatal industrial accidents, consistent with mass society theory. Improvements in industrial safety evidently await a more communitarian approach to economic and political life, when occupational health will become a national political priority.

Worker's Rights. For 1982, the percentage of nonleftist political parties explained from 10 to 29 percent of the variance in the right of unions to federate within LDCs, though a smaller parliamentary majority topped the predictors for the full sample, explaining 29 percent of the variance (Table 6.26, a, b). For 1986, the only consistent predictor was the percentage of direct taxes, which accounted for only 5 to 6 percent of the variance (Table 6.26, c, d). The best predictor for the full sample was a small parliamentary majority, and the percentage of nonleftists in parliament best predicted the right of LDC unions to federate; each explained nearly 30 percent of the variance. The size of nonleftist parties added 10 percent to the full sample for 1982. Regressing 1982 C variables onto the right of unions to federate in 1986, a similar pattern emerged (Table 6.26, e, f). Among 1982 C variables, a consistent predictor of increased right of unions to federate from 1982 to 1986 was a high percentage of direct as opposed to indirect taxes, but the explained variance was only 7 percent (Table 6.26, g, h). Regressing changes in C variables onto improvements in the right of unions to federate, a reduction in domestic conflict deathrates and increased voter turnout each consistently accounted for just under 10 percent of the variance (Table 6.26, i, j). Consistent with the theories of liberal democracy and power elitism, most centrist democracies allow unions to federate, provided the country is not involved in internal war.

Welfare Rights. For 1982, television sets per capita explained about half the variance in family allowance benefits for the full sample, while heart disease deathrates topped predictors for LDCs with 31 percent of the explained variance (Table 6.27, a, b). For 1986, per capita spending on welfare was the best predictor for both samples, with similar percentages (Table 6.27, c, d). When

1982 C variables were regressed onto 1986 family allowance coverages, the results for 1982 reappeared (Table 6.27, e, f). High levels of inflation in 1982, however, accounted for 17 to 18 percent of increased coverage in family allowance benefits from 1982 to 1986 (Table 6.27, g, h). Regressions involving changes in C variables showed that decreased urbanization, possibly due to suburbanization, explained 5 ,to 8 percent of the variance in increased family allowance benefits (Table 6.27, i, j). Social democracy theory is consistent with these results.

Children's Rights. For 1982, newspaper circulation per capita accounted for 40 percent of the variance in the percentage of children immunized against diphtheria, tetanus, and whooping cough for the full sample, but only 6 percent for the LDC sample. For less developed countries, the per capita health budget accounted for 46 percent of the variance (Table 6.28, a, b). Similar results emerged when 1982 C variables were regressed onto immunization rates in 1986 (Table 6.28, e, f). For 1986, energy consumption per capita explained nearly half the variance, and the foreign investment rate added 7 percent to the explained variance (Table 6.28, c, d). Regressing 1982 C variables onto improved immunization rates, there were three consistent predictors: the percentage of GNP due to military imports, percentage of Western arms imports, and income inequality, each accounting for 5 to 12 percent of the variance (Table 6.28, g, h). Among changes in C variables from 1982 to 1986, three variables consistently explained increased immunization rates: increased percentages of the population in the army, increased official violence against the population, and decreased imports of Western arms; each contributed about 10 percent of the explained variance (Table 6.28, i, j). Although an economistic explanation is possible if we focus on the largest amounts of explained variance, social democracy theory is consistent with all the results for LDCs. Since improvements are linked to militarization, the explanation appears to be that militarized regimes want a healthy population.

Decent Standard of Living. Per capita energy consumption explained 63 to 74 percent of the variance in the percentage of housing units with safe drinking water for 1982 and 1986 (Table 6.29, a, b, c, d). Energy consumption in 1982 also explained the increased provision of safe water four years later, explaining about two-thirds of the variance (Table 6.29, e, f). Using 1982 C variables, countries with lower direct taxes in 1982 most increased the volume of safe water by 1986; the explained variance was about 11 percent (Table 6.29, g, h). Increased per capita GNP growth rates consistently accounted for 5 percent of the variance in increased availability of homes with safe running water (Table 6.29, i, j). Economistic theorists should be pleased with these results, as the data show a trickledown of safe water from increased economic growth and from a reduction in the burden of direct taxes.

Health Rights. Newspaper circulation per capita explained about three-fourths of the variance in levels of life expectancy for 1982 and 1986 (Table 6.30, a, b, c, d). The same finding applied to the regression of 1982 newspaper circulation per capita on life expectancy in 1986 (Table 6.30, e, f). Increased life expectancy from 1982 to 1986, however, occurred within countries that in 1982 had larger percentages of nonleftists in parliament; about one-sixth of the variance was explained by this variable (Table 6.30, g, h). Decreases in the percentage of the population in the armed forces for 1982 and 1986 accounted for about 10 percent of the variance in increased life expectancy over the same years (Table 6.30, i, j). Reversing these findings, life expectancy is lower where elites restrict information and mobilize to fight wars abroad, sacrificing the lives of the youth to remain in power. Liberal democracy theory is again the other side of the coin from power elite theory in explaining these results.

Educational Rights. With the exception of LDCs for 1982, energy consumption per capita accounted for about two-thirds of the variance in percentage of secondary school enrollment (Table 6.31, a, c, d, e, f). Newspaper circulation per capita explained half the variance in LDC secondary school enrollment rates for 1982 (Table 6.31, b). Improved secondary enrollment was explained by other variables. Using 1982 C variables, the most consistent predictors, each accounting for 6 to 10 percent of the variance in increased secondary enrollment, were the percentage of arms purchased from Western countries and percentage of GNP devoted to military spending (Table 6.31, g, h). Decreased Western arms imports from 1982 to 1986 explained about 10 percent of the variance in increased secondary enrollment (Table 6.31, i, j). Economism best squares with the data for the full sample, but liberal democracy theory applies to LDCs. Military spending indicators provide ambiguous results.

Cultural Rights: Percentage of Registered Public Library Users. Communication density variables were most prominent in regressions on the level of library use. For 1982, somewhat more than one-third of the variance was explained by telephones per capita for the full sample and by television sets per capita for LDCs (Table 6.32, a, b). Percentage of leftist parties added 9 percent to both regressions. For 1986, newspaper circulation per capita was the best predictor, accounting for 12 to 22 percent of the variance (Table 6.32, c, d). Among C variables for 1982, there was no consistent predictor of library usage in 1986 or improvements in library use from 1982 to 1986 (Table 6.32, e, f, g, h). Countries that ended civil wars by 1986, however, increased library use; the explained variance was 19 percent (Table 6.32, i, j). The results support the theory of liberal democracy, insofar as an information infrastructure and a stable social order serve as wellsprings for high levels of cultural rights attainments. When power elites send their youth off to war, public libraries have many empty seats.

Cultural Rights: Artistic Freedom. Political variables provided the best explanation for the extent of artistic freedom around the world. For 1982, the percentage of nonleftist parties was the most consistent predictor, accounting for 13 percent of the variance in the full sample and 33 percent for LDCs (Table 6.33, a, b). The smallness of the majority party was the best predictor for the full sample, accounting for 27 percent of the variance. For 1986, smallness of the majority party was again the best predictor for the full sample, accounting for about one-fourth of the variance in extent of artistic freedom (Table 6.33, c). Lower military spending, which topped the predictors for LDCs at 23 percent of the variance, contributed 8 percent more to the regression for the full sample (Table 6.33, c, d). The percentage of nonleftist parties added 13 percent to the explained variance for LDCs. Nonleftist parties and lower military spending in 1982 were consistent predictors of artistic freedom in 1986; for the full sample, the two variables each explained 8 percent of the variance, but for LDCs non-leftist parties accounted for 25 percent and military spending 14 percent (Table 6.33, e, f). The best predictor of artistic freedom in 1986 for the full sample was smallness of the majority party in 1982, which raked in 27 percent of the variance. Among C variables for 1982, countries other than former British colonies (presumably because British colonies already had exemplary artistic freedom) topped the predictors; the explained variance was about 16 percent (Table 6.33, g, h). Among measures of changes in C variables from 1982 to 1986, decreased U.S. military aid consistently accounted for about 8 percent of the variance (Table 6.33, i, j). Thus, liberal democracy theory best explains levels and increases in attainments of cultural rights.

International Assistance Obligations. The most consistent predictors of GDP devoted to foreign aid for 1982 were GNP and newspaper circulation per capita; the former accounted for 28 to 56 percent of the variance, the latter 7 to 19 percent (Table 6.34, a, b). For 1986, per capita spending on health accounted for almost half the variance in the full sample; for the few LDC aid providers, education spending per capita explained 16 percent of the variance (Table 6.34, c, d). Among C variables for 1982, the most consistent predictors of foreign aid levels in 1986, jointly accounting for 19 to 35 percent of the combined variance, were GNP and newspaper circulation per capita (Table 6.34, e, f). Lower percentages of arms imports in 1982 accounted for about one-fourth of increased foreign aid from 1982 to 1986 (Table 6.34, g, h). Reduced arms imports had the same effect on increased foreign aid from 1982 to 1986, though increased foreign conflict deathrate added almost 10 percent more to the explained variance (Table 6.34, i, j). Liberal democracy theory is consistent with most of the results.

Minority Rights. There was some divergence in regressions on the percentage of the population subject to economic discrimination. Although U.S. civilian aid as a percentage of GNP was consistently related in 1982, the amount of explained variance was only 5 to 7 percent (Table 6.35, a, b). For the full sample, heart disease deathrate accounted for 13 percent of the variance; for LDCs, the best predictor was smallness of the parliamentary majority, with 16 percent. For 1986, Gurr's measures of grievances explained about one-third of the variance in the percentage subjected to economic discrimination; the nature of the grievances was economic for the full sample but political for LDCs (Table 6.35, c, d). Consistently, both foreign conflict deathrates and ethnolinguistic heterogeneity in 1982 explained about one-fifth of the variance in the percentage of victims of economic discrimination in 1986 (Table 6.35, e, f). The percentage of Moslems in 1982 was the best predictor of increased economic discrimination from 1982 to 1986, explaining 13 to 16 percent of the variance (Table 6.35, g, h). A high percentage of indirect tax revenues in 1982 added about 10 percent more to the explained variance. A reduction in foreign conflict deaths from 1982 to 1986 best explained decreased economic discrimination over the same time period, accounting for 16 to 17 percent of the variance (Table 6.35, i, j). The signs point to group conflict and power elite theories as explanations of minority discrimination, as the mobilization of protest appears to be counterproductive.

Women's Rights. Newspaper circulation per capita was the most prominent predictor of the percentage of females in elementary education. For 1982, the explained variance was 34 to 39 percent, and years of nonmilitary rule added 6 to 7 percent to the equation (Table 6.36, a, b). For 1986, newspaper circulation accounted for 19 percent of the variance for LDCs, though the percentage of the workforce outside agriculture was the best predictor for the full sample, explaining 26 percent of the variance (Table 6.36, c, d). For both samples, lower percentage of Moslems added about 10 percent more to the explained variance. Newspaper circulation in 1982 explained 21 to 28 percent of the variance in female primary enrollment in 1986, and lower percentage of Moslems contributed 7 to 8 percent more (Table 6.36, e, f). C variables for 1982 failed to account for much more than 5 percent of the variance for increased female primary enrollment from 1982 to 1986; the only consistent predictor was a decrease in trade export dependency (Table 6.36, g, h). Changes in C variables also explained little of the variance in increased female primary school enrollment in the 1980s; for the full sample, decreased foreign investment was the best predictor, whereas a decrease in domestic violence deathrates best predicted an upturn in the presence of females in primary schools (Table 6.36, i, j). Liberal democratic and power elite theories are supported, but cultural relativism should be invoked to explain why Islamic countries fail to respect women's rights.

There are some definite differences between developed and developing countries, based on results derived from the two samples. In general, LDCs need a free economy, free elections, and a free press before attaining a minimum level of economic and social rights; the main hindrance is lack of domestic political stability, often due to ethnic heterogeneity, which prompts nervous governments into diverting funds toward military spending. Developed countries that have these positive attributes can continue to perfect the delivery of services to more citizens to the extent that they continue to prosper economically and become welfare states.

Implications

Economic and social rights are generally higher and improve best under conditions of social democracy; they should have economic growth, centrist politics, a strong information infrastructure, and more revenues for governments to aid the less fortunate. In some cases, nevertheless, a purely developmentalist explanation for economic attainments emerged from the quantitative analyses. Improved terms of trade, consumer spending per capita, safe drinking water piped into homes, and percentage of school-age children in secondary school were best explained by economic attainment variables, especially among developed countries. Among LDC governments that strive to establish legitimate rule over diverse peoples, as soon as a country has the political stability to develop a liberal democracy, economic growth provides the wherewithal for progress in economic and social human rights.

CONCLUSION

Although civil and political rights are quite distinct from most economic and social rights, neither predicting the other, both have common antecedents. The existence of a liberal democracy, with a competitive economy, a vast information infrastructure, and a multiparty system, evidently ensures that governments will improve both types of human rights. Civil and political rights develop for the mainstream first. As the role of the military declines, minority ethnic groups receive the same rights as the majority. As a welfare state emerges, women's rights are increasingly respected. Granting of various rights to gays and Lesbians follows the conferring of minority and women's rights. For economic and social rights, liberal democracy awaits political stability, which in turn may be elusive so long as civil and political rights are denied to the diverse peoples that inhabit many LDCs.

NOTE

1. Once again, the procedure was to use defaults from the program designed by the Statistical Analysis System Institute (1982:chapter 6). For a discussion of alternative methods, see R. R. Hocking (1976). Means were inserted for missing data.

Chapter 7

CONCLUSION

As the new U.N. High Commissioner for Human Rights takes office, the results of this study need to be considered seriously from several points of view. The findings have dispelled several misconceptions about which kinds of countries support human rights, and how improvements in human rights can be advanced most effectively. Previous theories of human rights need to be corrected. Finally, several important policy recommendations flow from the study.

EMPIRICAL FINDINGS

The analysis of some fifty civil and political rights, ninety-one economic and social rights, and fifty-seven variables predicted to account for levels of human rights has been remarkably smooth. Previous findings have been placed into context.

First of all, most civil and political rights are empirically distinct from economic and social rights. Civil and political rights neither precede nor follow increases in economic and social rights. Instead, the two sets of rights develop independently. Any correlation between civil-political and social-economic rights is spurious, because both sets of human rights attainments have a common underlying precondition. The precondition for development of basic human rights is the attainment of the economic and political pluralism of a centrist liberal democracy. The end of military rule, which can emerge as a country's information infrastructure expands, is essential before human rights can make substantial improvements. Human rights are complementary, not zerosum, so improvements in one area do not entail a risk of lesser attainments elsewhere.

Civil and political rights, in turn, consist of two types. Mainstream groups are likely to gain as arbitrary state power gives way to freedom of expression and judicial rights (as guaranteed by the First Amendment to the U.S. Constitution); in due course, other forms of civil and political rights, such as the right to privacy and the right to vote, emerge. While these basic rights are being secured, nonmainstream groups tend to be ignored. In due course, as the government abandons military options against minorities, the status of minorities improves. As the government develops a welfare state, women's rights improve. Finally, when minorities and women enjoy victories in their struggle for equal civil and political rights, gays and Lesbians begin to cash in.

Meanwhile, most economic and social rights are interrelated forms of quality of life. Among nonmainstream groups, left out of general advances in economic and social rights, are protesting workers and separatists, whose actions tend to be suppressed by the military or the police. Economic and social rights attainments increase as economies grow, as several legitimate political parties arise, and as the information infrastructure broadens. When countries become welfare states, women's economic and social rights become more secure.

The comprehensive quantitative analysis presented herein serves to clarify previous studies. It is useful, therefore, to compare any results with the summary of previous studies in Table 2.1 regarding both major types of human rights, as noted below.

Civil and Political Rights

Consistent with previous studies, my findings identify a strong association between arms imports and violations of many forms of civil and political rights. Although a few scholars reported no correlation between civil wars and other forms of domestic violence and nonobservance of civil-political rights, results herein strongly support most studies in finding a close connection. Contrary to two of three previous investigations, economic dependence is associated with many violations of civil and political rights. Ethnic diversity, rather than being associated with regime coerciveness in general, predicts problems of separatism. Although previous studies found no clear relationship between civil-political rights and participation in war, the factor analyses and regressions of chapters 4–6 find that human rights suffer in time of war. It was no surprise, however, to discover that countries with *laissez faire* economies tend to extend more civil-political rights than countries that impose restrictions on economic freedom; similarly, military rule and military spending are associated with extensive abuses of civil-political rights. Predominantly Moslem countries had poorer civil-political rights, as expected, but mostly in regard to women's rights. No previous study examined the effect of progressive taxation, but countries with a higher percentage of indirect taxes had better civil-political rights than those raising revenues primarily from direct taxes. Communication variables, such as per capita radios and television sets, were, as expected, predictors of higher civil-political rights attainments. Previous doubts about the effect of regime instability should be laid to rest; countries with a history of military coups tend to restrict civil and political rights, and they deal particularly harshly with women. A few studies found that countries that derive higher percentages of their GNP from trade are more respectful of civil-political rights, and results herein provide corroboration. The scholarly controversy surrounding the impact of U.S. economic and military aid will doubtless continue, but during the two years of the Reagan administration studied (1982 and 1986), both forms of U.S. aid were associated with serious deficiencies in overall civil-political rights, especially minority rights, although U.S. aid was much lower to countries that committed acts of government terror and suppressed women's rights. Finally, though few previous studies took note, welfare spending is a strong correlate of civil-political rights.

Despite these clear findings, my study fails to find close links between civil-political rights and percentages of Catholics and Protestants, economic development, equality, economic growth per capita, investment, former status as a British colony, GNP per capita, levels of government spending, urbanization, and voting habits. Some repressive Third World countries had impressive levels of economic activity, and former Communist countries had high voter turnout and large percentages of support for leftist and socialist parties, thereby confounding replications of previous studies. That civil-political rights fail to increase monotonically with economic development or GNP per capita is not a new finding, but a nearly complete washout of the linkage is extraordinary.

Economic and Social Rights

Once again, the previously overlooked variables of arms imports and domestic violence correlate negatively with human rights. Previous conflicting results on the role of economic development, economic growth, economic equality, and GNP per capita should be updated, since there is no doubt that these variables are central to the advancement of economic-social rights. Ethnic diversity, military rule, and military spending yielded contradictory correlations with economic-social rights in earlier studies, but are consistent negative correlates in this study. Islamic countries provide a decent amount of foreign aid, but otherwise the percentage of Moslems loaded negatively on the main economic-social rights factor. Consistent with previous analyses, regime instability spells trouble for several forms of economic and social rights. Unionization largely washed out of the analysis, contrary to two previous studies. Urbanization was a central element of the main economic and social rights factors, as expected. Voter turnout had a positive loading on economic and social rights factors, and percentage of leftists in parliament had a negative loading. Welfare spending contributed some variance in explaining some economic and social rights, but was far less prominent than in previous studies.

Not all puzzling findings in previous studies could be clarified. Although economic dependence is negatively related to some forms of economic and social rights, and trade dependence has a positive correlation, the overall judgment remains inconclusive. Economic-social rights are also largely independent of percentages of Catholics and Protestants, levels of government spending, and progressive taxation.

Some variables had not been specifically correlated with economic and social rights in previous analyses. Communication variables (radios, televisions, etc.) were important predictors of economic-social rights herein. External aggression and foreign investment turned out to be negatively related to a wide spectrum of economic and social rights in this study. Former British colonies had little to crow about. U.S. aid was associated with economic freedom but not with social rights.

One can go to the interstices of the findings and contemplate many more complexities, of course. These are the principal results of the exploratory multivariate analyses. As usual, quantitative analysis has many rough edges that are smoothed at the peril of the researcher.[1]

THEORETICAL IMPLICATIONS

Many typologies of human rights were found to be empirically ungrounded. The Muskie-Vance distinction between *freedom from violations of the human person* (torture, arbitrary arrest or imprisonment, summary execution, and denial of due process), *economic and social rights* (food, shelter, education, and health care), and *civil and political rights* (freedom of thought, expression, assembly, travel, and participation in politics) was largely vindicated (Muskie 1980; Vance 1977). But the empirically more important dichotomy between *mainstream rights* and the *rights of nonmainstream groups* cuts across their trichotomy.

Among a dozen or so theories of human rights development, most were discarded or had limited explanatory power. *Trade-off theory*, which posits that gains in some human rights will entail losses in economic or political stability, was unambiguously rejected by this study. *Relativists*, who expect no cross-national patterns in human rights attainments, received little support from this analysis. The percentage of Islamic persons in a country, however, accounted for some of the lack of progress in minority rights, women's rights, and worker's rights, but other factors were more important. Within less developed countries (LDCs), the percentage of Catholics was the best predictor of respect for the privacy of gays and Lesbians, but otherwise Catholicism and Protestantism were of little consequence in the empirical analysis.

Liberal democracy theory received overwhelming support. Civil and political rights are respected in countries with political pluralism, and economic and social rights are enjoyed wherever economic and political pluralism are found with a high level of media or telephone usage. The few exceptions are noted in connection with other theories, as noted below.

Social democracy theory adds communitarian tenets to liberal democracy theory. Larger per capita welfare expenditures were prominent along with indicators of liberal democracy in regard to two civil and political rights, namely, women's rights and the rights of gays and Lesbians. Among economic and social rights, welfare spending explained much of the variance in family allowance benefits,

LDC consumer spending per capita, and the percentage of infants immunized in LDCs.

Economism, which argues that the level of economic prosperity unlocks advancements in human rights, did not receive much support in this study. Per capita electricity consumption explained a large portion of the variance in percentage of children immunized, percentage of dwellings with safe drinking water, percentage enrolled in secondary schools, and percentage of GNP allocated to foreign aid, but other factors were responsible as well.

Developmentalism, which assigns primacy to both level of prosperity and efforts at economic development as conducive to human rights, did not explain the level of civil and political rights. In regard to economic and social rights, there was considerable progress when countries had a higher or faster growing GNP per capita and higher levels of foreign investment. On the other hand, economic growth predicted lower levels of consumer spending, and a high level of foreign investment was related to lack of occupational safety.

Mobilization theory expects progress in human rights to result from struggles by groups suffering discrimination. Contrary to this theory, Gurr's (1993) measures of grievances accounted for considerable variance in the percentage of separatists out of the total population of a country and the percentage suffering economic discrimination. There was no evidence that demonstrations of worker solidarity, such as strikes, had any impact upon improving human rights attainments.

Group conflict theory receives limited support. When the heterogeneous ethnic groups of a country seek to articulate considerable economic, political, and social grievances, they do so in the context of discrimination and separatism, but the success of such articulation of demands is limited within poorer countries.

Power elite theory turned out to be vindicated as well, since a failure of human rights advancements in times of external and internal conflicts, when leaders are under more pressure to stay in charge, is also a failure of democracy. "Disappearances," for example, occurred in countries with a lot of arms imports, domestic violence, and government-initiated violence. Other forms of civil and political violence appeared to impact power elites, whose responses were to increase the number of countries proscribed for external travel, restrictions on the right to teach ideas and receive information, limitations on the right to vote, mail censorship, star chamber proceedings (instead of civilian, public trials), indefinite detention, a lack of prominent women in politics, and prohibitions on the right of adults to consensual sex. Among economic and social rights, power elite theory evidently explains the practice of compulsory work permits and labor conscription, prohibitions on the right of unions to federate, lower life expectancy, reduced use of public libraries, increased ethnic economic discrimination, and decreases in female enrollment in schools. On the other hand, militarized societies evidently found a way to immunize many more children against common childhood diseases in the 1980s.

Marxian theories explained little. Measures of inequality and trade dependency did not emerge prominently in the multivariate analyses.

Frustration-aggression theory predicts that economic downswings are the wellspring for crackdowns on human rights. There was a worldwide recession in the early 1980s, but a recovery by the mid-1980s, so there was insufficient information to test this theory.

Freudian theory blames industrialization for outbursts of barbarism. Since agriculturally based societies respect fewer human rights than urban-industrial societies, Freudian theory was rejected herein.

Mass society theory, finally, assumes a connection between too rapid economic growth and such vicissitudes of employment instability as deaths from cancer, heart disease, and suicide, which exist in a condition of social turmoil that makes elites reluctant to respect human rights. The data showed, however, that rapid economic growth explained improvements in terms of trade, and that countries with higher heart disease deathrates conferred more generous welfare benefits.

In sum, the most satisfactory theoretical explanation for the findings comes from a combination of *liberal democratic* and *power elite theories*. When power elites desperately cling to positions of influence, the human rights of the masses seem of little consequence. As poorer countries receive economic aid to build up their infrastructure, especially in the field of communications, a more competitive economy spills over into competitive politics. A liberal democracy can then emerge, whence basic human rights will be granted to mainstream groups in the population. As dissident minorities and workers benefit from prosperity, and the government abandons violence against declining separatism, minority rights are established. When the economy booms, a welfare state is possible, and rights are extended to women. Ultimately, the rights of gays and Lesbians are respected after minorities' economic and social rights and after women's civil and political rights reach a plateau.

POLICY IMPLICATIONS

Data Collection on Human Rights

Although many provisions in the basic international agreements on human rights have yet to be measured, efforts to collect data on human rights need not try to focus on every possible indicator. Charles Humana's list of some forty civil and political rights is impressive but largely redundant empirically, since factor analyses found fewer than ten dimensions. The same can be said concerning economic and social rights, although there were a lot of missing data in U.N. statistical yearbooks.

Clumsy composite measures, such as a "social welfare index," likewise appear to be a waste of time; one indicator will usually suffice. In order to study problems and trends, more parsimony is warranted in future efforts.

At the same time, these remarks should not discourage human rights organizations from compiling lists of political prisoners. The aim of this study is to find ways to promote general progress on human rights. Microanalytic investigations of specific abuses, which stimulated this microanalytic study, are needed, too.[2]

Sanctions Against Human Rights Violators?

Perhaps the most controversial question is whether the study suggests that withholding aid is a useful tool in promoting human rights. The data clearly show that human rights advance as a country develops economically, builds a communication infrastructure, and has competitive political parties. Economic aid usually is articulated toward the first two of these three goals, though aid to political parties is usually covert and, when later revealed, can easily boomerang.[3] In view of the centrality of economic development for promoting economic and social rights and communications development in advancing civil and political rights, withholding economic aid can only retard the advance of human rights. Although humanitarian aims justify pressuring notorious violators of human rights to release political prisoners, stop police torture of suspects, and the like, the analysis herein does not support blanket sanctions against notorious human rights violators.

Strategies for Improving Human Rights

A successful strategy to promote human rights should begin with an assessment of where a country is today. LDCs with ethnolinguistic heterogeneity, which tend to be under military rule, need to develop communications and economic pluralism through foreign aid, provided that the aid finances an information infrastructure, provides aid to education so that a more literate population will emerge, and insists on a privatization of the economy that promotes economic pluralism.

Another implication of this study is that Amnesty International and similar organizations might support a macroagenda. Regarding disappearances and summary executions, the underlying condition is emergency rule; efforts to get governments to restore normalcy will facilitate an end to such government terrorism. Similarly, to stop indefinite detention and torture, the appropriate strategy appears to be that of promoting a legal system that provides many checks on the possibility of arbitrary actions by those in authority. The task of promoting constitutional rule ultimately falls upon leaders of loyal opposition parties to insist on multiparty elections with secret ballots. A loyal opposition, in turn, is more likely in countries that have economic pluralism.

In short, a demand for "free and fair elections" is meaningless unless the economic and social interests represented in a multiparty parliament are diverse. Too often, economically poor countries hold elections, but parliamentarians later represent their own personal interests. Since such governments tend to be corrupt, military coups are frequent. One definition of democracy is a form of government in which parliament serves as a channel for legislators to design compromises on behalf of pluralistic societal interests. Since truly representative democracy is the form of government most favorable to human rights, conditional foreign aid can best be based on the carrot of additional support for progress rather than on the stick of sanctions that cut back economic assistance to developing countries for human rights failures.

Foreign aid should not be conditioned prematurely on progress in the rights of minorities, women, and workers, according to the analysis presented herein. Since regimes are likely to provide basic human rights to the mainstream before nonmainstream groups, aid donors should apply pressure on recipient countries to establish an umbrella of general guarantees similar to the U.S. Bill of Rights before trying to put special groups under the same umbrella. Since minority rights improve as economic aspects of liberal democracy emerge, the appropriate strategy is to provide aid for power grids, printing presses, telephone lines, elementary textbooks, and professionalism in broadcasting. For the working class, the perfection of democracy, such as high voter turnout and many centrist political parties, is crucial, but none of these conditions will exist until economic pluralism exists. When democratic states have sufficient economic prosperity to adopt social welfare legislation, women's rights are advanced. When progress in minority rights and women's rights is assured, gays and Lesbians will be accorded more decent treatment. Historically, trade union rights came first, leading to the establishment of welfare states, and the efforts of Martin Luther King, Jr., paved the way for advances in the rights of women and, much later, gays and Lesbians. This study suggests that minorities and trade unionists should pursue separate but simultaneous struggles for their rights, whereas women, gays, and Lesbians will benefit most by first working for the success of these two struggles, and later stressing their own agendas.

A possible wild card in this outline of steps toward improving human rights is that some Islamic countries may, for cultural reasons, resist such a unilinear path. Nevertheless, based on the data in this study, Egypt and Turkey appear to be pursuing human rights progress along these lines today.

CONCLUSION

Early in this study, three questions were posed. In reply to the question, "Which countries are most likely to violate human rights?" the data point to poor, undemocratic countries. "What accounts for improvements in human rights?" The response is that human rights improve when countries achieve solid economic progress, have an informed citizenry, end military rule, and become liberal and later social democracies. "Where can pressure be applied to encourage countries to improve human rights?" The best strategy appears to be to provide aid in order to build a communication and economic infrastructure that will lay the foundations for a more pluralistic economy and polity.

Since the denial of basic human rights is a desperate strategy for maintaining power in poor countries, advocates of human rights should urge more economic aid to the poorer parts of the world so that the infrastructure for a free flow of ideas and economic largesse for better social conditions can be established. Advocacy organizations that focus on particular abuses of the moment should be congratulated for successful efforts to free prisoners of conscience and similar short-term measures. For the long run, human rights can best be advanced by creating the preconditions for a liberal, prosperous democracy.

NOTES

1. A task for the future is to undertake path analysis to test the causal connections between the variables, as suggested in this chapter.

2. Regarding Singapore's odd record of human rights, the explanation provided herein is that caning, indefinite detention, and police torture will remain until a genuinely competitive two- or multi-party system emerges.

3. Huntington (1968:23–27) has urged precisely this form of aid and corresponding cuts in economic aid. For the pitfalls of political aid of this sort, see Irving Horowitz (1967).

Appendix A ⸻⸻⸻⸻⸻⸻⸻⸻⸻⸻⸻⸻

INTERNATIONAL COVENANT ON CIVIL AND POLITICAL RIGHTS

PREAMBLE

The States Parties to the present Covenant,

Considering that, in accordance with the principles proclaimed in the Charter of the United Nations, recognition of the inherent dignity and of the equal and inalienable rights of all members of the human family is the foundation of freedom, justice and peace in the world,

Recognizing that these rights derive from the inherent dignity of the human person,

Recognizing that, in accordance with the Universal Declaration of Human Rights, the ideal of free human beings enjoying civil and political freedom and freedom from fear and want can only be achieved if conditions are created whereby everyone may enjoy his civil and political rights, as well as his economic, social, and cultural rights,

Considering the obligation of States under the Charter of the United Nations to promote universal respect for, and observance of, human rights and freedoms,

Realizing that the individual, having duties to other individuals and to the community to which he belongs, is under a responsibility to strive for the promotion and observance of the rights recognized in the present Covenant,

Agree upon the following articles:

PART I
Article 1

1. All peoples have the right of self-determination. By virtue of that right they freely determine their political status and freely pursue their economic, social and cultural development.

2. All peoples may, for their own ends, freely dispose of their natural wealth and resources without prejudice to any obligations arising out of international economic cooperation, based upon the principle of mutual benefit, and international law. In no case may a people be deprived of its own means of subsistence.

3. The States parties to the present Covenant, including those having responsibility for the administration of Non-Self-Governing and Trust Territories, shall promote the real-

ization of the right of self-determination, and shall respect that right, in conformity with the provisions of the Charter of the United Nations.

PART II

Article 2

1. Each State Party to the present Covenant undertakes to respect and to ensure to all individuals within its territory and subject to its jurisdiction the rights recognized in the present Covenant, without distinction of any kind, such as race, color, sex, language, religion, political or other opinion, national or social origin, property, birth or other status.

2. Where not already provided for by existing legislative or other measures, each State Party to the present Covenant undertakes to take the necessary steps, in accordance with its constitutional processes and with the provisions of the present Covenant, to adopt such legislative or other measures as may be necessary to give effect to the rights recognized in the present Covenant.

3. Each State Party to the present Covenant undertakes:

(a) To ensure that any person whose rights of freedom as herein recognized are violated shall have an effective remedy, notwithstanding that the violation has been committed by persons acting in an official capacity;

(b) To ensure that any person claiming such a remedy shall have his right thereto determined by competent judicial, administrative or legislative authorities, or by any other competent authority provided for by the legal system of the State, and to develop the possibilities of judicial remedy;

(c) To ensure that the competent authorities shall enforce such remedies when granted.

Article 3

The States Parties to the present Covenant undertake to ensure the equal right of men and women to the enjoyment of all civil and political rights set forth in the present Covenant.

Article 4

1. In time of public emergency which threatens the life of the nation and the existence of which is officially proclaimed, the States Parties to the present Covenant may take measures derogating from their obligations under the present Covenant to the extent strictly required by the exigencies of the situation, provided that such measures are not inconsistent with their other obligations under international law and do not involve discrimination solely on the ground of race, color, sex, language, religion or social origins.

2. No derogation from articles 6, 7, 8 (paragraphs 1 and 2), 11, 15, 16, and 18 may be made under this provision.

3. Any State Party to the present Covenant availing itself of the right of derogation shall immediately inform the other States Parties to the present Covenant, through the intermediary of the Secretary-General of the United Nations, of the provisions from which it was actuated. A further communication shall be made, through the same intermediary, on the date on which it terminates such derogation.

Article 5

1. Nothing in the present Covenant may be interpreted as implying for any State, group or person any right to engage in any activity or perform any act aimed at the destruction of any of the rights and freedom recognized herein or at their limitation to greater extent than is provided for in the present Covenant.

2. There shall be no restriction upon or derogation from any of the fundamental human rights recognized or existing in any State Party to the present Covenant pursuant to law,

conventions, regulations or custom on the pretext that the present Covenant does not recognize such rights or that it recognizes them to a lesser extent.

PART III
Article 6

1. Every human being has the inherent right to life. This right shall be protected by law. No one shall be arbitrarily deprived of his life.

2. In countries which have not abolished the death penalty, sentence of death may be imposed only for the most serious crimes in accordance with the law in force at the time of the commission of the crime and not contrary to the provisions of the present Covenant and to the Convention on the Prevention and Punishment of the Crime of Genocide. This penalty can only be carried out pursuant to a final judgment rendered by a competent court.

3. When deprivation of life constitutes the crime of genocide, it is understood that nothing in this article shall authorize any State Party to the present Covenant to derogate in any way from any obligation assured under the provisions of the Convention on the Prevention and Punishment of the Crime of Genocide.

4. Anyone sentenced to death shall have the right to seek pardon or commutation of the sentence. Amnesty, pardon or commutation of the sentence of death may be granted in all cases.

5. Sentence of death shall not be imposed for crimes committed by persons below eighteen years of age and shall not be carried out on pregnant women.

6. Nothing in this article shall be invoked to delay or to prevent the abolition of capital punishment by any State Party to the present Covenant.

Article 7

1. No one shall be subjected to torture or to cruel, inhuman or degrading treatment or punishment. In particular, no one shall be subjected without his free consent to medical or scientific experimentation.

Article 8

1. No one shall be held in slavery; slavery and the slave trade in all their forms shall be prohibited.

2. No one shall be held in servitude.

3. (a) No one shall be required to perform forced or compulsory labor;

(b) Paragraph 3(a) shall not be held to preclude, in countries where imprisonment with hard labor may be imposed as a punishment for a crime, the performance of hard labor in pursuance of a sentence to such punishment by a competent court;

(c) For the purpose of this paragraph the term ''forced or compulsory labor'' shall not include:

(i) Any work or service, not referred to in subparagraph (b), normally required of a person who is under detention in consequence of a lawful order of a court, or of a person during conditional release from such detention;

(ii) Any service of a military character and, in countries where conscientious objection is recognized, any national service required by law of conscientious objectors;

(iii) Any service exacted in cases of emergency or calamity threatening the life or well-being of the community;

(iv) Any work or service which forms part of normal civil service obligations.

Article 9

1. Everyone has the right to liberty and security of person. No one shall be subjected

to arbitrary arrest or detention. No one shall be deprived of his liberty except on such grounds and in accordance with such procedures as are established by law.

2. Anyone who is arrested shall be informed, at the time of arrest, of the reasons for his arrest and shall be promptly informed of any charges against him.

3. Anyone arrested or detained on a criminal charge shall be brought promptly before a judge or other officer authorized by law to exercise judicial power and shall be entitled to trial within a reasonable time or to release. It shall not be the general rule that persons awaiting trial shall be detained in custody, but release may be subject to guarantees to appear for trial, at any other stage of the judicial proceedings, and, should occasion arise, for execution of the judgment.

4. Anyone who is deprived of his liberty by arrest or detention shall be entitled to take proceedings before a court, in order that the court may decide without delay on the lawfulness of his detention and order his release if the detention is not lawful.

5. Anyone who has been the victim of unlawful arrest or detention shall have an enforceable right to compensation.

Article 10

1. All persons deprived of their liberty shall be treated with humanity and with respect for the inherent dignity of the human person.

2. (a) Accused persons shall, save in exceptional circumstances, be segregated from convicted persons and shall be subject to separate treatment appropriate to their status as unconvicted persons;

(b) Accused juvenile persons shall be separated from adults and brought as speedily as possible for adjudication.

3. The penitentiary system shall comprise treatment of prisoners the essential aim of which shall be their reformation and social rehabilitation. Juvenile offenders shall be segregated from adults and be accorded treatment appropriate to their age and legal status.

Article 11

No one shall be imprisoned merely on the ground of inability to fulfill a contractual obligation.

Article 12

1. Everyone lawfully within the territory of a State shall, within that territory, have the right to liberty of movement and freedom to choose his residence.

2. Everyone shall be free to leave any country, including his own.

3. The above-mentioned rights shall not be subject to any restrictions except those which are provided by law, are necessary to protect national security, public order, public health or morals or the rights and freedoms of others, and are consistent with the other rights recognized in the present Covenant.

4. No one shall be arbitrarily deprived of the right to enter his own country.

Article 13

An alien lawfully in the territory of a State Party to the present Covenant may be expelled therefrom only in pursuance of a decision reached in accordance with law and shall, except where compelling reasons of national security otherwise require, be allowed to submit the reasons against his expulsion and to have his case reviewed by, and be represented for the purpose before, the competent authority of a person or persons especially designated by the competent authority.

Article 14

1. All persons shall be equal before the courts and tribunals. In the determination of any criminal charge against him, or of his rights and obligations in a suit of law, everyone

shall be entitled to a fair and public hearing by a competent, independent and impartial tribunal established by law. The press and the public may be excluded from all or part of a trial for reasons of morals, public order or national security in a democratic society, or when the interest of the private lives of the parties so requires, or to the extent strictly necessary in the opinion of the court in special circumstances where publicity would prejudice the interests of justice; but any judgment rendered in a criminal case or in a suit at law shall be made public except where the interest of juvenile persons otherwise requires or the proceedings concern matrimonial disputes or the guardianship of children.

2. Everyone charged with a criminal offence shall have the right to be presumed innocent until proved guilty according to law.

3. In the determination of any criminal charge against him, everyone shall be entitled to the following minimum guarantees, in full equality:

(a) To be informed promptly and in detail in a language which he understands of the nature and cause of the charge against him;

(b) To have adequate time and facilities for the preparation of his defense and to communicate with counsel of his own choosing;

(c) To be tried without undue delay;

(d) To be tried in his presence, and to defend himself in person or through legal assistance of his own choosing; to be informed, if he does not have legal assistance, of this right; and to have legal assistance assigned to him, in any case where the interests of justice so require, and without payment by him in any such case if he does not have sufficient means to pay for it;

(e) To examine, or have examined, the witnesses against him and to obtain the attendance and examination of witnesses on his behalf under the same conditions as witnesses against him;

(f) To have the free assistance of an interpreter if he cannot understand or speak the language used in court;

(g) Not to be compelled to testify against himself or to confess guilt.

4. In the case of juvenile persons, the procedure shall be such as will take account of their age and the desirability of promoting their rehabilitation.

5. Everyone convicted of a crime shall have the right to his conviction and sentence being reviewed by a higher tribunal according to law.

6. When a person has by a final decision been convicted of a criminal offense and when subsequently his conviction has been reversed or he has been pardoned on the ground that a new or newly discovered fact shows conclusively that there has been a miscarriage of justice, the person who has suffered punishment as a result of such conviction shall be compensated according to law, unless it is proved that the nondisclosure of the unknown fact in time is wholly or partly attributable to him.

7. No one shall be liable to be tried or punished against for an offense for which he has already been finally convicted or acquitted in accordance with the law and penal procedure of each country.

Article 15

1. No one shall be held guilty of any criminal offense on account of any act or omission which did not constitute a criminal offense, under national or international law, at the time when it was committed. Nor shall a heavier penalty be imposed than the one that was applicable at the time when the criminal offense was committed. If, subsequent to the commission of the offense, provision is made by law for the imposition of the lighter penalty, the offender shall benefit thereby.

2. Nothing in this article shall prejudice the trial and punishment of any person for any act or omission which, at the time when it was committed, was criminal according to the general principles of law recognized by the community of nations.

Article 16

Everyone shall have the right to recognition everywhere as a person before the law.

Article 17

1. No one shall be subjected to arbitrary or unlawful interference with his privacy, family, home or correspondence, nor to unlawful attacks on his honor and reputation.

2. Everyone has the right to the protection of the law against such interference or attacks.

Article 18

1. Everyone shall have the right to freedom of thought, conscience and religion. This right shall include freedom to have or to adopt a religion or belief of his choice, and freedom, either individually or in community with others and in public or private, to manifest his religion or belief in worship, observance, practice and teaching.

2. No one shall be subject to coercion which would impair his freedom to have or to adopt a religion or belief of his choice.

3. Freedom to manifest one's religion or beliefs may be subject only to such limitations as are prescribed by law and are necessary to protect public safety, order, health, or morals or the fundamental rights and freedoms of others.

4. The States Parties to the present Covenant undertake to have respect for the liberty of parents and, when applicable, legal guardians to ensure the religious and moral education of their children in conformity with their own convictions.

Article 19

1. Everyone shall have the right to hold opinions without interference.

2. Everyone shall have the right to freedom of expression; this right shall include freedom to seek, receive and impart information and ideas of all kinds, regardless of frontiers, either orally, in writing or in print, in the form of art, or through any other media of his choice.

3. The exercise of the rights provided for in paragraph 2 of this article carries with it special duties and responsibilities. It may therefore be subject to certain restrictions, but these shall only be such as are provided by law and are necessary:

(a) For respect of the rights or reputations of others.

(b) For the protection of national security or of public order, or of public health or morals.

Article 20

1. Any propaganda for war shall be prohibited by law.

2. Any advocacy of national, racial or religious hatred that constitutes incitement to discrimination, hostility or violence shall be prohibited by law.

Article 21

The right of peaceful assembly shall be recognized. No restrictions may be placed on the exercise of this right other than those imposed in conformity with the law and which are necessary in a democratic society in the interests of national security or public safety, public order, the protection of public health or morals or the protection of the rights and freedoms of others.

Article 22

1. Everyone shall have the right to freedom of association with others, including the right to form and join trade unions for the protection of his interests.

2. No restrictions may be placed on the exercise of this right other than those which are prescribed by law and which are necessary in a democratic society in the interests of national security or public safety, public order, the protection of public health or morals or the protection of the rights and freedoms of others. This article shall not prevent the imposition of lawful restrictions on members of the armed forces and of the police in their exercise of this right.

3. Nothing in this article shall authorize States Parties to the International Labor Organization Convention of 1948 concerning Freedom of Association and Protection of the Right to Organize to take legislative measures which would prejudice, or to apply the law in such a manner as to prejudice the guarantees provided for in that Convention.

Article 23

1. The family is the natural and fundamental group unit of society and is entitled to protection by society and the State.

2. The right of men and women of marriageable age to marry and to found a family shall be recognized.

3. No marriage shall be entered into without the free and full consent of the intending spouses.

4. States Parties to the present Covenant shall take appropriate steps to ensure equality of rights and responsibilities of spouses as to marriage, during marriage and at its dissolution. In the case of dissolution, provision shall be made for the necessary protection of any children.

Article 24

1. Every child shall have, without any discrimination as to race, color, sex, language, religion, national or social origin, property or birth, the right to such measures of protection as are required by his status as a minor, on the part of his family, society and the State.

2. Every child shall be registered immediately after birth and shall have a name.

3. Every child has the right to acquire a nationality.

Article 25

Every citizen shall have the right and the opportunity, without any of the distinctions mentioned in article 2 and without unreasonable restrictions:

(a) To take part in the conduct of public affairs, directly or through freely chosen representatives;

(b) To vote and to be elected at genuine periodic elections which shall be by universal and equal suffrage and shall be held by secret ballot, guaranteeing the free expression of the will of the electors;

(c) To have access, on general terms of equality, to public service in his country.

Article 26

All persons are equal before the law and are entitled without any discrimination to the equal protection of the law. In this respect, the law shall prohibit any discrimination and guarantee to all persons equal and effective protection against discrimination on any ground such as race, color, sex, language, religion, political or other opinion, national or social origin, property, birth or other status.

Article 27

In those States in which ethnic, religion or linguistic minorities exist, persons belonging to such minorities shall not be denied the right in community with the other members of their group, to enjoy their own culture, to profess and practice their own religion, or to use their own language.

PART IV
Article 28

1. There shall be established a Human Rights Committee (hereafter referred to in the present Covenant as the Committee). It shall consist of eighteen members and shall carry out the functions hereinafter provided.

2. The Committee shall be composed of nationals of the States Parties to the present Covenant who shall be persons of high moral character and recognized competence in the field of human rights, consideration being given to the usefulness of the participation of some persons having legal experience.

3. The members of the Committee shall be elected and shall serve in their personal capacity.

Article 29

1. The members of the Committee shall be elected by secret ballot from a list of persons possessing the qualifications prescribed in article 28 and nominated for the purpose by the State Parties to the present Covenant.

2. Each State Party to the present Covenant may nominate not more than two persons. These persons shall be nationals of the nominating State.

3. A person shall be eligible for renomination.

Article 30

1. The initial election shall be held no later than six months after the date of the entry into force of the present Covenant.

2. At least four months before the date of each election to the Committee, other than an election to fill a vacancy declared in accordance with article 34, the Secretary-General of the United Nations shall address a written invitation to the States Parties to the present Covenant to submit their nominations for membership of the Committee within three months.

3. The Secretary-General of the United Nations shall prepare a list in alphabetical order of all the persons thus nominated, with an indication of the States Parties which have nominated them, and shall submit it to the States Parties to the present Covenant no later than one month before the date of each election.

4. Elections of the members of the Committee shall be held at a meeting of the States Parties to the present Covenant convened by the Secretary-General of the United Nations at the Headquarters of the United Nations. At that meeting, for which two-thirds of the States Parties to the present Covenant shall constitute a quorum, the persons elected to the Committee shall be those nominees who obtain the largest number of votes and an absolute majority of the votes of the representatives of States Parties present and voting.

Article 31

1. The Committee may not include more than one national of the same State.

2. In the election of the Committee, consideration shall be given to equitable geographic distribution of membership and to the representation of the different forms of civilization and of the principal legal systems.

Article 32

1. The members of the Committee shall be elected for a term of four years. They shall be eligible for re-election if renominated. However, the terms of nine of the members elected at the first election shall expire at the end of two years; immediately after the first election, the names of these nine members shall be chosen by lot by the Chairman of the meeting referred to in article 30, paragraph 4.

2. Elections at the expiry of office shall be held in accordance with the proceeding articles of this part of the present Covenant.

Article 33

1. If, in the unanimous opinion of the other members, a member of the Committee has ceased to carry out his functions for any cause other than absence of a temporary character, the Chairman of the Committee shall notify the Secretary-General of the United Nations, who shall then declare the seat of that member to be vacant.

2. In the event of the death or the resignation of a member of the Committee, the Chairman shall immediately notify the Secretary-General of the United Nations, who shall declare the seat vacant from the date of death or the date on which the resignation takes effect.

Article 34

1. When a vacancy is declared in accordance with article 33 and if the term of office of the member to be replaced does not expire within six months of the declaration of the vacancy, the Secretary-General of the United Nations shall notify each of the States Parties to the present Covenant, which may within two months submit nominations in accordance with article 29 for the purpose of filling the vacancy.

2. The Secretary-General of the United Nations shall prepare a list in alphabetical order of the persons thus nominated and shall submit it to the States Parties to the present Covenant. The election to fill the vacancy shall then take place in accordance with the relevant provisions of this part of the present Covenant.

3. A member of the Committee elected to fill a vacancy declared in accordance with article 33 shall hold office for the remainder of the term of the member who vacated the seat on the Committee under the provisions of that article.

Article 35

The members of the Committee shall, with the approval of the General Assembly of the United Nations, receive emoluments from United Nations resources on such terms and conditions as the General Assembly may decide, having regard to the importance of the Committee's responsibilities.

Article 36

The Secretary-General of the United Nations shall provide the necessary staff and facilities for the effective performance of the functions of the Committee under the present Covenant.

Article 37

1. The Secretary-General of the United Nations shall convene the initial meeting of the Committee at the Headquarters of the United Nations.

2. After its initial meeting, the Committee shall meet at such times as shall be provided in its rules of procedure.

3. The Committee shall normally meet at the Headquarters of the United Nations or at the United Nations Office at Geneva.

Article 38

Every member of the Committee shall, before taking up his duties, make a solemn declaration in open committee that he will perform his functions impartially and conscientiously.

Article 39

1. The Committee shall elect its officers for a term of two years. They may be re-elected.

2. The Committee shall establish its own rules of procedure, but these rules shall provide *inter alia*, that:

(a) Twelve members shall constitute a quorum;

(b) Decisions of the Committee shall be made by a majority vote of the members present.

Article 40

1. The States Parties to the present Covenant undertake to submit reports on the measures they have adopted which give effect to the rights recognized herein and on the progress made in the enjoyment of those rights:

(a) Within one year of the entry into force of the present Covenant for the States Parties concerned;

(b) Thereafter whenever the Committee so requests.

2. All reports shall be submitted to the Secretary-General of the United Nations, who shall transmit them to the Committee for consideration. Reports shall indicate the factors and difficulties, if any, affecting the implementation of the present Covenant.

3. The Secretary-General of the United Nations may, after consultation with the Committee, transmit to the specialized agencies concerned copies of such parts of the reports as may fall within their field of competence.

4. The Committee shall study the reports submitted by the States Parties to the present Covenant. It shall transmit its reports, and such general comments as it may consider appropriate, to the States Parties. The Committee may also transmit to the Economic and Social Council these comments along with the copies of the reports it has received from States Parties to the present Covenant.

5. The States Parties to the present Covenant may submit to the Committee observations on any comments that may be made in accordance with paragraph 4 of this article.

Article 41

1. A State Party to the present Covenant may at any time declare under this article that it recognized the competence of the Committee to receive and consider communications to the effect that a State Party claims that another State Party is not fulfilling its obligations under the present Covenant. Communications under this article may be received and considered only if submitted by a State Party which has made a declaration recognizing in regard to itself the competence of the Committee. No communication shall be received by the Committee if it concerns a State Party which has not made such a declaration. Communications received under this article shall be dealt with in accordance with the following procedure:

(a) If a State Party to the present Covenant considers that another State Party is not giving effect to the provisions of the present Covenant, it may, by written communication, bring the matter to the attention of that State Party. Within three months after the receipt of the communication the receiving State shall afford the State which sent the communication an explanation or any other statement in writing clarifying the matter, which should include, to the extent possible and pertinent, reference to domestic procedures and remedies taken, pending, or available in the matter.

(b) If the matter is not adjusted to the satisfaction of both States Parties concerned within six months after the receipt by the receiving State of the initial communication, either State shall have the right to refer the matter to the Committee, by notice given to the Committee and to the other State.

(c) The Committee shall deal with a matter referred to it only after it has ascertained that all available domestic remedies have been invoked and exhausted in the matter, in conformity with the generally recognized principles of international law. This shall not be the rule where the application of the remedies is unreasonably prolonged.

(d) The Committee shall hold closed meetings when examining communications under this article.

(e) Subject to the provision of sub-paragraph (c), the Committee shall make available its good offices to the States Parties concerned with a view to a friendly solution of the matter on the basis of respect for human rights and fundamental freedoms as recognized in the present Covenant.

(f) In any matter referred to it, the Committee may call upon the States Parties concerned, referred to in sub-paragraph (b), to supply any relevant information.

(g) The States Parties concerned, referred to in sub-paragraph (b), shall have the right to be represented when the matter is being considered in the Committee and to make submissions orally and/or in writing.

(h) The Committee shall, within twelve months after the date of receipt of notice under sub-paragraph (b), submit a report:

(i) If a solution within the terms of sub-paragraph (e) is reached, the Committee shall confine its report to a brief statement of the facts and of the solution reached;

(ii) If a solution within the terms of sub-paragraph (e) is not reached, the Committee shall confine its report to a brief statement of the facts; the written submissions and record of the oral submissions made by the States Parties concerned shall be attached to the report.

In every matter, the report shall be communicated to the States Parties concerned.

2. The provisions of this article shall come into force when ten States Parties to the present Covenant have made declarations under paragraph 1 of this article. Such declarations shall be deposited by the States Parties with the Secretary-General of the United Nations, who shall transmit copies thereof to the other States Parties. A declaration may be withdrawn at any time by notification to the Secretary-General. Such a withdrawal shall not prejudice the consideration of any matter which is the subject of a communication already transmitted under this article; no further communication by any State Party shall be received after the notification of withdrawal of the declaration has been received by the Secretary-General, unless the State Party concerned has made a new declaration.

Article 42

1. (a) If a matter referred to the Committee in accordance with article 41 is not resolved to the satisfaction of the States Parties concerned, the Committee may, with the prior consent of the States Parties concerned, appoint an *ad hoc* Conciliation Commission (hereinafter referred to as the Commission). The good offices of the Commission shall be made available to the States Parties concerned with a view to an amicable solution of the matter on the basis of respect for the present Covenant;

(b) The Commission shall consist of five persons acceptable to the States Parties concerned. If the States Parties concerned fail to reach agreement within three months on all or part of the composition of the Commission, the members of the Commission concerning whom no agreement has been reached shall be elected by secret ballot by a two-thirds majority vote of the Committee from among its members.

2. The members of the Commission shall serve in their personal capacity. They shall not be nationals of the States Parties concerned, or of a State not party to the present Covenant, or of a State Party which has not made a declaration under article 41.

3. The Commission shall elect its own Chairman and adopt its own rules of procedure.

4. The meetings of the Commission shall normally be held at the Headquarters of the

United Nations or at the United Nations Office at Geneva. However, they may be held at such other convenient places as the Commission may determine in consultation with the Secretary-General of the United Nations and the States Parties concerned.

5. The secretariat provided in accordance with article 36 shall also service the commissions appointed under this article.

6. The information received and collated by the Committee shall be made available to the Commission and the Commission may call upon the States Parties concerned to supply any other relevant information.

7. When the Commission has fully considered the matter, but in any event not later than twelve months after having been seized of the matter, it shall submit to the Chairman of the Committee a report for communication to the States Parties concerned:

(a) If the Commission is unable to complete its consideration of the matter within twelve months, it shall confine its report to a brief statement of the status of its consideration of the matter;

(b) If an amicable solution to the matter on the basis of respect of human rights as recognized in the present Covenant is reached, the Commission shall confine its report to a brief statement of the facts and of the solution reached;

(c) If a solution within the terms of sub-paragraph (b) is not reached, the Commissioner's report shall embody its findings on all questions of fact relevant to the issues between the States Parties concerned and its views on the possibilities of an amicable solution of the matter. This report shall also contain the written submissions and a record of the oral submissions made by the States Parties concerned;

(d) If the Commission's report is submitted under sub-paragraph (c), the States Parties concerned shall, within three months of the receipt of the report, notify the Chairman of the Committee whether or not they accept the contents of the report of the Commission.

8. The provisions of this article are without prejudice to the responsibilities of the Committee under article 41.

9. The States Parties concerned shall share equally all the expenses of the members of the Commission in accordance with estimates to be provided by the Secretary-General of the United Nations.

10. The Secretary-General of the United Nations shall be empowered to pay the expenses of the members of the Commission, if necessary, before reimbursement by the States Parties concerned, in accordance with paragraph 9 of this article.

Article 43

The members of the Committee, and of the *ad hoc* conciliation commissions which may be appointed under article 42, shall be entitled to the facilities, privileges and immunities of experts on mission for the United Nations as laid down in the relevant sections of the Convention on the Privileges and Immunities of the United Nations.

Article 44

The provisions for the implementation of the present Covenant shall apply without prejudice to the procedures prescribed in the field of human rights by or under the constituent instruments and the conventions of the United Nations and of the specialized agencies and shall not prevent the States Parties to the present Covenant from having recourse to other procedures for settling a dispute in accordance with general or special international agreements in force between them.

Article 45

The Committee shall submit to the General Assembly of the United Nations, through the Economic and Social Council, an annual report on its activities.

PART V
Article 46

Nothing in the present Covenant shall be interpreted as impairing the provisions of the Charter of the United Nations and of the constitutions of the specialized agencies which define the respective responsibilities of the various organs of the United Nations and of the specialized agencies in regard to the matters dealt within the present Covenant.

Article 47

Nothing in the present Covenant shall be interpreted as impairing the inherent right of all peoples to enjoy and utilize fully and freely their natural wealth and resources.

PART VI
Article 48

1. The present Covenant is open for signature by any State Member of the United Nations or member of any of its specialized agencies, by any State Party to the Statute of the International Court of Justice, and by any other State which has been invited by the General Assembly of the United Nations to become a party to the present Covenant.

2. The present Covenant is subject to ratification. Instruments of ratification shall be deposited with the Secretary-General of the United Nations.

3. The present Covenant shall be open to accession by any State referred to in paragraph 1 of this article.

4. Accession shall be effected by the deposit of an instrument of accession with the Secretary-General of the United Nations.

5. The Secretary-General of the United Nations shall inform all States which have signed this Covenant or acceded to it of the deposit of each instrument of ratification or accession.

Article 49

1. The present Covenant shall enter into force three months after the date of the deposit with the Secretary-General of the United Nations of the thirty-fifth instrument of ratification or instrument of accession.

2. For each State ratifying the present Covenant or acceding to it after the deposit of the thirty-fifth instrument of ratification or instrument of accession, the present Covenant shall enter into force three months after the date of the deposit of its own instrument of ratification or instrument of accession.

Article 50

The provisions of the present Covenant shall extend to all parts of federal States without any limitations or exceptions.

Article 51

1. Any State Party to the present Covenant may propose an amendment and file it with the Secretary-General of the United Nations. The Secretary-General of the United Nations shall thereupon communicate any proposed amendments to the States Parties to the present Covenant with a request that they notify him whether they favor a conference of States Parties for the purpose of considering and voting upon the proposals. In the event that at least one third of the States Parties favors such a conference, the Secretary-General shall convene the conference under the auspices of the United Nations. Any amendment adopted by a majority of the States Parties present and voting at the conference shall be submitted to the General Assembly of the United Nations for approval.

2. Amendments shall come into force when they have been approved by the General Assembly of the United Nations and accepted by a two-thirds majority of the States Parties to the present Covenant in accordance with their respective constitutional processes.

3. When amendments come into force, they shall be binding on those States Parties which have accepted them, other States Parties still being bound by the provisions of the present Covenant and any earlier amendment which they have accepted.

Article 52

Irrespective of the notifications made under article 48, paragraph 5, the Secretary-General of the United Nations shall inform all States referred to in paragraph 1 of the same article of the following particulars:

(a) Signatures, ratifications and accessions under article 48;

(b) The date of the entry into force of the present Covenant under article 49 and the date of the entry into force of any amendments under article 51.

Article 53

1. The present Covenant, of which the Chinese, English, French, Russian and Spanish texts are equally authentic, shall be deposited in the archives of the United Nations.

2. The Secretary-General of the United Nations shall transmit certified copies of the present Covenant to all States referred to in article 48.

Appendix B _____

INTERNATIONAL COVENANT ON ECONOMIC, SOCIAL, AND CULTURAL RIGHTS

PREAMBLE

The States Parties to the present Covenant,

Considering that, in accordance with the principles proclaimed in the Charter of the United Nations, recognition of the inherent dignity and of the equal and inalienable rights of all members of the human family is the foundation of freedom, justice and peace in the world,

Recognizing that these rights derive from the inherent dignity of the human person,

Recognizing that, in accordance with the Universal Declaration of Human Rights, the ideal of free human beings enjoying freedom from fear and want can only be achieved if conditions are created whereby everyone may enjoy his economic, social and cultural rights, as well as his civil and political rights,

Considering the obligation of States under the Charter of the United Nations to promote universal respect for, and observance of, human rights and freedoms,

Realizing that the individual, having duties to other individuals and to the community to which he belongs, is under a responsibility to strive for the promotion and observance of the rights recognized in the present Covenant,

Agree upon the following articles:

PART I

Article 1

1. All peoples have the right of self-determination. By virtue of that right they freely determine their political status and freely pursue their economic, social and cultural development.

2. All peoples may, for their own ends, freely dispose of their natural wealth and resources without prejudice to any obligations arising out of international economic cooperation, based upon the principle of mutual benefit, and international law. In no case may a people be deprived of its own means of subsistence.

3. The States Parties to the present Covenant, including those having responsibility for the administration of Non-Self-Governing and Trust Territories, shall promote the

realization of the right of self-determination, and shall respect that right, in conformity with the provisions of the Charter of the United Nations.

PART II
Article 2

1. Each State Party to the present Covenant undertakes to take steps, individually and through international assistance and cooperation, especially economic and technical, to the maximum of its available resource, with a view to achieving progressively the full realization of the rights recognized in the present Covenant by all appropriate means, including particularly the adoption of legislative measures.

2. The States Parties to the present Covenant undertake to guarantee that the rights enunciated in the present Covenant will be exercised without distinction of any kind as to race, color, sex, language, religion, political or other opinion, national or social origin, property, birth or other status.

3. Where not already provided for by existing legislative or other measures, each State Party to the present Covenant undertakes to take the necessary steps, in accordance with its constitutional processes and with the provisions of the present Covenant, to adopt such legislative or other measures as may be necessary to give effect to the rights recognized in the present Covenant.

4. Developing countries, with due regard to human rights and their national economy, may determine to what extent they would guarantee the economic rights recognized in the present Covenant to non-nationals.

Article 3

The States Parties to the present Covenant undertake to ensure the equal right of men and women to the enjoyment of all economic, social and cultural rights set forth in the present Covenant.

Article 4

The States Parties to the present Covenant recognize that, in the enjoyment of those rights provided by the State in conformity with the present Covenant, the State may subject such rights only to such limitations as are determined by law only insofar as this may be compatible with the nature of these rights and solely for the purpose of promoting the general welfare in a democratic society.

Article 5

1. Nothing in the present Covenant may be interpreted as implying for any State, group or person any right to engage in any activity or to perform any act aimed at the destruction of any of the rights or freedoms recognized herein, or at their limitation to a greater extent than is provided for in the present Covenant.

2. No restriction or derogation from any of the fundamental human rights recognized or existing in any country in virtue of law, conventions, regulations or custom shall be admitted on the pretext that the present Covenant does not recognize such rights or that it recognized them to a lesser extent.

PART III
Article 6

1. The States Parties to the present Covenant recognize the right to work, which includes the right of everyone to the opportunity to gain his living by work which he freely chooses or accepts, and will take appropriate steps to safeguard this right.

2. The steps to be taken by a State Party to the present Covenant to achieve the full realization of this right shall include technical and vocational guidance and training programs, policies and techniques to achieve steady economic, social and cultural devel-

opment and full and productive employment under conditions safeguarding fundamental political and economic freedoms to the individual.

Article 7

The States Parties to the present Covenant recognize the right of everyone to the enjoyment of just and favorable conditions of work which ensure, in particular:

(a) Remuneration which provides all workers, as a minimum, with:

(i) Fair wages and equal remuneration for work of equal value without distinction of any kind, in particular women being guaranteed conditions of work not inferior to those enjoyed by men, with equal pay for equal work;

(ii) A decent living for themselves and their families in accordance with the provisions of the present Covenant;

(b) Safe and healthy working conditions;

(c) Equal opportunity for everyone to be promoted in his employment to an appropriate higher level, subject to considerations other than those of seniority and competence;

(d) Rest, leisure and reasonable limitation of working hours and periodic holidays with pay, as well as remuneration for public holidays.

Article 8

1. The States Parties to the present Covenant undertake to ensure:

(a) The right of everyone to form trade unions and join the trade union of his choice, subject only to the rules of the organization concerned, for the promotion and protection of his economic and social interests. No restrictions may be placed on the exercise of this right other than those prescribed by law and which are necessary in a democratic society in the interests of national security or public order or for the protection of the rights and freedoms of others;

(b) The right of trade unions to establish national federations or confederations and the right of the latter to form or join international trade-union organizations;

(c) The right of trade unions to function freely subject to no limitations other than those prescribed by law and which are necessary in a democratic society in the interests of national security or public order or for the protection of the rights and freedoms of others;

(d) The right to strike, provided that it is exercised in conformity with the laws of the particular country.

2. This article shall not prevent the imposition of lawful restrictions on the exercise of these rights by members of the armed forces or of the police or of the administration of the State.

3. Nothing in this article shall authorize State Parties to the International Labor Organization Convention of 1948 concerning Freedom of Association and Protection of the Right to Organize to take legislative measures which would prejudice, or apply the law in such a manner as would prejudice, the guarantees provided for in that Convention.

Article 9

The States Parties to the present Covenant recognize the right of everyone to social security, including social insurance.

Article 10

The States Parties to the present Covenant recognize that:

1. The widest possible protection and assistance should be accorded to the family, which is the natural and fundamental group unit of society, particularly for its establish-

ment and while it is responsible for the care and education of dependent children. Marriage must be entered into with the free consent of the intending spouses.

2. Special protection should be accorded to mothers during a reasonable period before and after childbirth. During such period working mothers should be accorded paid leave or leave with adequate social security benefits.

3. Special measures of protection and assistance should be taken on behalf of all children and young persons without any discrimination for reasons of parentage or other conditions. Children and young persons should be protected from economic and social exploitation. Their employment in work harmful to their morals or health or dangerous to life or likely to hamper their normal development should be punishable by law. States should also set age limits below which the paid employment of child labor should be prohibited and punishable by law.

Article 11

1. The States Parties to the present Covenant recognize the right of everyone to an adequate standard of living for himself and his family, including adequate food, clothing and housing, and to the continuous improvement of living conditions. The States Parties will take appropriate steps to ensure the realization of this right, recognizing to this effect the essential importance of international cooperation based on free consent.

2. The States Parties of the present Covenant, recognizing the fundamental right of everyone to be free from hunger, shall take, individually and through international cooperation, the measures, including specific programs, which are needed:

(a) To improve methods of production, conservation and distribution of food by making full use of technical and scientific knowledge, by disseminating knowledge of the principles of nutrition and by developing or reforming agrarian systems in such a way as to achieve the most efficient development and utilization of natural resources;

(b) Taking into account the problems of both food-importing and food-exporting countries, to ensure an equitable distribution of world food supplies in relation to need.

Article 12

1. The States Parties to the present Covenant recognize the right of everyone to the enjoyment of the highest attainable standard of physical and mental health.

2. The steps taken by the States Parties to the present Covenant to achieve the full realization of this right shall include those necessary for:

(a) The provision for the reduction of the stillbirthrate and of infant mortality and for the healthy development of the child;

(b) The improvement of all aspects of environmental and industrial hygiene;

(c) The prevention, treatment and control of epidemic, endemic, occupational and other diseases;

(d) The creation of conditions which would assure to all medical service and medical attention in the event of sickness.

Article 13

1. The States Parties to the present Covenant recognize the right to everyone to education. They agree that education shall be directed to the full development of the human personality and the sense of its dignity, and shall strengthen the respect for human rights and fundamental freedoms. They further agree that education shall enable all persons to participate effectively in a free society, promote understanding, tolerance and friendship among all nations and all racial, ethnic or religious groups, and further the activities of the United Nations for the maintenance of peace.

2. The States Parties to the present Covenant recognize that, with a view to achieving the full realization of this right:

(a) Primary education shall be compulsory and available free to all;

(b) Secondary education in its different forms, including technical and vocational secondary education, shall be made generally available and accessible to all by every appropriate means, and in particular by the progressive introduction of free education;

(c) Higher education shall be made equally accessible to all, on the basis of capacity, by every appropriate means, and in particular by the progressive introduction of free education;

(d) Fundamental education shall be encouraged or intensified as far as possible for those persons who have not received or completed the whole period of their primary education;

(e) The development of a system of schools at all levels shall be actively pursued, an adequate fellowship system shall be established, and the material conditions of teaching staff shall be continuously improved.

3. The States Parties to the present Covenant undertake to have respect for the liberty of parents and, when applicable, legal guardians to choose for their children schools, other than those established by the public authorities, which conform to such minimum educational standards as may be laid down or approved by the State and to ensure the religious and moral education of their children in conformity with their own convictions.

4. No part of this article shall be construed so as to interfere with the liberty of individuals and bodies to establish and direct educational institutions, subject always to the observance of the principles set forth in paragraph 1 of this article and to the requirement that the education given in such institutions shall conform to such minimum standards as may be laid down by the State.

Article 14

Each State Party to the present Covenant which, at the time of becoming a Party, has not been able to secure in its metropolitan territory or other territories under its jurisdiction compulsory primary education, free of charge, undertakes, within two years, to work out and adopt a detailed plan of action for the progressive implementation, within a reasonable number of years, to be fixed in the plan, of the principle of compulsory education free of charge for all.

Article 15

1. The States Parties to the present Covenant recognize the right of everyone:

(a) To take part in cultural life;

(b) To enjoy the benefits of scientific progress and its applications;

(c) To benefit from the protection of the moral and material interests resulting from any scientific, literary or artistic production of which he is the author.

2. The steps to be taken by the States Parties to the present Covenant to achieve the full realization of this right shall include those necessary for the conservation, the development and the diffusion of science and culture.

3. The States Parties to the present Covenant undertake to respect the freedom indispensable for scientific research and creative activity.

4. The States Parties to the present Covenant recognize the benefits to be derived from the encouragement and development of international contacts and cooperation in the scientific and cultural fields.

PART IV
Article 16

1. The States Parties to the present Covenant undertake to submit in conformity with this part of the Covenant reports on the measures which they have adopted and the progress made in achieving the observance of the rights recognized herein.

2. (a) All reports shall be submitted to the Secretary-General of the United Nations, who shall transmit copies to the Economic and Social Council for consideration in accordance with the provisions of the present Covenant;

(b) The Secretary-General of the United Nations shall also transmit to the specialized agencies copies of the reports, or any relevant parts therefrom, from States Parties to the present Covenant which are also members of these specialized agencies insofar as these reports, or parts therefrom, relate to any matters which fall within the responsibilities of the said agencies in accordance with their constitutional instruments.

Article 17

1. The States Parties to the present Covenant shall furnish their reports in stages, in accordance with a program to be established by the Economic and Social Council within one year of the entry into force of the present Covenant after consultation with the States Parties and the specialized agencies concerned.

2. Reports may indicate factors and difficulties affecting the degree of fulfillment of obligations under the present Covenant.

3. Where relevant information has previously been furnished to the United Nations or to any specialized agency by any State Party to the present Covenant, it will not be necessary to reproduce that information, but a precise reference to the information so furnished will suffice.

Article 18

Pursuant to its responsibilities under the Charter of the United Nations in the field of human rights and fundamental freedoms, the Economic and Social Council may make arrangements with the specialized agencies in respect of their reporting to it on the progress made in achieving the observance of the provisions of the present Covenant falling within the scope of their activities. These reports may include particulars of decisions and recommendations on such implementation adopted by their competent organs.

Article 19

The Economic and Social Council may transmit to the Commission on Human Rights for study and general recommendation or, as appropriate, for information that reports concerning human rights submitted by States in accordance with article 16 and 17, and those concerning human rights submitted by the specialized agencies in accordance with article 18.

Article 20

The States Parties to the present Covenant and the specialized agencies concerned may submit comments to the Economic and Social Council on any general recommendation under article 19 or reference to such general recommendation in any report of the Commission on Human Rights or any documentation referred to therein.

Article 21

The Economic and Social Council may submit from time to time to the General Assembly reports with recommendations of a general nature and a summary of the information received from the States Parties to the present Covenant and the specialized agencies on the measures taken and the progress made in achieving general observance of the rights recognized in the present Covenant.

Article 22

The Economic and Social Council may bring to the attention of other organs of the United Nations, their subsidiary organs and specialized agencies concerned with furnishing technical assistance any matters arising out of the reports referred to in this part of the present Covenant which may assist such bodies in deciding, each within its field of competence, on the advisability of international measures likely to contribute to the effective progressive implementation of the present Covenant.

Article 23

The States Parties to the present Covenant agree that international action for the achievement of the rights recognized in the present Covenant includes such methods as the conclusion of conventions, the adoption of recommendations, the furnishing of technical assistance and the holding of regional meetings and technical meetings for the purpose of consultation and study organized in conjunction with the Governments concerned.

Article 24

Nothing in the present Covenant shall be interpreted as impairing the provision of the Charter of the United Nations and of the constitutions of the specialized agencies which define the respective responsibilities of the various organs of the United Nations, and of the specialized agencies in regard to the matters dealt with in the present Covenant.

Article 25

Nothing in the present Covenant shall be interpreted as impairing the inherent right of all peoples to enjoy and utilize fully and freely their natural wealth and resources.

PART V

Article 26

1. The present Covenant is open for signature by any State Member of the United Nations or member of any of its specialized agencies, by any State Party to the Statute of the International Court of Justice, and by any other State which has been invited by the General Assembly of the United Nations to become a party to the present Covenant.

2. The present Covenant is subject to ratification. Instruments of ratification shall be deposited with the Secretary-General of the United Nations.

3. The present Covenant shall be open to accession by any State referred to in paragraph 1 of this article.

4. Accession shall be effected by the deposit of an instrument of accession with the Secretary-General of the United Nations.

5. The Secretary-General of the United Nations shall inform all States which have signed this Covenant or acceded to it of the deposit of each instrument of ratification or accession.

Article 27

1. The present Covenant shall enter into force three months after the date of the deposit with the Secretary-General of the United Nations of the thirty-fifth instrument of ratification or instrument of accession.

2. For each State ratifying the present Covenant or acceding to it after the deposit of the thirty-fifth instrument of ratification or instrument of accession, the present Covenant shall enter into force three months after the date of the deposit of its own instrument of ratification or instrument of accession.

Article 28

The provisions of the present Covenant shall extend to all parts of federal States without any limitations or exceptions.

Article 29

1. Any State Party to the present Covenant may propose an amendment and file it with the Secretary-General of the United Nations. The Secretary-General of the United Nations shall thereupon communicate any proposed amendments to the States Parties to the present Covenant with a request that they notify him whether they favor a conference of States Parties for the purpose of considering and voting upon the proposals. In the event that at least one third of the States Parties favors such a conference, the Secretary-General shall convene the conference under the auspices of the United Nations. Any amendment adopted by a majority of the States Parties present and voting at the conference shall be submitted to the General Assembly of the United Nations for approval.

2. Amendments shall come into force when they have been approved by the General Assembly of the United Nations and accepted by a two-thirds majority of the States Parties to the present Covenant in accordance with their respective constitutional processes.

3. When amendments come into force, they shall be binding on those States Parties which have accepted them, other States Parties still being bound by the provisions of the present Covenant and any earlier amendment which they have accepted.

Article 30

Irrespective of the notifications made under article 26, paragraph 5, the Secretary-General of the United Nations shall inform all States referred to in paragraph 1 of the same article of the following particulars:

(a) Signatures, ratifications and accessions under article 26;

(b) The date of the entry into force of the present Covenant under article 27 and the date of the entry into force of any amendments under article 29.

Article 31

1. The present Covenant, of which the Chinese, English, French, Russian and Spanish texts are equally authentic, shall be deposited in the archives of the United Nations.

2. The Secretary-General of the United Nations shall transmit certified copies of the present Covenant to all States referred to in article 26.

Appendix C _____

FIGURES AND TABLES

Figure 4.1
Civil and Political Rights: Cluster Analysis for 1982 Data

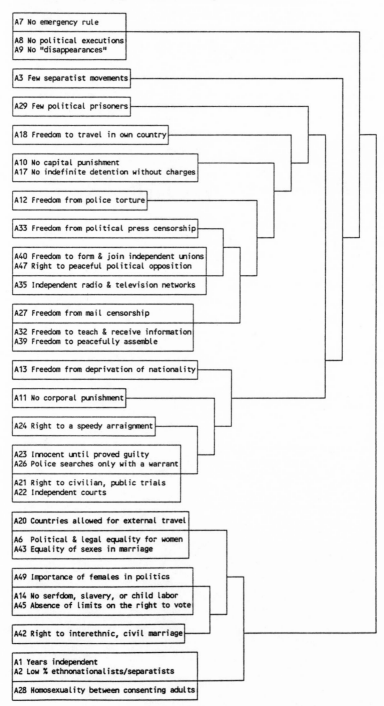

Figure 4.1 (continued)

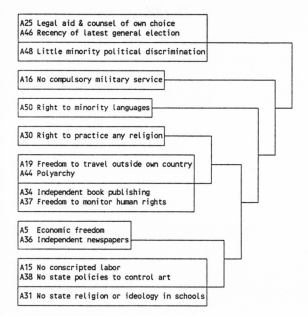

Figure 4.2
Civil and Political Rights: Cluster Analysis for 1986 Data

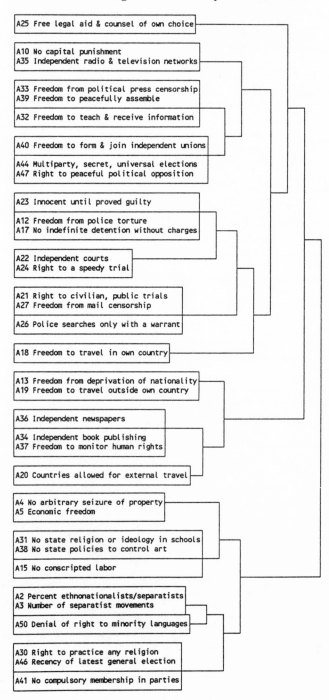

Figure 4.2 (continued)

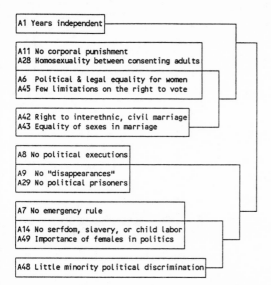

Figure 4.3
Economic and Social Rights: Cluster Analysis for 1982 Data

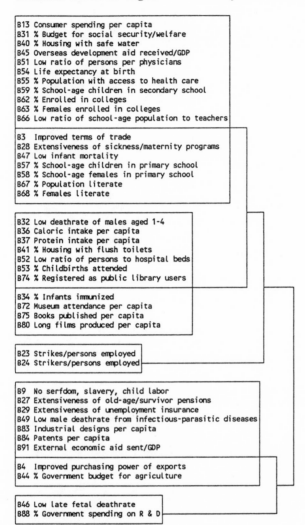

B13 Consumer spending per capita
B31 % Budget for social security/welfare
B40 % Housing with safe water
B45 Overseas development aid received/GDP
B51 Low ratio of persons per physicians
B54 Life expectancy at birth
B55 % Population with access to health care
B59 % School-age children in secondary school
B62 % Enrolled in colleges
B63 % Females enrolled in colleges
B66 Low ratio of school-age population to teachers

B3 Improved terms of trade
B28 Extensiveness of sickness/maternity programs
B47 Low infant mortality
B57 % School-age children in primary school
B58 % School-age females in primary school
B67 % Population literate
B68 % Females literate

B32 Low deathrate of males aged 1-4
B36 Caloric intake per capita
B37 Protein intake per capita
B41 % Housing with flush toilets
B52 Low ratio of persons to hospital beds
B53 % Childbirths attended
B74 % Registered as public library users

B34 % Infants immunized
B72 Museum attendance per capita
B75 Books published per capita
B80 Long films produced per capita

B23 Strikes/persons employed
B24 Strikers/persons employed

B9 No serfdom, slavery, child labor
B27 Extensiveness of old-age/survivor pensions
B29 Extensiveness of unemployment insurance
B49 Low male deathrate from infectious-parasitic diseases
B83 Industrial designs per capita
B84 Patents per capita
B91 External economic aid sent/GDP

B4 Improved purchasing power of exports
B44 % Government budget for agriculture

B46 Low late fetal deathrate
B88 % Government spending on R & D

Figure 4.3 (continued)

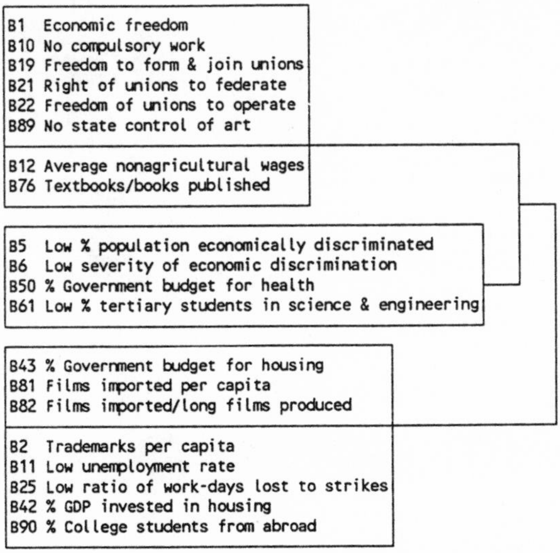

```
B1   Economic freedom
B10  No compulsory work
B19  Freedom to form & join unions
B21  Right of unions to federate
B22  Freedom of unions to operate
B89  No state control of art

B12  Average nonagricultural wages
B76  Textbooks/books published

B5   Low % population economically discriminated
B6   Low severity of economic discrimination
B50  % Government budget for health
B61  Low % tertiary students in science & engineering

B43  % Government budget for housing
B81  Films imported per capita
B82  Films imported/long films produced

B2   Trademarks per capita
B11  Low unemployment rate
B25  Low ratio of work-days lost to strikes
B42  % GDP invested in housing
B90  % College students from abroad
```

Figure 4.3 (continued)

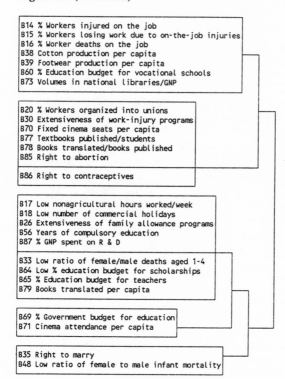

B14 % Workers injured on the job
B15 % Workers losing work due to on-the-job injuries
B16 % Worker deaths on the job
B38 Cotton production per capita
B39 Footwear production per capita
B60 % Education budget for vocational schools
B73 Volumes in national libraries/GNP

B20 % Workers organized into unions
B30 Extensiveness of work-injury programs
B70 Fixed cinema seats per capita
B77 Textbooks published/students
B78 Books translated/books published
B85 Right to abortion

B86 Right to contraceptives

B17 Low nonagricultural hours worked/week
B18 Low number of commercial holidays
B26 Extensiveness of family allowance programs
B56 Years of compulsory education
B87 % GNP spent on R & D

B33 Low ratio of female/male deaths aged 1-4
B64 Low % education budget for scholarships
B65 % Education budget for teachers
B79 Books translated per capita

B69 % Government budget for education
B71 Cinema attendance per capita

B35 Right to marry
B48 Low ratio of female to male infant mortality

Figure 4.4
Economic and Social Rights: Cluster Analysis for 1986 Data

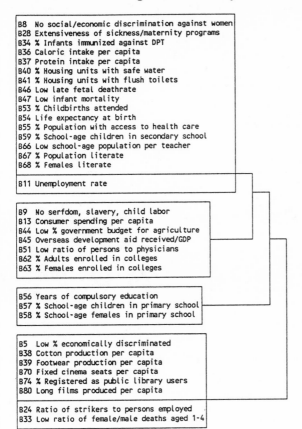

Figure 4.4 (continued)

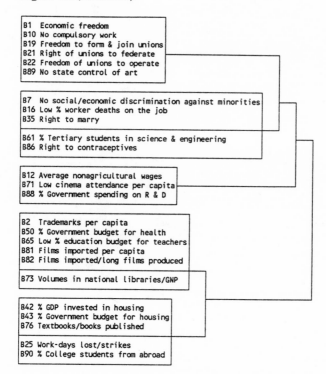

Figure 4.4 (continued)

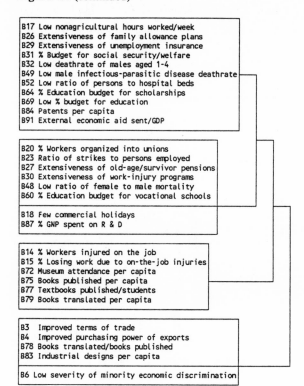

Figure 4.5
Civil, Political, Economic, and Social Rights: Cluster Analysis for 1982 Data

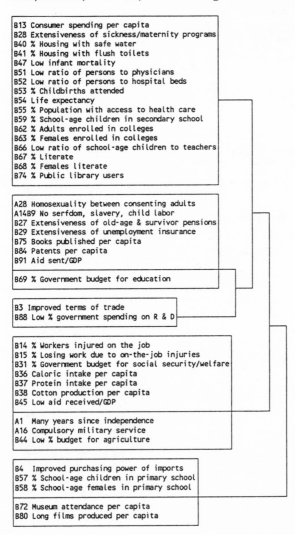

Figure 4.5 (continued)

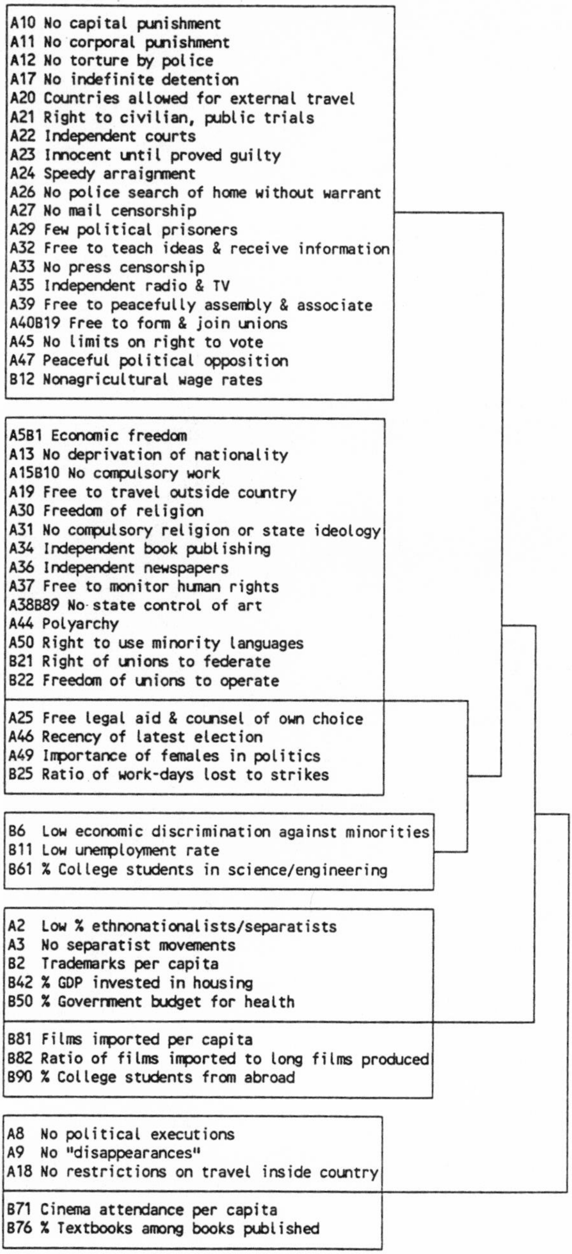

```
A10 No capital punishment
A11 No corporal punishment
A12 No torture by police
A17 No indefinite detention
A20 Countries allowed for external travel
A21 Right to civilian, public trials
A22 Independent courts
A23 Innocent until proved guilty
A24 Speedy arraignment
A26 No police search of home without warrant
A27 No mail censorship
A29 Few political prisoners
A32 Free to teach ideas & receive information
A33 No press censorship
A35 Independent radio & TV
A39 Free to peacefully assembly & associate
A40B19 Free to form & join unions
A45 No limits on right to vote
A47 Peaceful political opposition
B12 Nonagricultural wage rates
```

```
A5B1 Economic freedom
A13 No deprivation of nationality
A15B10 No compulsory work
A19 Free to travel outside country
A30 Freedom of religion
A31 No compulsory religion or state ideology
A34 Independent book publishing
A36 Independent newspapers
A37 Free to monitor human rights
A38B89 No state control of art
A44 Polyarchy
A50 Right to use minority languages
B21 Right of unions to federate
B22 Freedom of unions to operate
```

```
A25 Free legal aid & counsel of own choice
A46 Recency of latest election
A49 Importance of females in politics
B25 Ratio of work-days lost to strikes
```

```
B6  Low economic discrimination against minorities
B11 Low unemployment rate
B61 % College students in science/engineering
```

```
A2  Low % ethnonationalists/separatists
A3  No separatist movements
B2  Trademarks per capita
B42 % GDP invested in housing
B50 % Government budget for health
```

```
B81 Films imported per capita
B82 Ratio of films imported to long films produced
B90 % College students from abroad
```

```
A8  No political executions
A9  No "disappearances"
A18 No restrictions on travel inside country
```

```
B71 Cinema attendance per capita
B76 % Textbooks among books published
```

Figure 4.5 (continued)

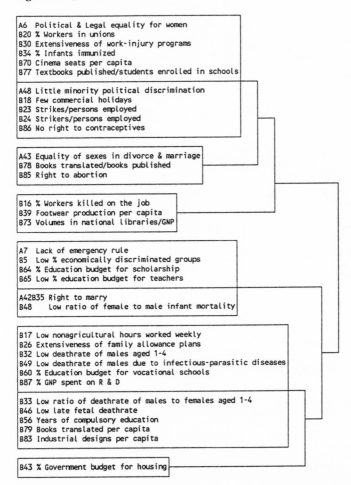

```
A6  Political & Legal equality for women
B20 % Workers in unions
B30 Extensiveness of work-injury programs
B34 % Infants immunized
B70 Cinema seats per capita
B77 Textbooks published/students enrolled in schools
```

```
A48 Little minority political discrimination
B18 Few commercial holidays
B23 Strikes/persons employed
B24 Strikers/persons employed
B86 No right to contraceptives
```

```
A43 Equality of sexes in divorce & marriage
B78 Books translated/books published
B85 Right to abortion
```

```
B16 % Workers killed on the job
B39 Footwear production per capita
B73 Volumes in national libraries/GNP
```

```
A7  Lack of emergency rule
B5  Low % economically discriminated groups
B64 % Education budget for scholarship
B65 Low % education budget for teachers
```

```
A42B35 Right to marry
B48    Low ratio of female to male infant mortality
```

```
B17 Low nonagricultural hours worked weekly
B26 Extensiveness of family allowance plans
B32 Low deathrate of males aged 1-4
B49 Low deathrate of males due to infectious-parasitic diseases
B60 % Education budget for vocational schools
B87 % GNP spent on R & D
```

```
B33 Low ratio of deathrate of males to females aged 1-4
B46 Low late fetal deathrate
B56 Years of compulsory education
B79 Books translated per capita
B83 Industrial designs per capita
```

```
B43 % Government budget for housing
```

Figure 4.6
Civil, Political, Economic, and Social Rights: Cluster Analysis for 1986 Data

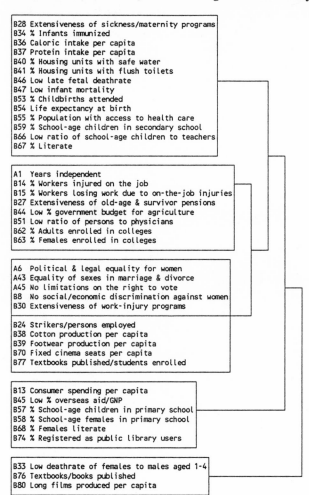

Figure 4.6 (continued)

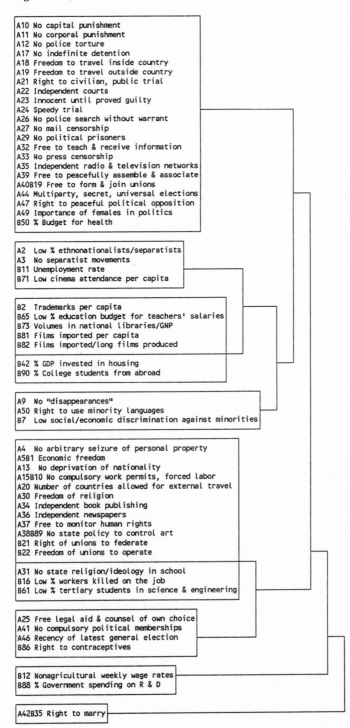

```
A10 No capital punishment
A11 No corporal punishment
A12 No police torture
A17 No indefinite detention
A18 Freedom to travel inside country
A19 Freedom to travel outside country
A21 Right to civilian, public trial
A22 Independent courts
A23 Innocent until proved guilty
A24 Speedy trial
A26 No police search without warrant
A27 No mail censorship
A29 No political prisoners
A32 Free to teach & receive information
A33 No press censorship
A35 Independent radio & television networks
A39 Free to peacefully assemble & associate
A40B19 Free to form & join unions
A44 Multiparty, secret, universal elections
A47 Right to peaceful political opposition
A49 Importance of females in politics
B50 % Budget for health
```

```
A2  Low % ethnonationalists/separatists
A3  No separatist movements
B11 Unemployment rate
B71 Low cinema attendance per capita
```

```
B2  Trademarks per capita
B65 Low % education budget for teachers' salaries
B73 Volumes in national libraries/GNP
B81 Films imported per capita
B82 Films imported/long films produced
```

```
B42 % GDP invested in housing
B90 % College students from abroad
```

```
A9  No "disappearances"
A50 Right to use minority languages
B7  Low social/economic discrimination against minorities
```

```
A4  No arbitrary seizure of personal property
A5B1 Economic freedom
A13  No deprivation of nationality
A15B10 No compulsory work permits, forced labor
A20 Number of countries allowed for external travel
A30 Freedom of religion
A34 Independent book publishing
A36 Independent newspapers
A37 Free to monitor human rights
A38B89 No state policy to control art
B21 Right of unions to federate
B22 Freedom of unions to operate
```

```
A31 No state religion/ideology in school
B16 Low % workers killed on the job
B61 Low % tertiary students in science & engineering
```

```
A25 Free legal aid & counsel of own choice
A41 No compulsory political memberships
A46 Recency of latest general election
B86 Right to contraceptives
```

```
B12 Nonagricultural weekly wage rates
B88 % Government spending on R & D
```

```
A42B35 Right to marry
```

Figure 4.6 (continued)

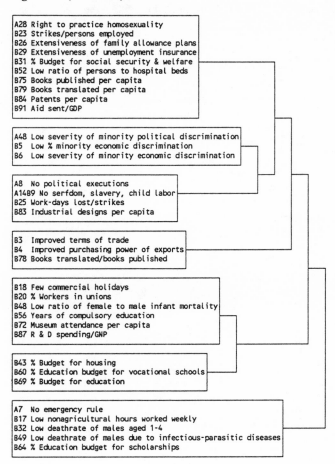

```
A28  Right to practice homosexuality
B23  Strikes/persons employed
B26  Extensiveness of family allowance plans
B29  Extensiveness of unemployment insurance
B31  % Budget for social security & welfare
B52  Low ratio of persons to hospital beds
B75  Books published per capita
B79  Books translated per capita
B84  Patents per capita
B91  Aid sent/GDP
```

```
A48  Low severity of minority political discrimination
B5   Low % minority economic discrimination
B6   Low severity of minority economic discrimination
```

```
A8   No political executions
A14B9 No serfdom, slavery, child labor
B25  Work-days lost/strikes
B83  Industrial designs per capita
```

```
B3   Improved terms of trade
B4   Improved purchasing power of exports
B78  Books translated/books published
```

```
B18  Few commercial holidays
B20  % Workers in unions
B48  Low ratio of female to male infant mortality
B56  Years of compulsory education
B72  Museum attendance per capita
B87  R & D spending/GNP
```

```
B43  % Budget for housing
B60  % Education budget for vocational schools
B69  % Budget for education
```

```
A7   No emergency rule
B17  Low nonagricultural hours worked weekly
B32  Low deathrate of males aged 1-4
B49  Low deathrate of males due to infectious-parasitic diseases
B64  % Education budget for scholarships
```

Figure 5.1
Cluster Analysis of Changes in Civil and Political Rights, 1982–1986

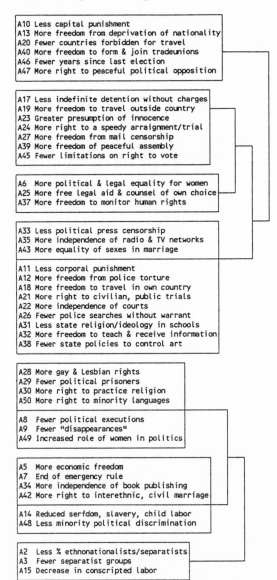

A10 Less capital punishment
A13 More freedom from deprivation of nationality
A20 Fewer countries forbidden for travel
A40 More freedom to form & join tradeunions
A46 Fewer years since last election
A47 More right to peaceful political opposition

A17 Less indefinite detention without charges
A19 More freedom to travel outside country
A23 Greater presumption of innocence
A24 More right to a speedy arraignment/trial
A27 More freedom from mail censorship
A39 More freedom of peaceful assembly
A45 Fewer limitations on right to vote

A6 More political & legal equality for women
A25 More free legal aid & counsel of own choice
A37 More freedom to monitor human rights

A33 Less political press censorship
A35 More independence of radio & TV networks
A43 More equality of sexes in marriage

A11 Less corporal punishment
A12 More freedom from police torture
A18 More freedom to travel in own country
A21 More right to civilian, public trials
A22 More independence of courts
A26 Fewer police searches without warrant
A31 Less state religion/ideology in schools
A32 More freedom to teach & receive information
A38 Fewer state policies to control art

A28 More gay & Lesbian rights
A29 Fewer political prisoners
A30 More right to practice religion
A50 More right to minority languages

A8 Fewer political executions
A9 Fewer "disappearances"
A49 Increased role of women in politics

A5 More economic freedom
A7 End of emergency rule
A34 More independence of book publishing
A42 More right to interethnic, civil marriage

A14 Reduced serfdom, slavery, child labor
A48 Less minority political discrimination

A2 Less % ethnonationalists/separatists
A3 Fewer separatist groups
A15 Decrease in conscripted labor

Figure 5.2
Cluster Analysis of Changes in Economic and Social Rights, 1982–1986

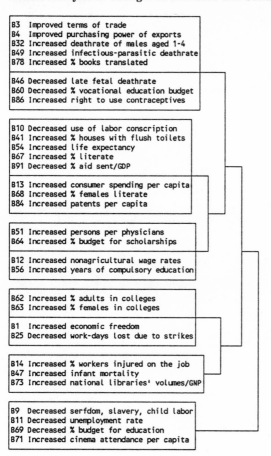

Figure 5.2 (continued)

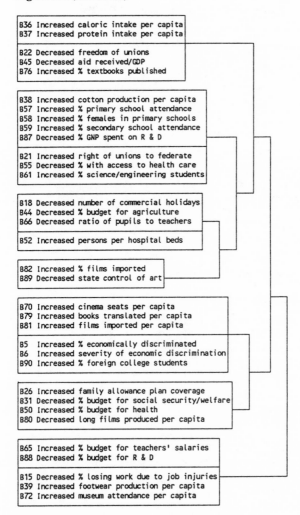

B36 Increased caloric intake per capita
B37 Increased protein intake per capita

B22 Decreased freedom of unions
B45 Decreased aid received/GDP
B76 Increased % textbooks published

B38 Increased cotton production per capita
B57 Increased % primary school attendance
B58 Increased % females in primary schools
B59 Increased % secondary school attendance
B87 Decreased % GNP spent on R & D

B21 Increased right of unions to federate
B55 Decreased % with access to health care
B61 Increased % science/engineering students

B18 Decreased number of commercial holidays
B44 Decreased % budget for agriculture
B66 Decreased ratio of pupils to teachers

B52 Increased persons per hospital beds

B82 Increased % films imported
B89 Decreased state control of art

B70 Increased cinema seats per capita
B79 Increased books translated per capita
B81 Increased films imported per capita

B5 Increased % economically discriminated
B6 Increased severity of economic discrimination
B90 Increased % foreign college students

B26 Increased family allowance plan coverage
B31 Decreased % budget for social security/welfare
B50 Increased % budget for health
B80 Decreased long films produced per capita

B65 Increased % budget for teachers' salaries
B88 Decreased % budget for R & D

B15 Decreased % losing work due to job injuries
B39 Increased footwear production per capita
B72 Increased museum attendance per capita

Figure 5.2 (continued)

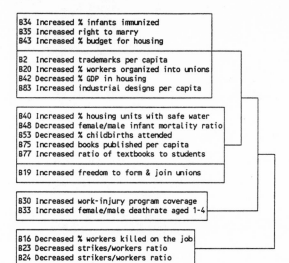

Figure 5.3
Cluster Analysis of Changes in Civil, Political, Economic, and Social Rights, 1982–1986

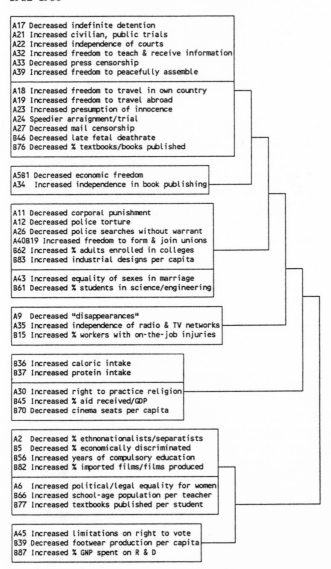

Figure 5.3 (continued)

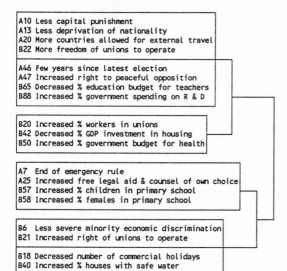

A10 Less capital punishment
A13 Less deprivation of nationality
A20 More countries allowed for external travel
B22 More freedom of unions to operate

A46 Few years since latest election
A47 Increased right to peaceful opposition
B65 Decreased % education budget for teachers
B88 Increased % government spending on R & D

B20 Increased % workers in unions
B42 Decreased % GDP investment in housing
B50 Increased % government budget for health

A7 End of emergency rule
A25 Increased free legal aid & counsel of own choice
B57 Increased % children in primary school
B58 Increased % females in primary school

B6 Less severe minority economic discrimination
B21 Increased right of unions to operate

B18 Decreased number of commercial holidays
B40 Increased % houses with safe water

Figure 5.3 (continued)

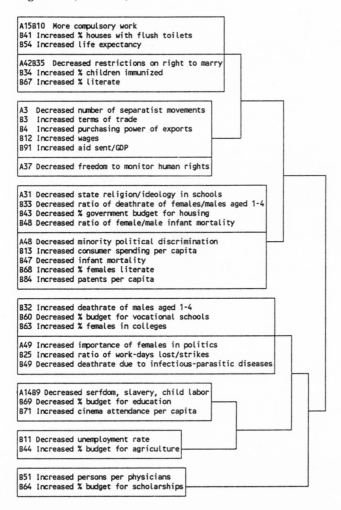

A15B10 More compulsory work
B41 Increased % houses with flush toilets
B54 Increased life expectancy

A42B35 Decreased restrictions on right to marry
B34 Increased % children immunized
B67 Increased % literate

A3   Decreased number of separatist movements
B3   Increased terms of trade
B4   Increased purchasing power of exports
B12 Increased wages
B91 Increased aid sent/GDP

A37 Decreased freedom to monitor human rights

A31 Decreased state religion/ideology in schools
B33 Decreased ratio of deathrate of females/males aged 1-4
B43 Decreased % government budget for housing
B48 Decreased ratio of female/male infant mortality

A48 Decreased minority political discrimination
B13 Increased consumer spending per capita
B47 Decreased infant mortality
B68 Increased % females literate
B84 Increased patents per capita

B32 Increased deathrate of males aged 1-4
B60 Decreased % budget for vocational schools
B63 Increased % females in colleges

A49 Increased importance of females in politics
B25 Increased ratio of work-days lost/strikes
B49 Decreased deathrate due to infectious-parasitic diseases

A14B9 Decreased serfdom, slavery, child labor
B69 Decreased % budget for education
B71 Increased cinema attendance per capita

B11 Decreased unemployment rate
B44 Increased % budget for agriculture

B51 Increased persons per physicians
B64 Increased % budget for scholarships

Figure 5.3 (continued)

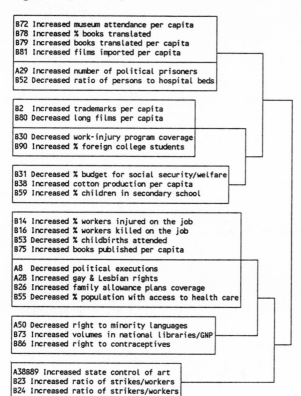

B72 Increased museum attendance per capita
B78 Increased % books translated
B79 Increased books translated per capita
B81 Increased films imported per capita

A29 Increased number of political prisoners
B52 Decreased ratio of persons to hospital beds

B2 Increased trademarks per capita
B80 Decreased long films per capita

B30 Decreased work-injury program coverage
B90 Increased % foreign college students

B31 Decreased % budget for social security/welfare
B38 Increased cotton production per capita
B59 Increased % children in secondary school

B14 Increased % workers injured on the job
B16 Increased % workers killed on the job
B53 Decreased % childbirths attended
B75 Increased books published per capita

A8 Decreased political executions
A28 Increased gay & Lesbian rights
B26 Increased family allowance plans coverage
B55 Decreased % population with access to health care

A50 Decreased right to minority languages
B73 Increased volumes in national libraries/GNP
B86 Increased right to contraceptives

A38889 Increased state control of art
B23 Increased ratio of strikes/workers
B24 Increased ratio of strikers/workers

Table 2.1

Correlates of Human Rights Observance

Independent Variables	Democracies (Political Rights)	Regime Coerciveness (Lack of Civil Rights)	Gastil/Humana Scales (Civil-Political Rights)	Quality of Life (Socioeconomic Rights)	Welfare Benefits (Socioeconomic Rights)
Arms imports	~ Arat	■ Boswell & Dixon ■ Wolpin		O Rosh	
% Catholic	~ Flanigan & Fogelman 1971b	O Wolpin	■ Park	■ Park	
Domestic Violence	~ Arat ~ Flanigan & Fogelman 1971b	■ Boswell & Dixon O Feierabend, Feierabend, Nesvold 1969b ■ Hibbs 1 London & Robinson 1 Muller & Seligson ■ Moaddel O Walton & Ragin ■ Wolpin	1 Timberlake & Williams	O Hibbs ~ Jackman 1975	~ Jackman 1975
Economic dependence		O Cingranelli & Pasquarello O Cingranelli & Wright ■ Moaddel		~ Rosh O Dixon	~ Rubison
Economic development (kwh/capita)	1 Arat ■ Bollen 1979, 1980, 1983 ■ Cutright 1965 ■ Cutright & Wiley ■ Frakt 1 Jackman 1975 ■ Lipset ■ Muller 1 Neubauer		■ Strouse & Claude ■ Timberlake & Williams	1 Jackman 1975	■ Cutright 1965 ■ Frakt 1 Jackman 1975 ■ Rubison
Economic equality	O Arat O Bollen & Grandjean O Bollen & Jackman ■ Cutright 1967a ■ Jackman 1975 ■ Muller ■ Rubison & Quinlan ■ Stack ■ Weede ■ Ziegler	O Boswell & Dixon ~ Moaddel	■ Park ■ Vorhies & Glahe	■ Park ■ Vorhies & Glahe	■ Rubison
Economic growth/capita	1 Feierabend, Feierabend, Nesvold 1969a ■ Bollen 1979	O Moaddel O Wolpin	O Strouse & Claude	■ Dixon ■ Hicks 1979 ~ Jackman 1975	~ Jackman 1975

150

Independent Variables	Democracies (Political Rights)	Regime Coerciveness (Lack of Civil Rights)	Gastil/Humana Scales (Civil-Political Rights)	Quality of Life (Socioeconomic Rights)	Welfare Benefits (Socioeconomic Rights)
Economic growth rate	~ Arat		■ Strouse & Claude		O Hicks 1988 O Jackman 1989
% Education spending			O Park	O Park ~ Spalding	
% Enrolled in educational institutions	O Banks 1972 ■ Cutright 1963 ■ Flanigan & Fogelman ■ Lipset ■ McCrone & Cnudde O Neubauer	~ Wolpin		■ Hicks 1979	
Ethnic diversity	~ Banks O Chan O Maoz & Abdolali O Maoz & Russett O Morgan & Campbell	■ Moaddel ■ Wolpin	O Jackman 1975	O Jackman 1975 ■ Park	
External Aggression		■ Feierabend, Feierabend, Bororiak ■ Wolpin	~ Haas ~ Rummel 1983 O Vincent O Weede 1984		
Foreign investmen/capita		■ Wolpin	■ Timberlake & Williams		
Former British colony	■ Bollen & Jackman 1985	O Boswell & Dixon ~ Mitchell & McCormick			
GNP		~ Feierabend, Feierabend, Bororiak	■ Banks 1985 O Conway O Strouse & Claude		
GNP/capita or National income/capita	■ Feierabend, Feierabend, Nesvold 1969a ■ Hewitt ■ Lipset ■ Nesvold	~ Boswell & Dixon ~ Feierabend, Feierabend, Bororiak ~ Mitchell & McCormick ■ Wolpin	■ Friedman ■ Gupta, Jongman, Schmid ■ Strouse & Claude ■ Ziegler	■ Hicks 1979 ■ Moon & Dixon 1985b ■ Pritchard ■ Rosh ■ Spalding ■ Ziegler	■ Ziegler

151

Table 2.1 (continued)

Independent Variables	Democracies (Political Rights)	Regime Coerciveness (Lack of Civil Rights)	Gastil/Humana Scales (Civil-Political Rights)	Quality of Life (Socioeconomic Rights)	Welfare Benefits (Socioeconomic Rights)
% Government spending	■ Banks 1972			O Jackman 1975 ~ Moon & Dixon 1985b	O Jackman 1975 ■ Rubison
Government spending/capita			■ Pritchard	■ Pritchard	
Laiserfaire capitalism	■ Ziegler	~■ Wolpin		■ Vorhies & Glahe	
Literacy rate	■ Cutright 1965 ■ Cutright & Wiley ■ Feierabend, Feierabend, Nesvold 1969a ■ Lipset ■ McCrone & Cnudde ■ Nesvold	~ Wolpin	■ Strouse & Claude ■ Vorhies & Glahe	■ Hicks 1979 ■ Moon & Dixon 1985b	■ Cutright 1965
Military rule	~ Adelman & Morris	■ Wolpin	~ Adelman & Morris ~ Conway ~ Gupta, Jongman, Schmit		
% Military spending		O Wolpin	~ Park	~ Park ■ Rosh	O Jackman 1975
% Moslems		■ Wolpin	~ Park	~ Park	
Periphery & semi-periphery status	~ Bollen 1983 ~ Bollen & Jackman 1985	O Boswell & Dixon			
Physicians/capita	■ Jackman 1975 ■ Lipset ■ Rosh				
Population growth				~ Jackman 1975	~ Jackman 1975
Progressive taxation				O Jackman 1975	O Jackman 1975
% Protestants	■ Bollen 1979 ■ Bollen & Jackman 1985	O Boswell & Dixon O Wolpin		■ Park	

Independent Variables	Democracies (Political Rights)	Regime Coerciveness (Lack of Civil Rights)	Gastil/Humana Scales (Civil-Political Rights)	Quality of Life (Socioeconomic Rights)	Welfare Benefits (Socioeconomic Rights)
Radios, TVs, newspapers/capita	■ Banks 1972 ■ Cutright 1963 ■ Lipset ■ McCrone & Cnudde ■ Nesvold ■ Neubauer	~ Wolpin	■ Strouse & Claude		~ Cutright 1965 ~1 Jackman 1975
Regime instability	~ Banks 1972 ~ Cutright 1965 ~1 Feierabend & Feierabend 1971b ~1 Feierabend, Feierabend, Nesvold 1969a ~ Hibbs ~ Nesvold	1 Feierabend & Feierabend O Feierabend, Feierabend, Nesvold 1969b ■ Hibbs 1 Marcus & Nesvold O Moaddel	~ Strouse & Claude	~ Feierabend & Feierabend ~1 Jackman 1975 ~ Nesvold	~ Cutright 1965 ~1 Jackman 1975
Trade/GNP	■ Banks 1972	~ Mitchell & McCormick		O Jackman 1975	O Jackman 1975 ~ Rubison
% Unionized	■ Adelman & Morris O Frakt	O Wolpin	■ Adelman & Morris	1 Jackman 1975	■ Frakt 1 Jackman 1975
% Urban population	■ Banks ■ Cutright 1963, 1965 1 Flanigan & Fogelman ■ Lipset ■ McCrone & Cnudde O Neubauer		■ Park	■ Park	■ Cutright 1965 ■ Spalding
% Urban workers	■ Cutright 1963 1 Flanigan & Fogelman ■ Lipset ■ Nesvold O Neubauer		■ Strouse & Claude	■ Spalding	■ Cutright 1967b
US economic aid/capita		O Carleton & Stohl ~ Poe & Sirirangsi ■ Schoultz 1981	■ Cingranelli & Pasquarello ~ Pasquarello ■ Poe O Stohl, Carleton, Johnson O Travis		

Table 2.1 (continued)

Independent Variables	Democracies (Political Rights)	Regime Coerciveness (Lack of Civil Rights)	Gastil/Humana Scales (Civil-Political Rights)	Quality of Life (Socioeconomic Rights)	Welfare Benefits (Socioeconomic Rights)
US military aid/capita		O Carleton & Stohl O Schoultz 1981 ■ Wolpin	O Cingranelli & Pasquarello ~ Pasquarello ~ Poe O Stohl, Carleton, Johnson ■ Travis		
Voter turnout	■ Neswold	~ Hibbs	O Ziegler		■ Cutright 1967b
% Votes for leftists				O Jackman 1975	O Jackman 1975
% Votes for socialists	■ Hewitt			O Jackman 1975	O Jackman 1975
% Welfare spending			■ Park	■ Dixon ■ Park	
Years since formation of democratic institutions	■ Bollen & Jackman 1989 ■ Flanigan & Fogelman 1971a		¶ Jackman 1975	¶ Jackman 1975	

Key:
- ■ = positive correlation
- ~ = negative correlation
- O = no correlation
- ~¶ = curvilinear relationship, negative
- ¶ = curvilinear relationship, positive

154

Table 3.1

Variable Names and Sources: Civil and Political Rights

Variables	Principal Data Sources
A1 Years independent since 1800 (minus years occupied by a foreign power)	Taylor & Hudson (1972:26-29)
A2 Percent of a country's population composed of ethnonationalists/separatists	Gurr & Gurr (1983); Gurr (1993)
A3 Number of separatist movements	Gurr & Gurr (1983); Gurr (1993)
A4 Freedom from arbitrary seizure of personal property (1986 only)	Humana (1987)
A5 Economic freedom	Gastil (1982:78-83;1986/87:74-75)
A6 Political & legal equality for women	Humana (1984,1987)
A7 Emergency constitutional suspensions that breach basic rights	Banks (1982/83,1986); USDOS-C (1982,1986)*
A8 Number of political executions	AI (1983,1987); USDOS-C (1982,1986)*
A9 Number of reported extrajudicial killings or "disappearances"	AI (1983,1987); USDOS-C (1982,1986)*
A10 Freedom from capital punishment by the state	Humana (1984,1987)
A11 Freedom from court sentences of corporal punishment	Humana (1984,1987)
A12 Freedom from torture or coercion by the state	Humana (1984,1987)
A13 Freedom from deprivation of nationality	Humana (1984,1987)
A14 Absence of serfdom, slavery, & child labor	Humana (1984,1987)
A15 Freedom from compulsory work permits & labor conscription	Humana (1984,1987)
A16 Freedom from compulsory military service (1982 only)	Humana (1984)
A17 Freedom from indefinite detention without charge	Humana (1984,1987)
A18 Freedom to travel in own country	Humana (1984,1987)
A19 Freedom to travel outside own country	Humana (1984,1987)
A20 Number of countries forbidden for external travel	Humana (1984,1987)
A21 Right to civilian, public trials	Humana (1984,1987)
A22 Independent courts	Humana (1984,1987)
A23 Right to be considered innocent until proved guilty	Humana (1984,1987)
A24 Right to a speedy arraignment (1982 only) trial (1986 only)	Humana (1984,1987)
A25 Right to free legal aid when necessary & counsel of own choice	USDOS-C (1982,1986)*
A26 Freedom from police searches of home without a warrant	Humana (1984,1987)
A27 Freedom from mail censorship	Humana (1984,1987)
A28 Right to practice homosexuality between consenting adults	Humana (1984,1987)
A29 Number of political prisoners	AI (1983,1987); USDOS-C (1982,1986)
A30 Right to practice any religion	Humana (1984,1987)
A31 Freedom from compulsory religion or state ideology in schools	Humana (1984,1987)
A32 Freedom to teach ideas and receive information	Humana (1984,1987)
A33 Freedom from political press censorship	Humana (1984,1987)
A34 Independent book publishing	Humana (1984,1987)
A35 Independent radio & television networks	Humana (1984,1987)
A36 Independent newspapers	Banks (1982/83,1986)*
A37 Freedom to monitor human rights violations	USDOS-C (1982,1986)*
A38 Freedom from deliberate state policies to control artistic works	Humana (1984,1987)
A39 Freedom to peacefully assemble and associate	Humana (1984,1987)

Table 3.1 (continued)

Variables	Principal Data Sources
A40 Freedom to form & join independent tradeunions	Humana (1984,1987)
A41 No compulsory membership in state organizations or parties (1986 only)	Humana (1987)
A42 Right to interracial, interreligious, or civil marriage	Humana (1984,1987)
A43 Equality of sexes in marriage (1986 only) & for divorce proceedings	Humana (1984,1987)
A44 Polyarchy (1982 only)/multiparty, secret, universal elections (1986 only)	Coppedge & Reineke (1988); Humana (1987)
A45 Limitations on the right to vote	Sivard (1982,1985)
A46 Years since latest general election	Banks (1982/83,1986)
A47 Right to peaceful political opposition	Humana (1984,1987)
A48 Severity of minority political discrimination	Gurr & Gurr (1983); Gurr (1993)
A49 Importance of females in politics	USDOS-C (1982,1986)*
A50 Right to publish & educate in minority languages	Humana (1984,1987)

<u>Key:</u> See end of Table 3.3.

156

Table 3.2

Variable Names and Sources: Economic and Social Rights

Variables		Principal Data Sources
B1	Economic freedom	Gastil (1982:78-83;1986/87:74-75)
B2	Trademarks applied for per capita	UNSY (1986/87)**
B3	Improvement in terms of trade	UNCTAD (1990); WT (1989/90)
B4	Improvement in purchasing power of exports	UNCTAD (1990); MDR (1989/90)
B5	Percent of population suffering economic discrimination	Gurr & Gurr (1983); Gurr (1993)
B6	Severity of minority economic discrimination	Gurr & Gurr (1983); Gurr (1993)
B7	No social and economic discrimination against minorities (1986 only)	Humana (1987)
B8	No social and economic discrimination against women (1986 only)	Humana (1987)
B9	Absence of serfdom, slavery, & child labor	Humana (1984,1987)
B10	Absence of compulsory work permits & labor conscription	Humana (1984,1987)
B11	Unemployment rate	ILO (1992); USCIA (1982-1988)
B12	Average nonagricultural weekly wage rates	ILO (1985-1991)***
B13	Consumer spending per capita	WT (1989/90)
B14	Percent of workers injured on the job	ILO (1992)
B15	Percent of workers losing work due to on-the-job injuries	ILO (1992)
B16	Percent of workers injured fatally on the job	ILO (1992)
B17	Average hours of work per week in nonagricultural activities	ILO (1992)
B18	Number of commercial holidays	USDOC (1981,1986)
B19	Freedom to form & join independent tradeunions	Humana (1984,1987)

Table 3.2 (continued)

Variables		Principal Data Sources
B20	Percent workers organized into unions	USCIA (1983,1986); USDOS-C (1982,1986)
B21	Right of unions to federate	USDOS-C (1982,1986)*
B22	Freedom of unions to operate	USDOS-C (1982,1986)*
B23	Ratio of strikes to persons employed	ILO (1992)
B24	Ratio of strikers to persons employed	ILO (1992)
B25	Ratio of work-days lost to number of strikes	ILO (1992)
B26	Extensiveness of family allowance plans	USDHHS (1983,1987)
B27	Extensiveness of old-age and survivor pensions	USDHHS (1983,1987)
B28	Extensiveness of sickness and/or maternity programs	USDHHS (1983,1987)
B29	Extensiveness of unemployment insurance	USDHHS (1983,1987)
B30	Extensiveness of work-injury programs	USDHHS (1983,1987)
B31	Percent of central government budget for social security & welfare	IMF (1988-1991)
B32	Deathrate of males aged 1-4	WHO (1990)
B33	Ratio of deathrate of females to males aged 1-4	WHO (1990)
B34	Percent of infants immunized against diphtheria, tetanus, & whooping cough	Sivard (1985,1989); UNDP (1990)
B35	Right to interracial, interreligious, or civil marriage	Humana (1984,1987)
B36	Caloric intake per capita	FAO (1990)**
B37	Protein intake per capita	FAO (1990)**
B38	Cotton woven fabric production per capita	UNSY (1988)**
B39	Nonrubber footwear production per capita	UNSY (1988)**
B40	Percent of housing units with safe water	Sivard (1985,1989)
B41	Percent of housing units with flush toilets	Sivard (1989)
B42	Percent gross domestic product invested in housing	SID (1982-1990)
B43	Percent of central government budget for housing	IMF (1988-1991)
B44	Percent of central government budget for agriculture	IMF (1988-1991)
B45	Overseas development aid received/gross domestic product	WDR (1982-1990)
B46	Late fetal deathrate	UNDY (1989)
B47	Infant mortality rate	Sivard (1985,1989)
B48	Ratio of female to male infant mortality	WHO (1983-1990)
B49	Deathrate due to infectious-parasitic diseases (males)	WHO (1983-1990)
B50	Percent government budget for health	IMF (1988-1991)
B51	Persons per physicians	Sivard (1985,1989)
B52	Persons per hospital beds	Sivard (1985,1989)
B53	Percent of childbirths attended	Sivard (1985,1989)
B54	Life expectancy at birth	Sivard (1985,1989)
B55	Percent of population with access to health care	SID (1982-1990)
B56	Years of compulsory education	UNESCO (1982-1991)
B57	Percent of school-age children in primary school	UNESCO (1982-1991)
B58	Percent of school-age females in primary school	UNESCO (1982-1991)

Variables		Principal Data Sources
B59	Percent of school-age children enrolled in secondary school	UNESCO (1982-1991)
B60	Percent of education budget for vocational schools	UNESCO (1982-1991)
B61	Percent of tertiary students in science & engineering	SID (1982-1990)
B62	Percent of adults enrolled in colleges	UNESCO (1982-1991)
B63	Percent of females enrolled in colleges	UNESCO (1982-1991)
B64	Percent of central government education budget for scholarships	UNESCO (1982-1991)
B65	Percent of central government education budget for teachers' salaries	UNESCO (1982-1991)
B66	School-age population per teacher	Sivard (1985, 1989)
B67	Percent of population literate	Sivard (1985); UNESCO (1991)
B68	Percent of females literate	UNESCO (1991); Sivard (1989)
B69	Percent of central government budget for education	IMF (1988-1991)
B70	Fixed cinema seats per capita	UNESCO (1982-1991)**
B71	Cinema attendance per capita	UNESCO (1982-1991)**
B72	Museum attendance per capita	UNESCO (1982-1991)**
B73	Ratio of volumes in national libraries to gross national product	UNESCO (1982-1991)**
B74	Percent of population registered as public library users	UNESCO (1982-1991)**
B75	Books published per capita	UNESCO (1982-1991)**
B76	Percent textbooks among all books published	UNESCO (1982-1991)
B77	Ratio of textbooks published to students enrolled in schools & colleges	UNESCO (1982-1991)
B78	Ratio of books translated to books published	UNESCO (1982-1991)
B79	Books translated per capita	UNESCO (1982-1991)**
B80	Long films produced per capita	UNESCO (1982-1991)
B81	Films imported per capita	UNESCO (1982-1991)**
B82	Ratio of films imported to long films produced	UNESCO (1982-1991)**
B83	Industrial designs applied for per capita	UNSY (1986/87)**
B84	Patents applied for per capita	UNSY (1986/87)**
B85	Right to early abortion (1982 only)	Humana (1984)
B86	Right to contraceptives	Humana (1984, 1987)
B87	Percent of GNP spent on R & D	UNESCO (1991)**
B88	Percent central government spending on R & D	UNESCO (1991); IMF (1988-1991)***
B89	Freedom from state policy to control artistic works	Humana (1984, 1987)
B90	Percent of college students from abroad	UNESCO (1991)
B91	External economic aid sent/gross domestic product	WDR (1982-1990)

Key: See end of Table 3.3.

159

Table 3.3
Variable Names and Sources: Predictor Variables

Variables	Principal Data Sources
C1 Per capita GNP	Sivard (1985,1989)
C2 GNP per capita growth rate	UNCTAD (1990)
C3 Percent of workforce employed in agriculture	SID (1982-1990)
C4 Energy consumption per capita	UNSY (1983/84-1988/89)**
C5 Percent of population living in cities	SID (1990)
C6 Newspaper circulation per capita	UNESCO (1982-1991)**
C7 Radios per capita	UNSY (1983/84-1988/89)
C8 Telephones per capita	UNSY (1983/84-1988/89)
C9 Television sets per capita	UNSY (1983/84-1988/89)
C10 Investment received/gross domestic product	WT (1982-1990)
C11 Dollar value of exports and imports/GNP	UNDOTSY (1982-1990)**
C12 Percent of trade with largest export partner	UNCTAD (1990)
C13 Percent of trade with largest import partner	UNCTAD (1990)
C14 Food import dependency (1986 only)	UNDP (1990)
C15 Income inequality (percent of income going to top 10 percent of population)	Taylor & Jodice (1983:134-136); WDR (1982-1990)
C16 Central government budget expenditures on education per capita	Sivard (1985,1989)
C17 Central government budget expenditures on health per capita	Sivard (1985,1989)
C18 Central government budget expenditures on welfare per capita	IMF (1988-1992)**
C19 Percentage of direct taxes collected	IMF (1988-1992)
C20 Rate of inflation	UNSY (1988/89)
C21 Votes cast/adults registered to vote	Keesing's (1980-1990)
C22 Number of political parties in parliament	Banks (1982/83,1986)
C23 Percent of seats held by largest political party or ruling coalition	Banks (1982/83,1986)
C24 Government revenues/GNP	IMF (1988-1992)
C25 Coups from 1960/years independent	Sivard (1982,1986); Taylor & Hudson (1972:26-29)
C26 Military-dominated government	Sivard (1982,1986)
C27 Years of military rule from 1960/years independent	Sivard (1982,1986)
C28 Official violence against citizens	Sivard (1982,1986)
C29 Years at civil war from 1960/years independent	Sivard (1982,1986); Taylor & Hudson (1972:26-29)
C30 Deathrate due to domestic violence	Sivard (1982,1986)
C31 Years in international war from 1960/years independent	Sivard (1982,1986); Taylor & Hudson (1972:26-29)
C32 Deathrate due to foreign conflict	Sivard (1982,1986)
C33 Percent of population in the armed forces	Sivard (1984,1989)
C34 Military budget/GNP	Sivard (1984,1989)
C35 Arms imports/GNP	Sivard (1985,1989)
C36 Arms imports/military budget	Sivard (1985,1989)
C37 Extent of minority political grievances (1986 only)	Gurr (1993)
C38 Extent of minority economic grievances (1986 only)	Gurr (1993)
C39 Extent of minority social grievances (1986 only)	Gurr (1993)

Variables		Principal Data Sources
C40	Number of terrorist incidents (1986 only)	USOCC (1983,1986)
C41	Percent budget for internal security (1986 only)	IMF (1992)
C42	Net arms exporting country (yes/no)	Sivard (1982,1986)
C43	Western arms imports/all arms imports	Sivard (1985,1989)
C44	US civilian aid/GNP	USAID (1982,1986)**
C45	US military aid/GNP	USAID (1982,1986)**
C46	Percent of troops abroad	Sivard (1982,1986)
C47	Foreign troops/domestic troops in country	Sivard (1982,1986)
C48	Western bloc troops in country/total troops in country (net)	Sivard (1982,1986)
C49	Former British colony	Banks (1982/83)
C50	Percent Protestant population	Europa (1982-1990)
C51	Percent Roman Catholic population	Europa (1982-1990)
C52	Percent Moslem population	Europa (1982-1990)
C53	Index of ethnolinguistic heterogeneity	USSR (1964)
C54	Percent leftists in parliament	Banks (1982/83,1986)
C55	Cancer deathrate (males)	WHO (1990)
C56	Heart disease deathrate (males)	WHO (1990)
C57	Suicide deathrate (males)	WHO (1990)

Key for Tables 3.1-3.3:

*	=	Haas codings from this source.
**	=	The denominator is from Sivard (1985, 1989).
***	=	Exchange rate conversions applied from UNSY (1988/89).
AI	=	Amnesty International, Report
Banks	=	Political Handbook of the World
FAO	=	Food and Agriculture Organization of the United Nations, Production Yearbook
ILO	=	International Labor Organization, Year Book of Labour Statistics
IMF	=	International Monetary Fund, Government Finance Statistics
SID	=	World Bank, Social Indicators of Development
UNCTAD	=	UN Conference on Trade and Development, Handbook of International Trade and Development Statistics
UNDOTSY	=	UN Statistical Office, Directions of Trade Statistics Yearbook
UNDP	=	UN Development Program, Human Development Report
UNDY	=	UN Statistical Office, Demographic Yearbook
UNESCO	=	UN Educational, Scientific, and Cultural Organization, Statistical Yearbook
UNSY	=	UN Statistical Office, Statistical Yearbook
USAID	=	US Department of State, Agency for International Development, U.S. Overseas Loans and Grants
USCIA	=	US Department of State, Central Intelligence Agency, World Fact Book
USDHHS	=	US Department of Health & Human Services, Social Security Administration, Social Security Programs Throughout the World
USDOC	=	US Department of Commerce, International Trade Administration (1981, 1986)
USOCC	=	US Department of State, Office of the Coordinator for Counterterrorism, Patterns of Global Terrorism
USDOS-C	=	US Department of State, Country Reports on Human Rights Practices
WHO	=	World Health Organization, Statistical Annual
WDR	=	World Bank, World Development Report
WT	=	World Bank, World Tables

Table 4.1

Civil and Political Rights: Factor Analysis for 1982 Data

Articles		Variables	1	2	3	4	5	6	7	8	9
1	A1	Years independent							.83		
	A2	Percent ethnonationalists/separatists				.86					
	A3	Number of separatist movements				.86					
2-3	A5	Economic freedom		.74							
	A6	Political & legal equality for women					.51	.43			
4	A7	Emergency rule									
6	A8	Political executions			.86					-.60	
	A9	"Disappearances"			.89						
7	A10	No capital punishment	.75								
	A11	No corporal punishment	.61					.62			
	A12	Freedom from police torture	.79								
	A13	Freedom from deprivation of nationality	.57								
8	A15	Absence of conscripted labor	.85								
	A16	No compulsory military service				.46					
9	A17	No indefinite detention without charges	.79								
12	A18	Freedom to travel in own country	.53						-.41		
	A19	Freedom to travel outside own country	.62	.62							
	A20	Countries forbidden for external travel	-.50						-.50		
14	A21	Right to civilian, public trials	.84								
	A22	Independent courts	.81								
	A23	Innocent until proved guilty	.86								
	A24	Right to a speedy arraignment	.77								
	A25	Free legal aid & counsel of own choice	.81								
17	A26	Police searches only with a warrant	.87								
	A27	Freedom from mail censorship	.41								
	A28	Homosexuality between consenting adults	-.75								
18	A29	Number of political prisoners						.49			
19	A30	Right to practice any religion		.69							
	A31	No state religion or ideology in schools		.73							
	A32	Freedom to teach & receive information	.76	.51							
	A33	Freedom from political press censorship	.77	.47							
	A34	Independent book publishing	.55	.50							
	A35	Independent radio & television networks	.71	.41							
	A36	Independent newspapers		.80							
	A37	Freedom to monitor human rights	.54	.69							
	A38	No state policies to control art		.79							
21-22	A39	Freedom to peacefully assemble	.79	.44							
	A40	Freedom to form & join independent unions	.76	.48							
23	A42	Right to interethnic, civil marriage					.83				

Articles	Variables	1	2	3	4	5	6	7	8	9
23	A43 Equality of sexes in marriage	.60					.43		-.41	
25	A44 Polyarchy	-.53	.64							
	A45 Limitations on the right to vote					-.40				
	A46 Years since latest general election						-.79			
	A47 Right to peaceful political opposition	.81								
	A48 Minority political discrimination									.66
	A49 Importance of females in politics					.67				
27	A50 Right to minority languages		.56		-.43					
	Percent Variance Explained	14.6	8.2	2.6	2.6	2.4	2.3	1.9	1.5	1.3

Note: Loadings below ±.40 omitted.
Variables with no loadings above ±.40 omitted.

Table 4.2
Civil and Political Rights: Factor Analysis for 1986 Data

Articles	Variables	1	2	3	4	5	6	7	8
1	A1 Years independent							.68	
	A2 Percent ethnonationalists/separatists				.91				
	A3 Number of separatist movements				.89				
2-3	A4 No arbitrary seizure of property	.66							
4	A5 Economic freedom	.56							
6	A6 Political & legal equality for women		.77						
	A7 Emergency rule			.47		.41			
	A8 Political executions					.75			
	A9 "Disappearances"					.81			
7	A10 No capital punishment	.72	.41						
	A11 No corporal punishment		.57						
	A12 Freedom from police torture	.72							
	A13 Freedom from deprivation of nationality	.64							.46
8	A14 No serfdom, slavery, or child labor	.59	.60						
	A15 Absence of conscripted labor	.81							
9	A17 No indefinite detention without charges	.59							
12	A18 Freedom to travel in own country	.59							
	A19 Freedom to travel outside own country	.78							

164

Articles	Variables	1	2	3	4	5	6	7	8
12	A20 Countries forbidden for external travel	-.69							
14	A21 Right to civilian, public trials	.87							
	A22 Independent courts	.85							
	A23 Innocent until proved guilty	.83							
	A24 Right to a speedy trial	.77							
	A25 Free legal aid & counsel of own choice	.40							.52
17	A26 Police searches only with a warrant	.76							
	A27 Freedom from mail censorship	.82							
18	A28 Homosexuality between consenting adults	.48	.60						
	A29 Number of political prisoners	-.65							
	A30 Right to practice any religion	.54		.46			.48		
19	A31 No state religion or ideology in schools	.52		.64					
	A32 Freedom to teach & receive information	.88							
	A33 Freedom from political press censorship	.86							
	A34 Independent book publishing	.88							
	A35 Independent radio & television networks	.77							
	A36 Independent newspapers	.71							
	A37 Freedom to monitor human rights	.77							
	A38 No state policies to control art	.59		.65					
21-22	A39 Freedom to peacefully assemble	.88							
	A40 Freedom to form & join independent unions	.90							
	A41 No compulsory membership in organizations	.43					.56		
23	A42 Right to interethnic, civil marriage		.56						-.50
	A43 Equality of sexes in marriage		.83						
25	A44 Multiparty, secret, universal elections	.88							
	A45 Limitations on the right to vote	-.46	-.59						
	A46 Years since latest general election						-.75		
	A47 Right to peaceful political opposition	.88							
	A48 Minority political discrimination		-.40		-.52				
	A49 Importance of females in politics	.41						.54	
27	A50 Right to minority languages	.42							
	Percent Variance Explained	18.7	4.7	3.1	2.7	2.4	2.2	1.8	1.4

Note: Loadings below ±.40 omitted.
Variables with no loadings above ±.40 omitted.

Table 4.3
Economic and Social Rights: Factor Analysis for 1982 Data

Articles	Variables	1	2	3	4	5	6	7	8
1	B1 Economic freedom	.47	.71						
	B2 Trademarks applied for per capita		.45						
2	B5 % Population suffering economic discrimination					.92			
	B6 Severity of minority economic discrimination					.89			
6	B9 Absence of serfdom, slavery, & child labor	.59							
7	B10 No compulsory work permits/labor conscription		.94						
	B12 Average nonagricultural weekly wage rates	.48	.42						
	B13 Consumer spending per capita	.81							
	B14 % Workers injured on the job	.65							
	B15 % Losing work due to on-the-job injuries	.74							
	B16 % Workers injured fatally on the job								
	B17 Nonagricultural work week in hours	-.55							
	B18 Number of commercial holidays						.82		.55
8	B19 Freedom to form & join independent unions		.81						
	B20 % Workers organized into unions	.41							
	B21 Right of unions to federate		.81						
	B22 Freedom of unions to operate		.83						
9	B26 Extensiveness of family allowance plans	.70							
	B27 Extensiveness of old-age/survivor pensions	.58							
	B28 Extensiveness of sickness/maternity programs	.63							
	B29 Extensiveness of unemployment insurance	.62							
	B31 % Budget for social security/welfare	.78	.45						
10	B32 Deathrate of males aged 1-4	-.80							
	B33 Ratio of deathrate of females/males aged 1-4				.43				
	B34 % Infants immunized against DPT	.70							
11	B36 Caloric intake per capita	.80							
	B37 Protein intake per capita	.81							
	B38 Cotton woven fabric production per capita	.40		.73					
	B39 Nonrubber footwear production per capita	.54		.68					
	B40 % Housing units with safe water	.84							
	B41 % Housing units with flush toilets	.84							
	B42 % Gross domestic product invested in housing				.77			.71	
	B43 % Central government budget for housing	-.44							
	B44 % Central government budget for agriculture	-.69							
	B45 Overseas development aid received/GDP							1.01	
12	B46 Late fetal deathrate								
	B47 Infant mortality rate	-.94							
	B48 Ratio of female to male infant mortality								.57
	B49 Infectious-parasitic diseases deathrate	.71							

Articles	Variables	1	2	3	4	5	6	7	8
12	B51 Persons per physicians	-.90							
	B52 Persons per hospital beds	-.83							
	B53 % Childbirths attended	.79							
	B54 Life expectancy at birth	.96							
	B55 % Population with access to health care	.75					-.43		
13	B56 Years of compulsory education	.53							
	B57 % School-age children in primary school	.73							
	B58 % School-age females in primary school	.79							
	B59 % School-age children in secondary school	.90							
	B60 % Education budget for vocational schools	.54							
	B61 % Tertiary students in science & engineering								.60
	B62 % Adults enrolled in colleges	.78							
	B63 % Females enrolled in colleges	.79							
	B64 % Education budget for scholarships								-.41
	B66 School-age population per teacher	-.78					-.54		
	B67 % Population literate	.92							
	B68 % Females literate	.90							
15	B70 Fixed cinema seats per capita	.48							
	B72 Museum attendance per capita	.65							
	B73 Volumes in national libraries/GNP			.46					
	B74 % Registered as public library users	.86							
	B75 Books published per capita	.57							
	B77 Textbooks published/students	.42							
	B79 Books translated per capita	.41							
	B80 Long films produced per capita	.41							
	B81 Films imported per capita				.89				
	B82 Films imported/long films produced				.57				
	B83 Industrial designs per capita	.48							
	B84 Patents per capita	.66							
	B85 Right to abortion	.40							
	B87 % GNP spent on R & D	.46							
16	B89 No state control of artistic works		.93						
	B91 External economic aid sent/GDP	.50							
	Percent Variance Explained	26.1	6.8	3.5	3.3	3.0	3.0	2.9	2.7

Note: Loadings below ±.40 omitted.
Variables with no loadings above ±.40 omitted.

167

Table 4.4
Economic and Social Rights: Factor Analysis for 1986 Data

Articles	Variables	1	2	3	4	5	6	7	8
1	B1 Economic freedom	.44							
	B2 Trademarks applied for per capita		.72						
	B3 Improvement in terms of trade		.43						
	B4 Improvement in purchasing power of exports			.87					
2	B5 % Population suffering economic discrimination			.80					
	B6 Severity of minority economic discrimination								.81
	B7 No social/economic discrimination against minorities								.75
	B8 No social/economic discrimination against women								-.70
6	B9 Absence of serfdom, slavery, & child labor	.63							
	B10 No compulsory work permits/labor conscription	.60							
7	B13 Consumer spending per capita		.90						
	B14 % Workers injured on the job	.79							
	B15 % Losing work due to on-the-job injuries	.62				.41			
	B16 % Workers injured fatally on the job	.65				.55			
8	B17 Nonagricultural work week in hours	-.49						-.43	
	B19 Freedom to form & join independent unions		.78						
	B21 Freedom of unions to operate		.84						
	B22 Right of unions to federate		.84						
9	B26 Extensiveness of family allowance plans	.56							
	B27 Extensiveness of old-age/survivor pensions	.53							
	B28 Extensiveness of sickness/maternity programs	.59							
	B29 Extensiveness of unemployment insurance	.52							
	B31 % Budget for social security/welfare	.63							
	B32 Deathrate of males aged 1-4	-.69							
10	B33 Ratio of deathrate of females/males aged 1-4						.52		
	B34 % Infants immunized against DPT	.79							
11	B36 Caloric intake per capita	.83							
	B37 Protein intake per capita	.81							
	B38 Cotton woven fabric production per capita	.54				.87			
	B39 Nonrubber footwear production per capita	.88				.48			
	B40 % Housing units with safe water	.68							
	B41 % Housing units with flush toilets								
	B42 % Gross domestic product invested in housing		.47						
12	B44 % Central government budget for agriculture	-.41							
	B45 Overseas development aid received/GDP	-.45							
	B46 Late fetal deathrate	-.79		-.49					
	B47 Infant mortality rate	-.96							
	B49 Infectious-parasitic diseases deathrate	-.70							
	B51 Persons per physicians	-.84							

Articles	Variables		1	2	3	4	5	6	7	8
12	B52	Persons per hospital beds	-.66							
	B53	% Childbirths attended	.74							
	B54	Life expectancy at birth	.90							
	B55	% Population with access to health care	.90							
13	B56	Years of compulsory education	.58							
	B57	% School-age children in primary school	.72							
	B58	% School-age females in primary school	.70							
	B59	% School-age children in secondary school	.90							
	B60	% Education budget for vocational schools	.54							
	B62	% Adults enrolled in colleges	.70							
	B63	% Females enrolled in colleges	.72							
	B65	% Education budget for teachers' salaries						-.41	-.41	
	B66	School-age population per teacher	-.88							
	B67	% Population literate	.88							
	B68	% Females literate	.85							
15	B71	Cinema attendance per capita		-.48	.50					
	B72	Museum attendance per capita						.61		
	B74	% Registered as public library users	.58							
	B75	Books published per capita	.61					.40		
	B77	Textbooks published/students	.42					.55		
	B79	Books translated per capita						.82		
	B81	Films imported per capita				.85				
	B82	Films imported/long films produced				.75				
	B83	Industrial designs per capita	.45		.42					
	B84	Patents per capita	.61		.43					
	B87	% GNP spent on R & D	.46	-.46	.50					
16	B88	% Government spending on R & D							.89	
	B89	No state control of artistic works		.83						
	B90	% College students from abroad				.58			.43	
	B91	External economic aid sent/GDP	.52							
		Percent Variance Explained	23.9	7.3	4.1	3.6	3.1	3.0	2.9	2.9

Note: Loadings below ±.40 omitted.
Variables with no loadings above ±.40 omitted.

169

Table 4.5
Civil, Political, Economic, and Social Rights: Factor Analyses for 1982 and 1986 Data

Articles		Variables	1982 Data		1986 Data	
			1	2	1	2
2-3	A5	Economic freedom	.47	.49	.61	
6	A6	Political & legal equality for women				.42
	A10	No capital punishment		.73	.69	
	A11	No corporal punishment		.60	.49	
	A12	Freedom from police torture		.69	.72	
	A13	Freedom from deprivation of nationality		.65	.71	
8	A14	No serfdom, slavery, or child labor	.58		.43	.53
	A15	Absence of conscripted labor		.82	.77	
9	A17	No indefinite detention without charges		.78	.81	
12	A18	Freedom to travel in own country		.66	.67	
	A19	Freedom to travel outside own country		.88	.87	
	A20	Countries forbidden for external travel			-.70	
14	A21	Right to civilian, public trials		.85	.85	
	A22	Independent courts		.87	.83	
	A23	Innocent until proved guilty		.79	.81	
	A24	Right to a speedy arraignment		.80	.81	
	A25	Free legal aid & counsel of own choice			.44	
17	A26	Police searches only with a warrant		.84	.82	
	A27	Freedom from mail censorship		.87	.86	
18	A28	Homosexuality between consenting adults			.44	.41
	A29	Number of political prisoners		-.61	-.66	
	A30	Right to practice any religion		.65	.71	
19	A31	No compulsory religion/state ideology in schools		.72	.68	
	A32	Freedom to teach & receive information		.93	.93	
	A33	Freedom from political press censorship		.90	.87	
	A34	Independent book publishing		.76	.92	
	A35	Independent radio & television networks		.83	.77	
	A36	Independent newspapers		.74	.75	
	A37	Freedom to monitor human rights		.84	.86	
	A38	No state policies to control art		.81	.77	
21-22	A39	Freedom to peacefully assemble		.91	.87	
	A40	Freedom to form & join independent unions		.91	.91	
	A41	No compulsory memberships in parties			.56	
23	A43	Equality of sexes in marriage		.87	.87	
25	A44	Polyarchy/free & fair elections		-.42	-.46	
	A45	Limitations on the right to vote		.90	.87	
	A47	Right to peaceful political opposition				.51

Articles		Variables	1982 Data		1986 Data	
			1	2	1	2
25	A49	Importance of females in politics		.46	.49	.49
27	A50	Right to minority languages		.47	.47	.47
1	B1	Economic freedom		.63	.61	.61
	B2	Trademarks applied for per capita		.49	.52	.43
2	B8	No social/economic discrimination against women	.58		.43	.62
6	B9	Absence of serfdom, slavery, & child labor		.82	.77	.53
	B10	No compulsory work permits/labor conscription		.59		
7	B12	Average nonagricultural weekly wage rates	.40			
	B13	Consumer spending per capita	.78			.73
	B14	% Workers injured on the job	.68			.67
	B15	% Losing work due to on-the-job injuries	.77			.70
	B17	Nonagricultural work week in hours	-.53			-.46
8	B19	Freedom to form & join independent unions	.43		.91	
	B20	% Workers organized into unions		.91		.41
	B21	Right of unions to federate	.75		.74	
	B22	Freedom of unions to operate	.87		.87	
9	B26	Extensiveness of family allowance plans	.70			.58
	B27	Extensiveness of old-age/survivor pensions	.57			.55
	B28	Extensiveness of sickness/maternity programs	.62			.59
	B29	Extensiveness of unemployment insurance	.56	.59	.46	.53
	B31	% Budget for social security/welfare	.75			.63
10	B32	Deathrate of males aged 1-4	-.80			-.64
	B34	% Infants immunized against DPT	.76			.77
11	B36	Caloric intake per capita	.83			.85
	B37	Protein intake per capita	.83			.83
	B38	Cotton woven fabric production per capita	.49			.42
	B39	Nonrubber footwear production per capita	.62			.59
	B40	% Housing units with safe water	.81			.89
	B41	% Housing units with flush toilets	.82			.66
	B42	% Gross domestic product invested in housing			.41	
	B44	% Central government budget for agriculture	-.44			-.43
	B45	Overseas development aid received/GDP	-.72			
12	B46	Late fetal deathrate				
	B47	Infant mortality rate	-.93			-.80
	B49	Infectious-parasitic diseases deathrate	-.74			-.94
	B50	% Government budget for health				-.66
	B51	Persons per physicians	-.91		.45	-.88

Table 4.5 (continued)

Articles	Variables	1982 Data 1	1982 Data 2	1986 Data 1	1986 Data 2
12	B52 Persons per hospital beds	-.83			-.67
	B53 % Childbirths attended	.78			.75
	B54 Life expectancy at birth	.95			.89
	B55 % Population with access to health care	.75			.90
13	B56 Years of compulsory education	.51			.59
	B57 % School-age children in primary school	.71			.68
	B58 % School-age females in primary school	.78			.64
	B59 % School-age children in secondary school	.89			.90
	B60 % Education budget for vocational schools	.55			.60
	B62 % Adults enrolled in colleges	.72	.62		.68
	B63 % Females enrolled in colleges	.74		.41	.72
	B66 School-age population per teacher	-.76			-.89
	B67 % Population literate	.90			.86
	B68 % Females literate	.86			.79
15	B70 Fixed cinema seats per capita	.53			.42
	B72 Museum attendance per capita	.66			.43
	B74 % Registered as public library users	.86			.52
	B75 Books published per capita	.55	.42		.58
	B77 Textbooks published/students	.43			.43
	B79 Books translated per capita	.41			
	B80 Long films produced per capita	.42			
	B83 Industrial designs per capita	.44	.41		.43
	B84 Patents per capita	.61	.48		.60
	B85 Right to abortion	.43			
	B87 % GNP spent on R & D	.50			
16	B89 No state control of artistic works	.47	.81	.77	.52
	B91 External economic aid sent/GDP				.51
	Percent Variance Explained	27.8	25.5	26.8	25.8

Note: Loadings below ±.40 omitted.
Variables with no loadings above ±.40 omitted.

172

Table 4.6
Predictor Variables: Factor Analysis for 1982 Data

Factors	1	2	3	4	5	6	7	8	9	10	11
C1 Per capita GNP	.94										
C2 GNP per capita growth rate										.78	
C3 % Workforce in agriculture	-.80										
C4 Energy consumption per capita	.90										
C5 % Population living in cities	.89										
C6 Newspaper circulation per capita	.83										
C7 Radios per capita	.76										
C8 Telephones per capita	.93										
C9 Television sets per capita	.88										
C10 Investment received/GDP											.83
C11 Exports and imports/GNP							.40				
C12 % Trade with largest export partner					.84						
C13 % Trade with largest import partner					.83						
C15 Income inequality	-.61										
C16 Education expenditures per capita	.92										
C17 Health expenditures per capita	.90										
C18 Welfare expenditures per capita	.92										
C19 Percentage of direct taxes collected							.61				
C20 Rate of inflation											
C21 Votes cast/registered to vote									.63	-.46	.51
C22 Political parties in parliament								-.41			
C23 % Seats held by largest coalition								.81			
C25 Coups from 1960/years independent		.48						-.76			
C26 Military-dominated government		.85									
C27 % Years of military rule from 1960		.84									
C28 Official violence against citizens		.74									
C29 % Years at civil war from 1960	-.45	.54									
C30 Deathrate due to domestic violence						.77				-.52	
C31 % Years at war from 1960			.63								
C32 Deathrate due to foreign conflict			.55						.42		
C33 % Population in the armed forces			.61		-.43						
C34 Military budget/GNP			.85								
C35 Arms imports/GNP			.68								
C36 Arms imports/military budget											
C42 Net arms exporting country (yes/no)						.60					
C44 US civilian aid/GNP									.75		
C45 US military aid/GNP									.80		
C46 Percent of troops abroad						.84					
C49 Former British colony							.73				

Table 4.6 (continued)

Factors	1	2	3	4	5	6	7	8	9	10	11
C50 Percent Protestant population	-.51										
C51 Percent Roman Catholic population							.47			-.45	
C52 Percent Moslem population			.41		.50						
C53 Ethnolinguistic heterogeneity					-.44		.51				
C54 Percent leftists in parliament				.63			-.40				
C55 Cancer deathrate (males)	.65			.55							
C56 Heart disease deathrate (males)	.57			.72							
C57 Suicide deathrate (males)				.78							
Percent Variance Explained	11.8	3.6	3.3	3.1	2.7	2.4	2.4	2.2	2.2	2.0	1.9

Note: Loadings below ±.40 omitted.
Variables with no loadings above ±.40 omitted.
"% Years" refers to the percentage of years since 1960.

174

Table 4.7
Predictor Variables: Factor Analysis for 1986 Data

Factors	1	2	3	4	5	6	7	8	9	10	11
C1 Per capita GNP	.96										
C2 GNP per capita growth rate					-.53						
C3 % Workforce in agriculture	-.91										
C4 Energy consumption per capita	.91										
C5 % Population living in cities	.83										
C6 Newspaper circulation per capita	.86										
C7 Radios per capita	.77										
C8 Telephones per capita	.87										
C9 Television sets per capita	.89										
C10 Investment received/GDP									.77		
C11 Exports and imports/GNP											.44
C12 % Trade with largest export partner								.90			
C13 % Trade with largest import partner								.83			
C14 Food import dependency					.47						
C15 Income Inequality	-.41			.41							
C16 Education expenditures per capita	.92										
C17 Health expenditures per capita	.88										
C18 Welfare expenditures per capita	.86										

Table 4.7 (continued)

Factors	1	2	3	4	5	6	7	8	9*	10	11
C19 Percentage of direct taxes collected											
C20 Rate of inflation										.78	
C21 Votes cast/registered to vote									-.47		
C22 Political parties in parliament		.76									.79
C23 % Seats held by largest coalition											-.72
C25 Coups from 1960/years independent									-.56		
C26 Military-dominated government						.79					
C27 % Years of military rule from 1960						.88					
C28 Official violence against citizens	-.60		.44								
C29 % Years at civil war from 1960	-.47		.44								
C31 % Years at war from 1960							.66				
C32 Deathrate due to foreign conflict						.89					
C33 % Population in the armed forces			.52								
C34 Military budget/GNP							.42				
C35 Arms imports/GNP					.75						
C36 Arms imports/military budget					.78						
C37 Minority political grievances				.80							
C38 Minority economic grievances				.91							
C39 Minority social grievances				.90							
C40 Number of terrorist incidents											.43
C41 Percent budget for internal security									-.44		
C42 Net arms exporting country (yes/no)							.76				
C44 US civilian aid/GNP						.65					
C45 US military aid/GNP						.90	.86				
C46 Percent of troops abroad								.46			
C49 Former British colony									-.42		
C50 Percent Protestant population										.53	
C51 Percent Roman Catholic population										.66	
C52 Percent Moslem population					.45				.46		
C53 Ethnolinguistic heterogeneity	-.53	.80									
C54 Percent leftists in parliament		.52									
C55 Cancer deathrate (males)	.47	.67									
C56 Heart disease deathrate (males)	.41	.41									
C57 Suicide deathrate (males)					-.46						
Percent Variance Explained	11.8	3.3	3.2	3.2	3.1	2.9	2.7	2.7	2.5	2.2	2.1

<u>Note:</u> Loadings below ±.40 omitted. Variables with no loadings above ±.40 omitted.
"% Years" refers to the percentage of years since 1960.

176

Table 5.1
Factor Analysis of Changes in Civil and Political Rights, 1982–1986

Articles	Variables	1	2	3	4	5	6	7	8	9
1	A2 Percent ethnonationalists/separatists				.82					
	A3 Number of separatist movements				.78					.78
4	A7 Emergency rule						.46			
6	A8 Political executions					.42				
	A9 "Disappearances"					.87				
	A10 No capital punishment		.76							
7	A12 Freedom from police torture		.49							
	A13 Freedom from deprivation of nationality					-.74				
8	A15 Absence of conscripted labor	.79		.70						
9	A17 No indefinite detention without charges	.41								
12	A18 Freedom to travel in own country			.66						
	A19 Freedom to travel outside own country			.59						
	A20 Countries forbidden for external travel		-.80							
14	A21 Right to civilian, public trials	.65								
	A23 Innocent until proved guilty	.74								
	A24 Right to a speedy arraignment/trial	.73								
17	A26 Police searches only with a warrant	.54								
	A27 Freedom from mail censorship	.68								
18	A29 Number of political prisoners	.43								
	A30 Right to practice any religion				.42					
19	A32 Freedom to teach & receive information					-.61				
	A34 Independent book publishing		.41					.84		
	A35 Independent radio & television networks		.58					.47		
21-22	A39 Freedom to peacefully assemble	.45								
	A40 Freedom to form & join independent unions						.71			
23	A42 Right to interethnic, civil marriage			.41						
	A43 Equality of sexes in marriage			.46						
25	A45 Limitations on the right to vote						-.59			
	A46 Years since latest general election									
	A47 Right to peaceful political opposition								.85	
27	A49 Importance of females in politics							.59		-.67
	A50 Right to minority languages									-.41
	Percent Variance Explained	4.6	3.2	2.5	2.5	2.4	2.2	2.0	1.8	1.7

Note: Loadings below ±.40 omitted.
Variables with no loadings above ±.40 omitted.

177

Table 5.2

Factor Analysis of Changes in Economic and Social Rights, 1982–1986

Articles	Variables	1	2	3	4	5	6	7	8
1	B3 Improvement in terms of trade		.83						
	B4 Improvement in purchasing power of exports		.81						
6	B10 No compulsory work permits/labor conscription						.84		
7	B13 Consumer spending per capita				.73				
10	B32 Deathrate of males aged 1-4		.49						
	B34 % Infants immunized against DPT								
	B35 Right to marry						-.55		
11	B36 Caloric intake per capita					.89	.41		
	B37 Protein intake per capita					.83			
	B41 % Housing units with flush toilets						-.48		
12	B46 Late fetal deathrate		-.45						-.41
	B49 Infectious-parasitic diseases deathrate		.56					.42	
	B54 Life expectancy at birth						-.64		
13	B56 Years of compulsory education								.87
	B57 % School-age children in primary school			.93					
	B58 % School-age females in primary school			.99					
	B62 % Adults enrolled in colleges							.87	
	B63 % Females enrolled in colleges							.93	
	B66 School-age population per teacher					.48			
	B68 % Females literate				.77				
15	B70 Fixed cinema seats per capita	.62							
	B72 Museum attendance per capita	.61							
	B78 Books translated/books published	.83							
	B79 Books translated per capita	.83							
	B81 Films imported per capita	.63							
	B82 Films imported/long films produced				-.63				.86
16	B84 Patents per capita				.45				
	B88 % Government spending on R & D								
	B91 External economic aid sent/GDP						.55		
	Percent Variance Explained	4.0	3.3	3.2	3.1	3.0	2.9	2.9	2.9

Note: Loadings below ±.40 omitted.
Variables with no loadings above ±.40 omitted.

Table 5.3

Factor Analysis of Changes in Civil, Political, Economic, and Social Rights, 1982–1986

Articles	Variables	1	2	3	4	5	6	7	8
1	A2 Percent ethnonationalists/separatists								-.49
	A3 Number of separatist movements								
6	A9 "Disappearances"				-.91		.40		
7	A10 No capital punishment	.46							
	A11 No corporal punishment	.43							
	A12 Freedom from police torture	.44							
	A13 Freedom from deprivation of nationality				.69				
8	A15 Absence of conscripted labor						.89		
9	A17 No indefinite detention without charges	.67							
12	A18 Freedom to travel in own country	.40							
	A20 Countries forbidden for external travel	-.64							
14	A21 Right to civilian, public trials	.64							
	A22 Independent courts	.59							
	A23 Innocent until proved guilty	.62							
17	A24 Right to a speedy arraignment/trial	.54							
	A27 Freedom from mail censorship	.61							
18	A31 No state religion or ideology in schools	.75						.80	
19	A32 Freedom to teach & receive information	.46							
	A33 Freedom from political press censorship	.86							
21-22	A39 Freedom to peacefully assemble	.63							
23	A43 Equality of sexes in marriage	.55							
25	A47 Right to peaceful political opposition								
1	B3 Improvement in terms of trade					.85			
	B4 Improvement in purchasing power of exports					.76			
2	B5 % Population suffering economic discrimination				.66				
10	B32 Deathrate of males aged 1-4					.46			
	B33 Ratio of deathrate of females/males aged 1-4	-.59							
11	B38 Cotton woven fabric production per capita			.43				.77	
12	B43 % Budget for housing							-.44	
	B46 Late fetal deathrate								
13	B49 Infectious-parasitic diseases deathrate					.61			
	B56 Years of compulsory education								
	B57 % School-age children in primary school			.98					
	B58 % School-age females in primary school			.96					
15	B65 % Education budget for teachers' salaries	-.45							
	B68 % Females literate				.63				
	B70 Fixed cinema seats per capita		.60						.80
	B72 Museum attendance per capita		.61						
	B73 Volumes in national library/GNP							-.42	

Table 5.3 (continued)

Articles	Variables	1	2	3	4	5	6	7	8
15	B76 % Textbooks among all books published	-.44							
	B78 Books translated/books published		.87						
	B79 Books translated per capita		.83						
	B80 Long films produced per capita							-.69	
	B81 Films imported per capita		.60						
	B82 Films imported/long films produced								.95
	B88 Government spending on R & D	.47							
Percent Variance Explained		8.2	4.3	3.9	3.8	3.7	3.4	3.4	3.4

Note: Loadings below ±.40 omitted.
       Variables with no loadings above ±.40 omitted.

180

Table 6.1

Factor Analysis of Civil and Political Rights and Predictor Variables, 1982

Variables	1	2	3	4	5	6	7	8	9	10	11
A1 Years independent										-.53	
A2 Percent ethnonationalists/separatists				.87							
A3 Number of separatist movements				.79							
A5 Economic freedom	.59										
A6 Political & legal equality for women						.71					
A8 Political executions							.78				
A9 "Disappearances"							.83				
A10 No capital punishment	.75										
A11 No corporal punishment	.61					.62					
A12 Freedom from police torture	.71										
A13 No deprivation of nationality	.68										
A14 No serfdom, slavery, or child labor		.62									
A15 Absence of conscripted labor	.76										
A16 No compulsory military service										.60	
A17 No indefinite detention	.80										
A18 Freedom to travel in own country	.66										
A19 Freedom to travel outside country	.88										
A21 Right to civilian, public trials	.86										
A22 Independent courts	.87										
A23 Innocent until proved guilty	.81										
A24 Right to a speedy arraignment	.81										
A26 Police searches only with a warrant	.85										
A27 Freedom from mail censorship	.90										
A29 Number of political prisoners	-.61										
A30 Right to practice any religion	.60										
A31 No state religion or ideology	.66										
A32 Freedom to teach & receive info	.92										
A33 Freedom from press censorship	.89										
A34 Independent book publishing	.74										
A35 Independent radio & TV networks	.83										
A36 Independent newspapers	.67										
A37 Freedom to monitor human rights	.75										
A38 No state policies to control art	.91										
A39 Freedom to peacefully assemble	.89										
A42 Right to interethnic, civil marriage					-.53						
A43 Equality of sexes in marriage			-.50			.65					
A44 Polyarchy	.86										
A45 Limitations on the right to vote	-.46					-.55					
A47 Peaceful political opposition	.89										

Table 6.1 (continued)

Variables	1	2	3	4	5	6	7	8	9	10	11
A49 Importance of females in politics	.45										
A50 Right to minority languages	.40					.43					
C1 Per capita GNP		.91		-.52							
C3 % Workforce in agriculture		-.75									
C4 Energy consumption per capita		.91									
C5 % Population living in cities		.82									
C6 Newspaper circulation per capita		.82									
C7 Radios per capita		.67									
C8 Telephones per capita		.89									
C9 Television sets per capita		.83									
C12 % Trade with largest export partner								.85			
C13 % Trade with largest import partner								.85			
C15 Income inequality		-.71									
C16 Education expenditures per capita		.87									
C17 Health expenditures per capita		.88									
C18 Welfare expenditures per capita		.90									
C20 Rate of inflation					.48					-.43	
C22 Political parties in parliament	.57										
C23 % Seats held by largest coalition	-.80										
C25 Coups from 1960/years independent			.49								
C26 Military-dominated government			.86								
C27 % Years of military rule from 1960			.85								
C28 Official violence against citizens			.68								
C29 % Years at civil war from 1960			.47								
C30 Deathrate due to domestic violence									.80		
C31 % Years at war from 1960							.58				
C32 Deathrate due to foreign conflict					.62						
C33 % Population in the armed forces					.48						
C34 Military budget/GNP	-.41										
C35 Arms imports/GNP											.62
C36 Arms imports/military budget									.57		.77
C42 Net arms exporting country (yes/no)		.41									
C44 US civilian aid/GNP					.70						
C45 US military aid/GNP					.86						
C46 Percent of troops abroad									.82		
C49 Former British colony											.70
C52 Percent Moslem population											
C53 Ethnolinguistic heterogeneity		-.44		.66							
C54 Percent leftists in parliament						.45					.47

Variables	1	2	3	4	5	6	7	8	9	10	11
C55 Cancer deathrate (males)		.77									
C56 Heart disease deathrate (males)		.77									
C57 Suicide deathrate (males)		.51									
Percent Variance Explained	22.9	13.8	4.7	3.3	3.2	3.1	3.1	3.0	2.8	2.7	2.6

Note: Loadings below ±.40 omitted.
Variables with no loadings above ±.40 omitted.
"% Years" refers to the percentage of years since 1960.

Table 6.2

Factor Analysis of Civil and Political Rights and Predictor Variables, 1986

Variables	1	2	3	4	5	6	7	8	9	10	11
A4 Freedom from property confiscation	.70										
A5 Economic freedom	.57		-.48								
A6 Political & legal equality for women			.59								
A8 Political executions								.72			
A9 "Disappearances"								.78			
A10 No capital punishment	.71										
A11 No corporal punishment	.48										
A12 Freedom from police torture	.74										
A13 No deprivation of nationality	.71										
A14 No serfdom, slavery, or child labor	.42	.59									
A15 Absence of conscripted labor	.74										
A17 No indefinite detentions	.81										
A18 Freedom to travel in own country	.66										
A19 Freedom to travel outside country	.87										
A20 Countries banned for external travel	-.70										
A21 Right to civilian, public trials	.85										
A22 Independent courts	.81										
A23 Innocent until proved guilty	.80										
A24 Right to a speedy arraignment	.79										
A25 Free legal aid & counsel	.44										
A26 Police searches only with a warrant	.82										
A27 Freedom from mail censorship	.87										

Variables		1	2	3	4	5	6	7	8	9	10	11
A28	Consensual adult homosexuality	.50	.41									
A29	Number of political prisoners	-.66										
A30	Right to practice any religion	.68										
A31	No state religion or ideology	.64										
A32	Freedom to teach & receive info	.93										
A33	Freedom from press censorship	.86										
A34	Independent book publishing	.90										
A35	Independent radio & TV networks	.79										
A36	Independent newspapers	.71		-.42								
A37	Freedom to monitor human rights	.84										
A38	No state policies to control art	.74										
A39	Freedom to peacefully assemble	.89										
A40	Freedom to form & join unions	.91										
A41	No compulsory memberships	.58										
A42	Right to interethnic, civil marriage			.41								
A43	Equality of sexes in marriage		.40	.59								
A44	Multiparty, secret elections	.89										
A45	Limitations on the right to vote	-.49		-.43								
A47	Right to loyal political opposition	.89										
A48	Minority political discrimination				.79							
A49	Importance of females in politics	.44										
A50	Right to minority languages	.46										
C1	Per capita GNP		.94									
C3	% Workforce in agriculture		-.88									
C4	Energy consumption per capita		.92									
C5	% Population living in cities		.82									
C6	Newspaper circulation per capita		.85									
C7	Radios per capita		.70									
C8	Telephones per capita		.83									
C9	Television sets per capita		.84									
C12	% Trade with largest export partner									.93		
C13	% Trade with largest import partner									.83		
C15	Income inequality		-.47									
C16	Education expenditures per capita		.91									
C17	Health expenditures per capita		.85									
C18	Welfare expenditures per capita		.82									
C21	Votes cast/registered to vote						.51					
C22	Political parties in parliament	.51		.58								
C23	% Seats held by largest coalition	-.73										

Table 6.2 (continued)

Variables	1	2	3	4	5	6	7	8	9	10	11
C25 Coups from 1960/years independent					.60						
C26 Military-dominated government					.77						
C27 % Years of military rule from 1960					.82						
C28 Official violence against citizens		-.49			.51						
C29 % Years at civil war from 1960											
C30 Deathrate due to domestic violence								.43			.41
C31 % Years at war from 1960						.41					
C32 Deathrate due to foreign conflict						.89					
C33 % Population in the armed forces						.54					
C34 Military budget/GNP	-.45										
C35 Arms imports/GNP										.71	
C36 Arms imports/military budget										.77	
C37 Minority political grievances				.78							
C38 Minority economic grievances				.90							
C39 Minority social grievances				.87							
C40 Terrorist incidents	.40										
C42 Net arms exporting country (yes/no)						.66					.79
C45 US military aid/GNP											
C46 Percent of troops abroad							.41				
C53 Ethnolinguistic heterogeneity		-.50									
C54 Percent leftists in parliament			.61								
C55 Cancer deathrate (males)		.46	.46								
C56 Heart disease deathrate (males)		.47	.64								
C57 Suicide deathrate (males)			.52								.79
Percent Variance Explained	24.6	13.6	4.8	4.4	3.7	3.2	3.0	2.8	2.8	2.7	2.5

Note: Loadings below ±.40 omitted.
Variables with no loadings above ±.40 omitted.
"% Years" refers to the percentage of years since 1960.

Table 6.3

Factor Analysis of Predictor Variables for 1982 and Civil and Political Rights for 1986

Variables	1	2	3	4	5	6	7	8	9	10	11
A2 Percent ethnonationalists/separatists							.92				
A3 Number of separatist movements							.87				
A4 Freedom from property confiscation	.69										
A5 Economic freedom	.56		-.51								
A6 Political & legal equality for women			.41								
A10 No capital punishment	.71										
A11 No corporal punishment	.48										
A12 Freedom from police torture	.74										
A13 No deprivation of nationality	.70										
A14 No serfdom, slavery, or child labor	.40	.60									
A15 Absence of conscripted labor	.72										
A17 No indefinite detention	.82										
A18 Freedom to travel in own country	.65										
A19 Freedom to travel outside country	.87										
A20 Countries banned for external travel	-.70										
A21 Right to civilian, public trials	.86										
A22 Independent courts	.82										
A23 Innocent until proved guilty	.81										
A24 Right to a speedy arraignment	.80										
A25 Free legal aid & counsel	.46										
A26 Police searches only with a warrant	.82										
A27 Freedom from mail censorship	.85										
A28 Consensual adult homosexuality	.49	.45									
A29 Number of political prisoners									.43		
A30 Right to practice any religion	.66										
A31 No state religion or ideology	.63										
A32 Freedom to teach & receive info	.92										
A33 Freedom from press censorship	.87										
A34 Independent book publishing	.89										
A35 Independent radio & TV networks	.80										
A36 Independent newspapers	.70		-.42								
A37 Freedom to monitor human rights	.83										
A38 No state policies to control art	.72										
A39 Freedom to peacefully assemble	.89										
A40 Freedom to form & join unions	.92										
A42 Right to interethnic, civil marriage	.57				.75						
A43 Equality of sexes in marriage		.44	.49		.50						
A44 Multiparty, secret elections	.89										
A45 Limitations on the right to vote	-.49				-.43						

Table 6.3 (continued)

Variables	1	2	3	4	5	6	7	8	9	10	11
A47 Right to loyal political opposition	.90										
A49 Importance of females in politics	.44										
A50 Right to minority languages	.43						-.43				
C1 Per capita GNP		.93									
C3 % Workforce in agriculture		-.79									
C4 Energy consumption per capita		.92									
C5 % Population living in cities		.86									
C6 Newspaper circulation per capita		.83									
C7 Radios per capita		.67									
C8 Telephones per capita		.89									
C9 Television sets per capita		.82									
C10 Investment received/GDP											.88
C12 % Trade with largest export partner								.87			
C13 % Trade with largest import partner								.89			
C14 Food import dependency					-.41						
C15 Income inequality		-.68									
C16 Education expenditures per capita		.88									
C17 Health expenditures per capita		.88									
C18 Welfare expenditures per capita	.46	.87									
C19 Percentage of direct taxes collected										.67	
C22 Political parties in parliament	.51										
C23 % Seats held by largest coalition	-.73										
C26 Military-dominated government				.87							
C27 % Years of military rule from 1960				.86							
C28 Official violence against citizens				.72							
C31 % Years at war from 1960									.77		
C32 Deathrate due to foreign conflict						.78					
C33 % Population in the armed forces						.54					
C34 Military budget/GNP						.43					
C35 Arms imports/GNP						.69					
C36 Arms imports/military budget						.44					
C42 Net arms exporting country (yes/no)		.41			.53				.81		
C46 Percent of troops abroad											
C49 Former British colony											
C50 Percent Protestant population										.67	
C52 Percent Moslem population					-.73					.47	
C53 Ethnolinguistic heterogeneity		-.50					.41				
C54 Percent leftists in parliament			.69								
C55 Cancer deathrate (males)		.70	.45								
C56 Heart disease deathrate (males)		.67	.64								
C57 Suicide deathrate (males)		.43	.71								
Percent Variance Explained	23.4	13.9	4.3	3.8	3.3	3.1	2.9	2.8	2.7	2.5	2.4

Note: Loadings below ±.40 omitted. Variables with no loadings above ±.40 omitted.

188

Table 6.4
Factor Analysis of Predictor Variables for 1982 and Changes in Civil and Political Rights, 1982–1986

Variables	1	2	3	4	5	6	7	8	9	10
A2 Percent ethnonationalists/separatists								.78		
A3 Number of separatist movements								.66		
A9 "Disappearances"					.81					
A11 No corporal punishment		.46								
A12 Freedom from police torture		.45								
A13 Freedom from deprivation of nationality					-.72					
A15 Absence of conscripted labor				-.48						
A17 No indefinite detention without charges		.81								
A18 Freedom to travel in own country		.54								
A19 Freedom to travel outside own country				-.49						
A20 Countries forbidden for external travel		-.44								
A21 Right to civilian, public trials		.70								
A22 Independent courts		.52								
A23 Innocent until proved guilty		.82								
A24 Right to a speedy arraignment		.73								
A26 Police searches only with a warrant		.55								
A27 Freedom from mail censorship		.59								
A28 Homosexuality between consenting adults										-.43
A30 Right to practice any religion								.48		
A31 No state religion or ideology in schools						-.79				
A32 Freedom to teach & receive information		.55								
A34 Independent book publishing								.56		
A35 Independent radio & television networks					-.55					
A37 Freedom to monitor human rights									.42	
A39 Freedom to peacefully assemble		.52								
A42 Right to interethnic, civil marriage				-.41						
A43 Equality of sexes in marriage	.48									
A45 Limitations on the right to vote			-.40							
C1 Per capita GNP	.97									
C3 % Workforce in agriculture	-.78									
C4 Energy consumption per capita	.93									
C5 % Population living in cities	.83									
C6 Newspaper circulation per capita	.88									
C7 Radios per capita	.74									
C8 Telephones per capita	.95									
C9 Television sets per capita	.88									
C11 Exports and imports/GNP						.73				
C12 % Trade with largest export partner							.85			
C13 % Trade with largest import partner							.80			

Table 6.4 (continued)

Variables	1	2	3	4	5	6	7	8	9	10
C14 Food import dependency	-.64									
C15 Income inequality	.92					.76				
C16 Education expenditures per capita	.93									
C17 Health expenditures per capita	.99									
C18 Welfare expenditures per capita									-.81	
C22 Political parties in parliament									.76	
C23 % Seats held by largest coalition										
C24 Government revenues/GNP					.77					
C25 Coups from 1960/years independent			.48							
C26 Military-dominated government			.85							
C27 % Years of military rule from 1960			.84							
C28 Official violence against citizens			.72							
C29 % Years at civil war from 1960	-.43									
C31 % Years at war from 1960										.70
C32 Deathrate due to foreign conflict				.76						
C33 % Population in the armed forces				.55						
C34 Military budget/GNP				.63						
C35 Arms imports/GNP				.80						
C36 Arms imports/military budget				.45						
C42 Net arms exporting country (yes/no)	.41									
C46 Percent of troops abroad										
C53 Ethnolinguistic heterogeneity	-.50							-.46		
C55 Cancer deathrate (males)	.76									.61
C56 Heart disease deathrate (males)	.71									.81
C57 Suicide deathrate (males)	.47									
Percent Variance Explained	13.8	6.1	4.3	4.1	3.3	3.2	3.0	2.9	2.9	2.7

<u>Note:</u> Loadings below ±.40 omitted. Variables with no loadings above ±.40 omitted.
"% Years" refers to the percentage of years since 1960.

Table 6.5

Factor Analysis of Changes in Civil and Political Rights and Predictor Variables, 1982–1986

Variables	1	2	3	4	5	6	7	8	9	10
A7 Emergency rule										.41
A8 Political executions				.92				.		
A9 "Disappearances"				.42		-.66		-.50		
A10 No capital punishment		.49								
A11 No corporal punishment		.43								
A12 Freedom from police torture		.49								
A13 Freedom from deprivation of nationality						.79				
A15 Absence of conscripted labor									.83	
A17 No indefinite detention without charges		.80								
A18 Freedom to travel in own country		.42								
A20 Countries forbidden for external travel		-.69								
A21 Right to civilian, public trials		.68								
A22 Independent courts		.57								
A23 Innocent until proved guilty		.71								
A24 Right to a speedy arraignment		.67								
A26 Police searches only with a warrant		.45								
A27 Freedom from mail censorship		.63								
A29 Number of political prisoners				.48						
A32 Freedom to teach & receive information		.67	-.48							
A35 Independent radio & television networks							.86			
A37 Freedom to monitor human rights		.72	-.42							
A39 Freedom to peacefully assemble										
A40 Freedom to form & join independent unions									.46	
A42 Right to interethnic, civil marriage	.42									
A43 Equality of sexes in marriage										
A46 Years since latest general election		.49								.83
A47 Right to peaceful political opposition							.77			
C1 Per capita GNP	.82									
C3 % Workforce in agriculture	.93									
C4 Energy consumption per capita	.90									
C6 Newspaper circulation per capita	.48									
C7 Radios per capita	.88									
C8 Telephones per capita								.42		
C9 Television sets per capita					-.42					
C11 Exports and imports/GNP						-.54				
C15 Income inequality									.49	
C16 Education expenditures per capita	.94									

191

Table 6.5 (continued)

Variables	1	2	3	4	5	6	7	8	9	10
C17 Health expenditures per capita	.93									
C18 Welfare expenditures per capita	.93									
C19 Percentage of direct taxes collected		-.43								
C21 Votes cast/registered to vote		-.43								
C22 Political parties in parliament										-.68
C24 Government revenues/GNP						.81				
C26 Military-dominated government			.83							
C27 % Years of military rule from 1960			.77							
C28 Official violence against citizens	-.53									
C29 % Years at civil war from 1960			.44							
C30 Deathrate due to domestic violence				.92						
C31 % Years at war from 1960								.74		
C32 Deathrate due to foreign conflict					-.88					
C33 % Population in the armed forces					-.90					
C34 Military budget/GNP					-.43			.45		
C35 Arms imports/GNP					.59					
C36 Arms imports/military budget	-.41									
C46 Percent of troops abroad								.71		
C55 Cancer deathrate (males)	.65									
C56 Heart disease deathrate (males)	-.44			.48						
C57 Suicide deathrate (males)			.64							
Percent Variance Explained	8.9	7.4	4.0	3.4	3.1	2.8	2.7	2.5	2.4	2.4

Note: Loadings below ±.40 omitted.
Variables with no loadings above ±.40 omitted.
"% Years" refers to the percentage of years since 1960.

Table 6.6
Regressions on "Disappearances" (A9)

Year of C Variables	Year of A Variable	Sample Size	Name of C Variable	Parameter Estimate	% Variance (Partial)	Probability (F Value)
a) 1982	1982	88	C35 Arms imports/GNP	40.04	.33	.0001
			C30 Domestic violence deathrate	484.49	.11	.0001
			C28 Government repression	1.42	.05	.0034
b) 1982	1982	LDCs	C35 Arms imports/GNP	29.40	.31	.0001
			C30 Domestic violence deathrate	813.26	.11	.0010
c) 1986	1986	88	C28 Government repression	.65	.21	.0001
			C31 % Years at war	1.04	.10	.0006
			C57 Suicide deathrate	.00	.06	.0072
d) 1986	1986	LDCs	C46 % Troops abroad	.30	.18	.0003
			C28 Government repression	.55	.11	.0023
			C37 Minority political grievances	.16	.08	.0067
e) 1982	1986	88	C29 % Years at civil war	2.16	.17	.0001
			C15 Income inequality	(0.00)	.06	.0149
f) 1982	1986	LDCs	C29 % Years at civil war	(1.58)	.14	.0018
			C24 Taxes/GNP	378.14	.08	.0132
			C46 % Troops abroad	.21	.07	.0150
			C53 Ethnolinguistic heterogeneity	.01	.07	.0116
g) 1982	1982-86	88	C24 Taxes/GNP	15545.37	.23	.0001
			C35 Arms imports/GNP	-1048.25	.13	.0001
			C21 % Voter turnout	-31.19	.07	.0123
h) 1982	1982-86	LDCs	C24 Taxes/GNP	19545.26	.26	.0001
			C35 Arms imports/GNP	-950.43	.14	.0002
			C8 Government repression	1.02	.08	.0020
i) 1982-86	1982-1986	88	C30 Domestic violence deathrate	116333.22	.19	.0001
			C24 Taxes/GNP	-20501.29	.12	.0002
			C3 % Workers in agriculture	-315.90	.16	.0001
			C35 Arms imports/GNP	-398.84	.07	.0007
j) 1982-86	1982-1986	LDCs	C30 Domestic violence deathrate	104952.83	.19	.0002
			C24 Taxes/GNP	-24110.60	.15	.0004
			C3 % Workers in agriculture	-341.37	.16	.0001
			C35 Arms imports/GNP	-601.28	.07	.0037

Note: C variables explaining less than 5% of the variance omitted.
Parentheses refer to variables later removed from the regression.
"% Years" refers to the percentage of years since 1960.

Table 6.7
Regressions on Number of Countries Prohibited for External Travel (A20)

Year of C Variables	Year of A Variable	Sample Size	Name of C Variable	Parameter Estimate	% Variance (Partial)	Probability (F Value)
a) 1982	1982	88	C27 % Years with military rule	.92	.22	.0001
			C23 % Seats held by majority	1.32	.08	.0028
			C1 Per capita GNP	.86	.08	.0007
b) 1982	1982	LDCs	C27 % Years with military rule	1.18	.17	.0001
			C49 Former British colony	813.26	.11	.0327
			C1 GNP per capita	1.09	.09	.0017
c) 1986	1986	88	C23 % Seats held by majority	2.54	.24	.0001
			C40 Terrorist incidents	-.29	.05	.0151
d) 1986	1986	LDCs	C56 Heart disease deathrate	.00	.16	.0008
			C23 % Seats held by majority	(1.02)	.09	.0082
			C10 Foreign investment/GDP	.00	.05	.0328
			C45 US military aid/GNP	-3.19	.05	.0310
e) 1982	1986	88	C23 % Seats held by majority	1.66	.26	.0001
			C10 Foreign investment/GDP	.00	.06	.0060
f) 1982	1986	LDCs	C56 Heart disease deathrate	.00	.21	.0001
			C51 % Roman Catholic	-.10	.07	.0153
			C45 US military aid/GNP	-3.60	.07	.0128
			C10 Foreign investment/GDP	.00	.07	.0065
			C31 % Years at war	1.66	.06	.0107
g) 1982	1982-86	88	C28 Government repression	-.53	.06	.0279
			C7 Radios per capita	(-.79)	.05	.0304
			C56 Heart disease deathrate	-.00	.16	.0001
h) 1982	1982-86	LDCs	C7 Radios per capita	-3.27	.13	.0023
			C14 Food import dependency	(.00)	.08	.0105
			C55 Cancer deathrate	.00	.08	.0074
i) 1982-86	1982-1986	88	C28 Government repression	.45	.08	.0072
			C19 % Direct taxes collected	1.71	.08	.0053
			C1 Per capita GNP	.35	.05	.0208
j) 1982-86	1982-1986	LDCs	C28 Government repression	.36	.11	.0050
			C19 % Direct taxes collected	1.40	.07	.0212
			C23 % Seats held by majority	2.30	.06	.0331

Note: C variables explaining less than 5% of the variance omitted.
Parentheses refer to variables later removed from the regression.
"% Years" refers to the percentage of years since 1960.

Table 6.8
Regressions on Teaching Ideas and Receiving Information (A32)

	Year of C Variables	Year of A Variable	Sample Size	Name of C Variable	Parameter Estimate	% Variance (Partial)	Probability (F Value)
a)	1982	1982	88	C23 % Seats held by majority	-3.94	.48	.0001
b)	1982	1982	LDCs	C23 % Seats held by majority	-4.43	.35	.0001
				C42 Arms exporter	(-.31)	.07	.0088
c)	1986	1986	88	C23 % Seats held by majority	-3.09	.43	.0001
				C27 % Years with military rule	(-.50)	.09	.0001
d)	1986	1986	LDCs	C23 % Seats held by majority	-3.94	.30	.0001
				C34 Military budget/GNP	-.58	.12	.0004
				C49 Former British colony	.70	.11	.0003
e)	1982	1986	88	C23 % Seats held by majority	(-1.66)	.40	.0001
				C35 Arms imports/GNP	(-5.38)	.08	.0005
f)	1982	1986	LDCs	C23 % Seats held by majority	-2.83	.24	.0001
				C34 Military budget/GNP	-.38	.14	.0003
				C49 Former British colony	.68	.08	.0042
				C31 % Years at war	-1.22	.05	.0145
g)	1982	1982-86	88	C28 Government repression	.45	.09	.0044
				C9 Television sets per capita	1.28	.05	.0510
				C23 % Seats held by majority	1.14	.06	.0152
h)	1982	1982-86	LDCs	C28 Government repression	.51	.11	.0061
				C23 % Seats held by majority	1.98	.08	.0152
				C51 % Roman Catholic	.11	.07	.0195
				C36 Arms imports/military budget	-.65	.05	.0336
i)	1982-86	1982-1986	88	C26 Military rule	-.40	.10	.0033
j)	1982-86	1982-1986	LDCs	C26 Military rule	(-.42)	.10	.0094

Note: C variables explaining less than 5% of the variance omitted.
Parentheses refer to variables later removed from the regression.
"% Years" refers to the percentage of years since 1960.

Table 6.9
Regressions on Limitations on the Right to Vote (A45)

	Year of C Variables	Year of A Variable	Sample Size	Name of C Variable	Parameter Estimate	% Variance (Partial)	Probability (F Value)
a)	1982	1982	88	C9 Television sets per capita	(-2.68)	.20	.0001
				C26 Military rule	.57	.08	.0030
				C52 % Moslem	.17	.07	.0038
b)	1982	1982	LDCs	C12 Trade export concentration	-.00	.11	.0057
				C26 Military rule	.57	.08	.0116
c)	1986	1986	88	C28 Government repression	.27	.36	.0001
				C23 % Seats held by majority	1.42	.12	.0001
d)	1986	1986	LDCs	C28 Government repression	.31	.22	.0001
				C22 Parties in parliament	-.07	.13	.0007
				C2 GNP per capita growth rate	-.00	.07	.0063
e)	1982	1986	88	C6 Newspaper readers per capita	-.18	.31	.0001
				C22 Parties in parliament	-.06	.09	.0059
f)	1982	1986	LDCs	C6 Newspaper readers per capita	-.23	.17	.0005
				C22 Parties in parliament	-.05	.09	.0059
g)	1982	1982-86	88	C28 Government repression	-.34	.10	.0030
				C7 Radios per capita	1.17	.07	.0486
				C25 Coups/years independent	-2.51	.07	.0061
h)	1982	1982-86	LDCs	C12 Trade export concentration	.00	.12	.0030
				C6 Newspaper readers per capita	-.15	.10	.0065
				C25 Coups/years independent	-1.80	.10	.0038
i)	1982-86	1982-1986	88	C25 Coups/years independent	4.87	.07	.0100
j)	1982-86	1982-1986	LDCs	C8 Telephones per capita	(-0.00)	.14	.0016
				C9 Television sets per capita	-9.21	.07	.0196
				C6 Newspaper readers per capita	-.24	.06	.0220
				C55 Cancer deathrate	.10	.05	.0335

Note: C variables explaining less than 5% of the variance omitted.
     Parentheses refer to variables later removed from the regression.

Table 6.10
Regressions on Freedom from Mail Censorship (A27)

	Year of C Variables	Year of A Variable	Sample Size	Name of C Variable	Parameter Estimate	% Variance (Partial)	Probability (F Value)
a)	1982	1982	88	C23 % Seats held by majority	-3.28	.46	.0001
				C4 KWH consumption per capita	-.38	.07	.0004
b)	1982	1982	LDCs	C23 % Seats held by majority	-4.24	.31	.0001
				C42 Arms exporter	-.76	.13	.0002
c)	1986	1986	88	C23 % Seats held by majority	-4.09	.44	.0001
				C27 % Years with military rule	-1.14	.11	.0001
				C39 Minority social grievances	-.61	.05	.0015
d)	1986	1986	LDCs	C34 Military budget/GNP	(.13)	.30	.0001
				C23 % Seats held by majority	-4.64	.13	.0003
				C14 Food import dependency	(.10)	.09	.0009
e)	1982	1986	88	C23 % Seats held by majority	-3.20	.40	.0001
				C34 Military budget/GNP	-.43	.11	.0001
				C28 Government repression	(-.22)	.05	.0024
f)	1982	1986	LDCs	C34 Military budget/GNP	-.46	.31	.0001
				C23 % Seats held by majority	-2.45	.13	.0002
				C14 Food import dependency	.00	.06	.0055
g)	1982	1982-86	88	none			
h)	1982	1982-86	LDCs	C36 Arms imports/military budget	-1.24	.06	.0456
				C22 Parties in parliament	-.06	.06	.0385
i)	1982-86	1982-1986	88	C29 % Years at civil war	-4.86	.17	.0001
				C9 Television sets per capita	-3.67	.06	.0121
j)	1982-86	1982-1986	LDCs	C29 % Years at civil war	-4.80	.19	.0002
				C56 Heart disease deathrate	-.00	.09	.0055
				C8 Telephones per capita	-.11	.06	.0216
				C55 Cancer deathrate	.13	.05	.0222

Note: C variables explaining less than 5% of the variance omitted.
Parentheses refer to variables later removed from the regression.

Table 6.11

Regressions on the Right to a Civilian, Public Trial (A21)

Year of C Variables	Year of A Variable	Sample Size	Name of C Variable	Parameter Estimate	% Variance (Partial)	Probability (F Value)
a) 1982	1982	88	C23 % Seats held by majority	-3.74	.35	.0001
			C33 % Population in army	(-19.17)	.08	.0006
			C3 % Agriculture workers	-1.83	.06	.0035
b) 1982	1982	LDCs	C23 % Seats held by majority	-2.81	.17	.0005
			C34 Military budget/GNP	-.24	.06	.0254
			C52 % Moslem	.18	.07	.0117
			C35 Arms imports/GNP	-16.08	.06	.0172
c) 1986	1986	88	C23 % Seats held by majority	-2.23	.32	.0001
			C28 Government repression	-.49	.14	.0001
			C40 Terrorist incidents	.83	.06	.0019
d) 1986	1986	LDCs	C23 % Seats held by majority	-2.45	.15	.0014
			C27 % Years with military rule	(-.67)	.11	.1061
			C40 Terrorist incidents	1.03	.06	.0597
			C12 Trade export concentration	.00	.07	.0718
			C10 Foreign investment/GDP	-.01	.06	.0559
e) 1982	1986	88	C23 % Seats held by majority	-3.12	.33	.0001
			C9 Television sets per capita	2.65	.08	.0009
			C34 Military budget/GNP	-.36	.06	.0030
f) 1982	1986	LDCs	C34 Military budget/GNP	-.37	.16	.0007
			C23 % Seats held by majority	-2.39	.08	.0129
g) 1982	1982-86	88	C25 Coups/years independent	-2.03	.09	.0059
			C36 Arms imports/military budget	-.60	.06	.0150
			C29 % Years at civil war	1.86	.06	.0153
h) 1982	1982-86	LDCs	C25 Coups/years independent	-2.32	.09	.0148
			C29 % Years at civil war	(.80)	.06	.0342
			C36 Arms imports/military budget	-1.73	.07	.0180
i) 1982-86	1982-1986	88	C29 % Years at civil war	-3.82	.23	.0001
			C31 % Years at war	1.93	.07	.0048
			C11 Trade/GNP	1.61	.06	.0061
j) 1982-86	1982-1986	LDCs	C29 % Years at civil war	-3.47	.23	.0001
			C31 % Years at war	1.79	.11	.0020
			C11 Trade/GNP	1.69	.06	.0157
			C57 Suicide deathrate	.02	.06	.0093

Note: C variables explaining less than 5% of the variance omitted.
Parentheses refer to variables later removed from the regression.
"% Years" refers to the percentage of years since 1960.

Table 6.12
Regressions on Freedom from Indefinite Detention (A17)

Year of C Variables	Year of A Variable	Sample Size	Name of C Variable	Parameter Estimate	% Variance (Partial)	Probability (F Value)
a) 1982	1982	88	C23 % Seats held by majority	-3.69	.39	.0001
			C17 Health spending per capita	.28	.14	.0001
b) 1982	1982	LDCs	C23 % Seats held by majority	-1.84	.18	.0003
			C45 US military aid/GNP	4.91	.09	.0065
			C42 Arms exporter	.07	.07	.0132
			C34 Military budget/GNP	-.19	.07	.0069
c) 1986	1986	88	C28 Government repression	-.50	.42	.0001
			C23 % Seats held by majority	-2.38	.16	.0001
d) 1986	1986	LDCs	C28 Government repression	-.44	.22	.0001
			C23 % Seats held by majority	-1.57	.14	.0004
			C24 Taxes/GNP	115.21	.08	.0034
e) 1982	1986	88	C9 Television sets per capita	(.90)	.32	.0001
			C23 % Seats held by majority	-1.84	.13	.0001
f) 1982	1986	LDCs	C34 Military budget/GNP	-.22	.12	.0039
			C48 % Western troops in country	.32	.06	.0316
			C18 Welfare spending per capita	.20	.07	.0150
			C44 US civilian aid/GNP	1.94	.06	.0267
			C43 % Arms imported from West	.09	.05	.0248
g) 1982	1982-86	88	C36 Arms imports/military budget	-.92	.06	.0241
h) 1982	1982-86	LDCs	C36 Arms imports/military budget	-1.10	.05	.0661
			C29 % Years at civil war	1.54	.05	.0547
i) 1982-86	1982-1986	88	C31 % Years at war	2.67	.13	.0006
j) 1982-86	1982-1986	LDCs	C31 % Years at war	2.77	.13	.0028
			C9 Television sets per capita	-13.36	.07	.0240

Note: C variables explaining less than 5% of the variance omitted.
Parentheses refer to variables later removed from the regression.
"% Years" refers to the percentage of years since 1960.

Table 6.13
Regressions on Percentage of Separatists (A2)

	Year of C Variables	Year of A Variable	Sample Size	Name of C Variable	Parameter Estimate	% Variance (Partial)	Probability (F Value)
a)	1982	1982	88	C53 Ethnolinguistic heterogeneity	.03	.42	.0001
b)	1982	1982	LDCs	C53 Ethnolinguistic heterogeneity	.03	.41	.0001
				C42 Arms exporter	.90	.08	.0027
c)	1986	1986	88	C37 Minority political grievances	.17	.15	.0002
				C54 % Leftwingers in parliament	2.11	.15	.0001
				C6 Newspaper readers per capita	-5.73	.06	.0045
d)	1986	1986	LDCs	C37 Minority political grievances	.23	.11	.0066
				C54 % Leftwingers in parliament	3.14	.17	.1711
				C34 Military budget/GNP	.21	.05	.0260
e)	1982	1986	88	C32 War deathrate	2902.17	.10	.0022
				C53 Ethnolinguistic heterogeneity	.02	.10	.0013
				C54 % Leftwingers in parliament	.39	.06	.0105
f)	1982	1986	LDCs	C32 War deathrate	2741.10	.12	.0039
				C53 Ethnolinguistic heterogeneity	.02	.09	.0100
				C42 Arms exporter	.56	.07	.0157
g)	1982	1982-86	88	C53 Ethnolinguistic heterogeneity	-.18	.29	.0001
h)	1982	1982-86	LDCs	C53 Ethnolinguistic heterogeneity	-.18	.30	.0001
				C21 % Voter turnout	.16	.06	.0216
i)	1982-86	1982-1986	88	C8 Telephones per capita	2.90	.16	.0001
				C3 % Agriculture workers	-50.45	.06	.0164
j)	1982-86	1982-1986	LDCs	C8 Telephones per capita	2.34	.18	.0004
				C3 % Agriculture workers	-74.31	.07	.0149
				C15 Income inequality	.15	.07	.0118
				C23 % Seats held by majority	-21.83	.08	.0069

Note: C variables explaining less than 5% of the variance omitted.

Table 6.14
Regressions on the Role of Women in Politics (A49)

Year of C Variables	Year of A Variable	Sample Size	Name of C Variable	Parameter Estimate	% Variance (Partial)	Probability (F Value)
a) 1982	1982	88	C34 Military budget/GNP	-.35	.14	.0003
			C18 Welfare spending per capita	.12	.09	.0012
			C22 Parties in parliament	.04	.07	.0074
b) 1982	1982	LDCs	C34 Military budget/GNP	-.30	.20	.0002
			C53 Ethnolinguistic heterogeneity	.01	.10	.0034
			C18 Welfare spending per capita	.12	.07	.0123
c) 1986	1986	88	C28 Government repression	-.43	.22	.0001
			C44 US civilian aid/GNP	1.98	.07	.0045
d) 1986	1986	LDCs	C28 Government repression	-.46	.17	.0005
			C21 % Voter turnout	-.01	.11	.0022
			C44 US civilian aid/GNP	2.11	.05	.0270
e) 1982	1986	88	C27 % Years with military rule	-1.26	.14	.0003
			C11 Trade/GNP	.92	.07	.0061
f) 1982	1986	LDCs	C44 US civilian aid/GNP	2.29	.13	.0030
			C42 Arms exporter	-.55	.07	.0188
			C25 Coups/years independent	-1.85	.08	.0096
g) 1982	1982-86	88	C45 US military aid/GNP	2.58	.11	.0018
			C23 % Seats held by majority	2.01	.06	.0176
h) 1982	1982-86	LDCs	C45 US military aid/GNP	3.44	.11	.0055
			C23 % Seats held by majority	2.65	.09	.0083
			C48 % Western troops in country	.22	.06	.0235
i) 1982-86	1982-1986	88	C24 Taxes/GNP	230.46	.08	.0061
			C3 % Agriculture workers	4.63	.13	.0004
			C56 Heart disease deathrate	.00	.07	.0067
			C29 % Years with civil war	-1.52	.05	.0123
j) 1982-86	1982-1986	LDCs	C24 Taxes/GNP	202.11.	.09	.0116
			C3 % Agriculture workers	5.11	.11	.0035
			C56 Heart disease deathrate	.00	.07	.0196

Note: C variables explaining less than 5% of the variance omitted.
      "% Years" refers to the percentage of years since 1960.

Table 6.15
Regressions on the Right to Consensual Adult Homosexuality (A28)

	Year of C Variables	Year of A Variable	Sample Size	Name of C Variable	Parameter Estimate	% Variance (Partial)	Probability (F Value)
a)	1982	1982	88	C9 Television sets per capita	3.83	.25	.0001
				C23 % Seats held by majority	(-1.19)	.05	.0120
b)	1982	1982	LDCs	C51 % Roman Catholic	.24	.14	.0021
				C13 Trade import concentration	-.00	.08	.0151
				C21 % Voter turnout	.02	.07	.0137
c)	1986	1986	88	C9 Television sets per capita	1.88	.31	.0001
				C23 % Seats held by majority	-3.19	.15	.0001
				C56 Heart disease deathrate	.00	.06	.0014
d)	1986	1986	LDCs	C51 % Roman Catholic	.24	.21	.0001
				C56 Heart disease deathrate	.00	.10	.0028
				C23 % Seats held by majority	-2.68	.08	.0050
e)	1982	1986	88	C19 % Budget for welfare	(.06)	.33	.0001
				C23 % Seats held by majority	-3.26	.11	.0001
				C47 % Foreign troops in country	.14	.07	.0009
				C35 Arms imports/GNP	-7.23	.05	.0018
f)	1982	1986	LDCs	C51 % Roman Catholic	.26	.21	.0001
				C47 % Foreign troops in country	.10	.07	.0132
				C12 Trade export concentration	-.00	.07	.0121
				C56 Heart disease deathrate	.00	.07	.0050
g)	1982	1982-86	88	none			
h)	1982	1982-86	LDCs	C24 Taxes/GNP	-181.23	.11	.0066
				C42 Arms exporter	-.55	.10	.0057
				C57 Suicide deathrate	.02	.08	.0089
				C23 % Seats held by majority	-2.87	.06	.0270
				C22 Parties in parliament	-.07	.06	.0199
i)	1982-86	1982-1986	88	C34 Military budget/GNP	-.26	.07	.0146
				C32 War deathrate	-1472.13	.07	.0084
j)	1982-86	1982-1986	LDCs	C46 % Troops abroad	-.13	.14	.0019
				C34 Military budget/GNP	-.23	.06	.0323

Note: C variables explaining less than 5% of the variance omitted.
Parentheses refer to variables later removed from the regression.

Table 6.16

Factor Analysis of Economic and Social Rights and Predictor Variables, 1982

Articles	Variables	1	2	3	4	5	6	7	8
1	B1 Economic freedom		.69						
6	B2 Trademarks applied for per capita	.48							
	B9 Absence of serfdom, slavery, & child labor	.61							
7	B10 No compulsory work permits/labor conscription		.89						
	B13 Consumer spending per capita	.62							
	B14 % Workers injured on the job	.48							.66
	B15 % Losing work due to on-the-job injuries	.48							.58
	B16 % Workers injured fatally on the job								.79
8	B19 Freedom to form & join independent unions		.77						
	B21 Right of unions to federate		.78						
	B22 Freedom of unions to operate		.80						
9	B26 Extensiveness of family allowance plans	.67							
	B27 Extensiveness of old-age/survivor pensions	.64							
	B28 Extensiveness of sickness/maternity programs	.64							
	B29 Extensiveness of unemployment insurance	.66							
	B30 Extensiveness of work-injury programs	.42	.41						
	B31 % Budget for social security/welfare	.71							
10	B32 Deathrate of males aged 1-4			-.78					
	B33 Ratio of deathrate of females/males aged 1-4			-.47					
	B34 % Infants immunized against DPT	.68							
	B35 Right to marry					-.41			
11	B36 Caloric intake per capita	.84							
	B37 Protein intake per capita	.83							
	B39 Nonrubber footwear production per capita	.46							
	B40 % Housing units with safe water	.85							
	B41 % Housing units with flush toilets	.70							
	B43 % Central government budget for housing							.56	
	B44 % Central government budget for agriculture	-.44							
	B45 Overseas development aid received/GDP	-.70							
12	B47 Infant mortality rate	-.86							
	B48 Ratio of female to male infant mortality					.48			
	B49 Infectious-parasite diseases deathrate		-.76						
	B51 Persons per physicians	-.91							
	B52 Persons per hospital beds	-.79							
	B53 % Childbirths attended	.55							
13	B54 Life expectancy	.91							
	B55 % Population with access to health care	.64							
	B56 Years of compulsory education	.43							
	B57 % School-age children in primary school	.55							

Table 6.16 (continued)

Articles	Variables	1	2	3	4	5	6	7	8
13	B58 % School-age females in primary school	.58							
	B59 % School-age children in secondary school	.90							
	B60 % Education budget for vocational schools	.43							
	B62 % Adults enrolled in colleges	.85							
	B63 % Females enrolled in colleges	.81							
	B66 School-age population per teacher	-.77							
	B67 % Population literate	.83							
	B68 % Females literate	.69							
15	B70 Fixed cinema seats per capita	.43							
	B72 Museum attendance per capita	.48							
	B74 % Registered as public library users	.57							
	B75 Books published per capita	.61							
	B81 Films imported per capita							.86	
	B82 Films imported/long films produced							.56	
	B84 Patents per capita	.57							
16	B89 Artistic freedom	.56	.86						
	B91 External economic aid sent/GDP	.89							
	C1 Per capita GNP								
	C3 Percent of workforce employed in agriculture	-.48							
	C4 Energy consumption per capita	.91							
	C5 Percent of population living in cities	.84							
	C6 Newspaper circulation per capita	.87							
	C7 Radios per capita	.73							
	C8 Telephones per capita	.89							
	C9 Television sets per capita	.83							
	C10 Investment received/gross domestic product							.43	
	C11 Dollar value of exports and imports/GNP							.52	
	C12 Percent of trade with largest export partner								.84
	C13 Percent of trade with largest import partner								.84
	C15 Income inequality	-.46							
	C16 Expenditures on education per capita	.87							
	C17 Expenditures on health per capita	.88							
	C18 Expenditures on welfare per capita	.83							
	C20 Rate of inflation					.49			
	C22 Number of political parties in parliament		.45						
	C23 Percent of seats held by largest political party		-.63						
	C25 Coups from 1960/years independent				.54				
	C26 Military-dominated government				.86				
	C27 Years of military rule from 1960/years independent				.87				

Articles Variables	1	2	3	4	5	6	7	8
C28 Official violence against citizens				.75				
C29 Years at civil war from 1960/years independent				.41				
C32 Deathrate due to foreign conflict					.51			
C33 Percent of population in the armed forces					.48			
C35 Arms imports/GNP						.78		
C36 Arms imports/military budget						.75		
C44 US civilian aid/GNP					.67			
C45 US military aid/GNP					.86			
C52 Percent Moslem population	-.43							
C53 Index of ethnolinguistic heterogeneity	-.54							
C54 Percent leftists in parliament		-.56						
C55 Cancer deathrate (males)			.84					
C56 Heart disease deathrate (males)			.74					
C57 Suicide deathrate (males)			.64					
Percent Variance Explained	30.5	7.9	4.6	3.6	3.3	3.2	3.0	3.0

<u>Note:</u> Loadings below ±.40 omitted.
    Variables with no loadings above ±.40 omitted.

Table 6.17

Factor Analysis of Economic and Social Rights and Predictor Variables, 1986

Articles	Variables	1	2	3	4	5	6	7	8
1	B1 Economic freedom	.48							
	B2 Trademarks applied for per capita		.66						
	B3 Improvement in terms of trade						.72		
	B4 Improvement in purchasing power of exports						.72		
2	B5 % Population suffering economic discrimination				.67				
	B6 Severity of minority economic discrimination				.81				
	B7 No social/economic discrimination against minorities				-.46				
	B8 No social/economic discrimination against women								
6	B9 Absence of serfdom, slavery, & child labor	.65							
	B10 No compulsory work permits/labor conscription	.59	.86						
7	B13 Consumer spending per capita	.60							
	B14 % Workers injured on the job	.50							

Articles	Variables	1	2	3	4	5	6	7	8
7	B15 % Losing work due to on-the-job injuries		.50						
8	B19 Freedom to form & join independent unions		.41	.79					
	B20 % Workers organized into unions		.42	.83					
	B21 Right of unions to federate								
	B22 Freedom of unions to operate		.80						
9	B26 Extensiveness of family allowance plans	.62							
	B27 Extensiveness of old-age/survivor pensions	.58							
	B28 Extensiveness of sickness/maternity programs	.61							
	B29 Extensiveness of unemployment insurance	.61							
	B31 % Budget for social security/welfare	.60							
10	B32 Deathrate of males aged 1-4			-.72					
	B34 % Infants immunized								
	B35 Right to marry	.69						-.54	
11	B36 Caloric intake per capita	.83							
	B37 Protein intake per capita	.81							
	B39 Nonrubber footwear production per capita	.45							
	B40 % Housing units with safe water	.89							
	B41 % Housing units with flush toilets	.68							
	B44 % Central government budget for agriculture	-.48							
	B45 Overseas development aid received/GDP	-.47							
12	B47 Infant mortality rate	-.90							
	B49 Infectious-parasite diseases deathrate			-.70					
	B51 Persons per physicians	-.91							
	B52 Persons per hospital beds	-.70							
	B53 % Childbirths attended	.61							
	B54 Life expectancy at birth	.93							
	B55 % Population with access to health care	.82							
13	B56 Years of compulsory education	.56							
	B57 % School-age children in primary school	.59							
	B58 % School-age females in primary school	.51							
	B59 % School-age children in secondary school	.90							
	B60 % Education budget for vocational schools	.47							
	B62 % Adults enrolled in colleges	.76							
	B63 % Females enrolled in colleges	.79							
	B64 % Education budget for scholarships			.44					
	B66 School-age population per teacher	-.87							
	B67 % Population literate	.82							
	B68 % Females literate	.75							
15	B75 Books published per capita	.50							

Table 6.17 (continued)

Articles Variables	1	2	3	4	5	6	7	8
15 B77 Textbooks published/students	.42							
B84 Patents per capita	.56							
16 B89 Artistic freedom		.84						
B91 External economic aid sent/GDP	.60							
C1 Per capita GNP	.92							
C2 Per capita GNP growth rate						.75		
C3 Percent of workforce employed in agriculture	-.91							
C4 Energy consumption per capita	-.92							
C5 Percent of population living in cities	.82							
C6 Newspaper circulation per capita	.89							
C7 Radios per capita	.71							
C8 Telephones per capita	.82							
C9 Television sets per capita	.83							
C10 Investment received/gross domestic product		-.41						
C12 Percent of trade with largest export partner						.87		
C13 Percent of trade with largest import partner						.82		
C16 Expenditures on education per capita	.86							
C17 Expenditures on health per capita	.86							
C18 Expenditures on welfare per capita	.72							
C22 Number of political parties in parliament		.48						
C23 Percent of seats held by largest political party		-.63						
C25 Coups from 1960/years independent					.62			
C26 Military-dominated government					.80			
C27 % Years with military rule					.84			
C28 Official violence against citizens	-.57							
C29 Years at civil war from 1960/years independent					.41			
C34 Military budget/GNP		-.47						
C35 Arms imports/GNP		-.42						
C37 Extent of minority political grievances				.85				
C38 Extent of minority economic grievances				.86				
C39 Extent of minority social grievances				.87				
C44 US civilian aid/GNP							.57	
C45 US military aid/GNP							.84	
C53 Index of ethnolinguistic heterogeneity	-.56	-.46						
C54 Percent leftists in parliament			.73					
C55 Cancer deathrate (males)			.77					
C56 Heart disease deathrate (males)			.74					
C57 Suicide deathrate (males)								
Percent Variance Explained	30.5	8.9	6.9	5.2	3.9	3.6	3.1	3.0

Note: Loadings below $\pm$.40 omitted.
Variables with no loadings above $\pm$.40 omitted.

Table 6.18
Factor Analysis of Predictor Variables for 1982 and Economic and Social Rights for 1986

Variables		1	2	3	4	5	6	7	8	9	10
B1	Economic freedom	.50									
B2	Trademarks applied for per capita		.72								
B3	Improvement in terms of trade					.68					
B4	Improvement in purchasing power of exports					.86					
B8	No female socioeconomic discrimination	.67									
B9	Absence of serfdom, slavery, & child labor	.63									
B10	No compulsory work permits		.85								
B13	Consumer spending per capita	.64									
B14	% Workers injured on the job	.47						.69			
B15	% Losing work due to on-the-job injuries	.57						.74			
B16	% Workers fatally injured on the job						.72				
B17	Nonagricultural work week in hours	.50							.42		
B19	Freedom to form & join independent unions		.82								
B20	% Workers organized into unions	.41									
B21	Right of unions to federate		.85								
B22	Freedom of unions to operate		.83								
B26	Extensiveness of family allowance plans	.67									
B27	Extensiveness of old-age/survivor pensions	.63									
B28	Extensiveness of sickness/maternity programs	.64									
B29	Extensiveness of unemployment insurance	.63									
B31	% Budget for social security/welfare	.76							.83		
B32	Deathrate of males aged 1-4	-.53									
B34	% Infants immunized against DPT	.72									
B35	Right to marry				.76						
B36	Caloric intake per capita	.85									
B37	Protein intake per capita	.85									
B38	Cotton woven fabric production per capita	.43									
B39	Nonrubber footwear production per capita	.89							.83		
B40	% Housing units with safe water	.72									
B41	% Housing units with flush toilets	.72									
B42	% Housing investment in GDP									.87	
B44	% Central government budget for agriculture	-.53									
B45	Overseas development aid received/GDP	-.41									
B46	Late fetal deathrate	-.75									
B47	Infant mortality rate	-.92									
B49	Infectious-parasitic diseases deathrate	-.61									
B51	Persons per physicians	-.74									
B52	Persons per hospital beds	-.58									
B53	% Childbirths attended	.72									

Table 6.18 (continued)

Variables	1	2	3	4	5	6	7	8	9	10
B54 Life expectancy at birth	.94									
B55 % Population with access to health care	.85									
B56 Years of compulsory education	.62									
B57 % School-age children in primary school	.67									
B58 % School-age females in primary school	.60							-.55		
B59 % School-age children in secondary school	.91									
B60 % Education budget for vocational schools	.62									
B62 % Adults enrolled in colleges	.73									
B63 % Females enrolled in colleges	.77									
B66 School-age population per teacher	-.80									
B67 % Population literate	.84									
B68 % Females literate	.82			.42						
B75 Books published per capita	.56									
B77 Textbooks published/students	.41									
B79 Books translated per capita	.40									
B80 Long films produced per capita									.75	
B81 Films imported per capita	.47					.57				
B83 Industrial designs per capita	.58				.51	.47				
B84 Patents per capita	.53									
B87 % GNP spent on R & D		-.47								
B89 No state control of artistic works		.82								
B90 % College students from abroad						.73				
B91 External economic aid sent/GDP						.86				
C1 Per capita GNP	.92									
C2 GNP per capita growth rate					.72					
C3 % Workforce employed in agriculture	-.79									
C4 Energy consumption per capita	.91									
C5 Percent of population living in cities	.81									
C6 Newspaper circulation per capita	.90									
C7 Radios per capita	.68									
C8 Telephones per capita	.89									
C9 Television sets per capita	.81									
C12 Percent trade with largest export partner										.46
C13 Percent trade with largest import partner										.85
C14 Food import dependency									.45	
C15 Income inequality	-.63									
C16 Expenditures on education per capita	.87									
C17 Expenditures on health per capita	.98									
C18 Expenditures on welfare per capita	.95									

Variables	1	2	3	4	5	6	7	8	9	10
C22 Number of political parties in parliament		.46								
C23 Percent of seats held by largest party		-.66								
C26 Military-dominated government			.91							
C27 Years of military rule/years independent			.87							
C28 Official violence against citizens			.79							
C29 Years at civil war/years independent			.46							
C34 Military budget/GNP				-.42						
C35 Arms imports/GNP				-.41						
C42 Net arms exporting country (yes/no)	.41									
C51 Percent Catholic population			.51							
C52 Percent Moslem population			-.72							
C53 Index of ethnolinguistic heterogeneity	-.57									
C54 Percent leftists in parliament		-.54								
C55 Cancer deathrate (males)	.71									
C56 Heart disease deathrate (males)	.65									
C57 Suicide deathrate (males)	.43									
Percent Variance Explained	34.7	9.2	5.4	4.1	4.1	3.4	3.4	3.4	3.3	3.3

<u>Note</u>: Loadings below ±.40 omitted.
        Variables with no loadings above ±.40 omitted.

Table 6.19
Factor Analysis of Predictor Variables for 1982 and Changes in Economic and Social Rights, 1982–1986

Variables	1	2	3	4	5	6	7	8	9	10
B3 Improvement in terms of trade				.79						
B4 Improvement in purchasing power of exports				.93						
B13 Consumer spending per capita	-.57									
B23 Ratio of strikes to persons employed			.89							
B24 Ratio of strikers to persons employed			.85							
B32 Deathrate of males aged 1-4	.57			.48						
B36 Caloric intake per capita										.86
B37 Protein intake per capita										.87
B38 Cotton production per capita							.40			
B42 % Housing investment/GDP								.51		

Variables	1	2	3	4	5	6	7	8	9	10
B46 Late fetal deathrate										
B49 Infectious-parasitic diseases deathrate	.43									
B57 % School-age children in primary school					.40					
B58 % School-age females in primary school							.94			
B60 % Education budget for vocational training					.58		.98			
B70 Fixed cinema seats per capita						.53				
B72 Museum attendance per capita						.45				
B78 Books translated/books published						.78				
B79 Books translated per capita						.83				
B80 Long films produced per capita								.62		
B81 Films imported per capita										
B83 Industrial designs per capita					.41	.52				
B84 Patents per capita	.58									
C1 GNP per capita	.97									
C2 GNP per capita growth rate				.48						
C3 Percent of workforce in agriculture	-.82									
C4 Energy consumption per capita	.92									
C5 Percent of population in cities	.86									
C6 Newspaper circulation per capita	.84									
C7 Radios per capita	.70									
C8 Telephones per capita	.95									
C9 Television sets per capita	.87									
C11 Dollar values of exports and imports/GNP								.75		
C12 Percent trade with largest export partner									.83	
C13 Percent trade with largest import partner									.89	
C14 Food import dependency								.67		
C15 Income inequality	-.60									
C16 Expenditures on education per capita	.94									
C17 Expenditures on health per capita	.94									
C18 Expenditures on welfare per capita	.98									
C21 Votes cast/adults registered to vote			-.51							
C22 Number of political parties in parliament			.52							
C23 Percent of seats held by largest party			-.55							
C25 Years with coups/years independent		.53								
C26 Military-dominated government		.87								
C27 Years of military rule/years independent		.87								
C28 Official violence against citizens		.72								
C29 Years at civil war/years independent	-.44									
C32 Deathrate due to foreign conflict				.42						

Table 6.19 (continued)

Variables	1	2	3	4	5	6	7	8	9	10
C33 Percent of population in the armed forces	-.50									
C36 Arms imports/military budget				.44						
C44 US civilian aid/GNP				-.41						
C45 US military aid/GNP				.69						
C53 Ethnolinguistic heterogeneity				.86						
C54 Percent leftists in parliament			-.56							
C55 Cancer deathrate (males)	.72									
C56 Heart disease deathrate (males)	.64									
Percent Variance Explained	15.8	4.8	4.5	4.1	3.8	3.7	3.6	3.5	3.4	3.3

Note: Loadings below ±.40 omitted.
Variables with no loadings above ±.40 omitted.

Table 6.20
Factor Analysis of Changes in Economic and Social Rights and Predictor Variables, 1982–1986

Variables	1	2	3	4	5	6	7	8	9	10
B2 Trademarks applied for per capita										
B3 Improvement in terms of trade				-.56	.80					
B4 Improvement in purchasing power of exports					.90					
B5 % Population with economic discrimination			-.42							
B10 No compulsory work permits			.46							
B12 Average nonagricultural weekly wages	.42									
B13 Consumer spending per capita	-.67									
B14 % Workers injured on the job										.91
B15 % Losing work due to on-the-job injuries										.58
B16 % Workers injured fatally on the job										.78
B23 Ratio of strikes to persons employed							.87			
B24 Ratio of strikers to persons employed							.85			
B31 % Budget for social security/welfare						.60				
B32 Deathrate of males aged 1-4	.55									
B33 Deathrate of females/males aged 1-4				-.62						
B42 % GDP invested in housing				.61						
B49 Infectious-parasitic diseases deathrate	.45									
B57 % School-age children in primary school								.95		

Table 6.20 (continued)

Variables	1	2	3	4	5	6	7	8	9	10
B58 % School-age females in primary school										
B62 % Adults enrolled in colleges								.96		
B63 % Females enrolled in colleges									.86	
B68 % Females literate	-.48								.89	
B70 Fixed cinema seats per capita		.77								
B72 Museum attendance per capita	.40	.45								
B75 Books published per capita		.41								
B76 % Textbooks among all books published						.43				
B78 Books translated/books published		.72								
B79 Books translated per capita		.70								
B80 Long films produced per capita				.58						
B81 Films imported per capita		.67								
B84 Patents per capita	.65									
B89 No state control of artistic works			.64							
B91 External economic aid sent/GDP				-.59						
C1 Per capita GNP	.82									
C4 Energy consumption per capita	.93									
C6 Newspaper circulation per capita	.89									
C7 Radios per capita	.42									
C8 Telephones per capita	.86									
C11 Dollar value of exports and imports/GNP			.41		.51					
C14 Food import dependency				.83						
C16 Expenditures on education per capita	.96									
C17 Expenditures on health per capita	.94									
C18 Expenditures on welfare per capita	.89									
C21 Votes cast/adults registered to vote	.42									
C26 Military-dominated government						.74				
C27 Years of military rule/years independent						.87				
C28 Official violence against citizens	-.49									
C32 Deathrate due to foreign conflict			.93							
C33 Percent of population in the armed forces			-.81							
C35 Arms imports/GNP			-.56							
C42 Arms exporter						.55				
C54 Percent leftists in parliament							-.50			
C55 Cancer deathrate (males)	.57									
C57 Suicide deathrate (males)						.42				
Percent Variance Explained	11.4	3.9	3.9	3.9	3.8	3.8	3.6	3.4	3.4	3.4

Note: Loadings below ±.40 omitted.
Variables with no loadings above ±.40 omitted.

Table 6.21
Regressions on Economic Freedom (B1)

	Year of C Variables	Year of B Variable	Sample Size	Name of C Variable	Parameter Estimate	% Variance (Partial)	Probability (F Value)
a)	1982	1982	88	C54 % Leftwingers in parliament	-3.88	.33	.0001
				C8 Telephones per capita	.87	.13	.0001
				C35 Arms imports/GNP	-17.29	.08	.0001
				C56 Heart disease deathrate	-.00	.05	.0015
b)	1982	1982	LDCs	C54 % Leftwingers in parliament	-3.43	.52	.0001
				C35 Arms imports/GNP	-19.72	.09	.0001
				C56 Heart disease deathrate	-.00	.05	.0021
c)	1986	1986	88	C54 % Leftwingers in parliament	-4.38	.40	.0001
				C35 Arms imports/GNP	-8.52	.12	.0001
				C19 % Direct taxes collected	2.83	.05	.0021
d)	1986	1986	LDCs	C54 % Leftwingers in parliament	-6.95	.50	.0001
				C35 Arms imports/GNP	-8.37	.10	.0002
e)	1982	1986	88	C54 % Leftwingers in parliament	-3.65	.35	.0001
				C35 Arms imports/GNP	-14.62	.13	.0001
				C23 % Seats held by majority	-3.23	.08	.0003
f)	1982	1986	LDCs	C54 % Leftwingers in parliament	-3.66	.50	.0001
				C30 Domestic violence deathrate	-29.15	.10	.0002
				C56 Heart disease deathrate	-.00	.05	.0035
g)	1982	1982-86	88	C20 Inflation rate	-.37	.07	.0152
h)	1982	1982-86	LDCs	C20 Inflation rate	-.42	.13	.0026
				C45 US military aid/GNP	1.66	.05	.0444
i)	1982-86	1982-1986	88	C5 % Urban population	.01	.06	.0269
j)	1982-86	1982-1986	LDCs	C21 % Voter turnout	.01	.06	.0387
				C24 Taxes/GNP	68.76	.05	.0351

Note: C variables explaining less than 5% of the variance omitted.

Table 6.22
Regressions on Improved Terms of Trade (B3)

	Year of C Variables	Year of B Variable	Sample Size	Name of C Variable	Parameter Estimate	% Variance (Partial)	Probability (F Value)
a)	1982	1982	88	C1 Per capita GNP	12.21	.20	.0001
				C52 % Moslem	(.62)	.12	.0002
				C10 Foreign investment/GDP	.04	.05	.0105
b)	1982	1982	LDCs	C1 Per capita GNP	17.37	.21	.0001
				C52 % Moslem	1.43	.12	.0015
c)	1986	1986	88	C2 GNP per capita growth rate	.11	.17	.0001
				C9 Television sets per capita	113.57	.08	.0028
				C5 % Urban population	(-.16)	.08	.0020
d)	1986	1986	LDCs	C2 GNP per capita growth rate	.14	.17	.0005
				C43 % Arms imports from West	9.06	.07	.0144
e)	1982	1986	88	C2 GNP per capita growth rate	.06	.17	.0001
				C55 Cancer deathrate	(.00)	.10	.0010
				C52 % Moslem	(-.67)	.06	.0575
				C9 Television sets per capita	193.56	.09	.0002
f)	1982	1986	LDCs	C2 GNP per capita growth rate	(.04)	.15	.0015
				C4 KWH consumption per capita	(-2.99)	.11	.0026
				C8 Telephones per capita	12.40	.10	.0432
				C1 Per capita GNP	-25.73	.06	.0134
				C25 Coups/years independent	-63.10	.05	.0155
				C12 Trade export concentration	-.03	.06	.0143
				C9 Television sets per capita	137.12	.05	.0042
g)	1982	1982-86	88	C35 Arms imports/GNP	-238.25	.14	.0003
				C2 GNP per capita growth rate	.09	.07	.0063
				C4 KWH consumption per capita	(-4.01)	.06	.0077
				C8 Telephones per capita	16.80	.16	.0001
				C42 Arms exporter	(5.59)	.06	.0035
h)	1982	1982-86	LDCs	C1 Per capita GNP	-29.86	.22	.0001
				C8 Telephones per capita	12.56	.22	.0001
				C9 Television sets per capita	119.38	.08	.0017
i)	1982-86	1982-1986	88	C11 Trade/GNP	75.80	.27	.0001
				C4 KWH consumption per capita	-11.58	.05	.0128
				C1 Per capita GNP	8.14	.06	.0078
j)	1982-86	1982-1986	LDCs	C11 Trade/GNP	84.54	.29	.0001
				C4 KWH consumption per capita	-13.65	.12	.0006

Note: C variables explaining less than 5% of the variance omitted.
Parentheses refer to variables later removed from the regression.

Table 6.23
Regressions on Freedom from Compulsory Work Permits (B10)

	Year of C Variables	Year of B Variable	Sample Size	Name of C Variable	Parameter Estimate	% Variance (Partial)	Probability (F Value)
a)	1982	1982	88	C54 % Leftwingers in parliament	-1.44	.30	.0001
				C23 % Seats held by majority	-2.22	.14	.0001
b)	1982	1982	LDCs	C54 % Leftwingers in parliament	-1.39	.44	.0001
				C56 Heart disease deathrate	-.00	.07	.0041
				C45 US military aid/GNP	2.80	.05	.0057
c)	1986	1986	88	C54 % Leftwingers in parliament	-.86	.20	.0001
				C34 Military budget/GNP	-.55	.13	.0001
				C11 Trade/GNP	2.68	.09	.0007
				C20 Inflation rate	.33	.05	.0050
				C29 % Years at civil war	-4.98	.10	.0035
d)	1986	1986	LDCs	C54 % Leftwingers in parliament	-1.46	.25	.0001
				C34 Military budget/GNP	-.41	.12	.0011
				C11 Trade/GNP	2.72	.08	.0048
				C20 Inflation rate	.30	.10	.0007
				C29 % Years at civil war	-4.98	.06	.0035
e)	1982	1986	88	C54 % Leftwingers in parliament	-1.28	.26	.0001
				C23 % Seats held by majority	-1.48	.12	.0002
				C29 % Years at civil war	-2.11	.08	.0007
f)	1982	1986	LDCs	C54 % Leftwingers in parliament	-1.52	.38	.0001
				C34 Military budget/GNP	-.47	.09	.0015
				C45 US military aid/GNP	7.37	.07	.0021
g)	1982	1982-86	88	C52 % Moslem	-.09	.15	.0002
				C15 Income inequality	-.00	.10	.0013
				C32 War deathrate	-938.22	.05	.0142
				C45 US military aid/GNP	2.18	.06	.0055
h)	1982	1982-86	LDCs	C52 % Moslem	-.08	.14	.0021
				C15 Income inequality	-.00	.12	.0017
				C45 US military aid/GNP	1.94	.06	.0055
i)	1982-86	1982-1986	88	C32 War deathrate	30.93	.19	.0001
				C6 Newspaper readers per capita	.08	.08	.0037
j)	1982-86	1982-1986	LDCs	C32 War deathrate	1789.60	.18	.0003
				C6 Newspaper readers per capita	.13	.08	.0125
				C15 Income inequality	.00	.05	.0343

Note: C variables explaining less than 5% of the variance omitted.
  "% Years" refers to the percentage of years since 1960.

Appendix C

Table 6.24
Regressions on Consumer Spending Per Capita (B13)

Year of C Variables	Year of B Variable	Sample Size	Name of C Variable	Parameter Estimate	% Variance (Partial)	Probability (F Value)
a) 1982	1982	88	C4 KWH consumption per capita	.29	.30	.0001
			C20 Inflation rate	.56	.07	.0032
			C53 Ethnolinguistic heterogeneity	-.01	.06	.0041
b) 1982	1982	LDCs	C18 Welfare spending per capita	.21	.38	.0001
			C16 Education spending per capita	.09	.12	.0003
			C34 Military budget/GNP	-.12	.11	.0001
c) 1986	1986	88	C3 % Agriculture workers	-.95	.34	.0001
d) 1986	1986	LDCs	C3 % Agriculture workers	-.83	.40	.0001
			C34 Military budget/GNP	(-1.11)	.06	.0087
e) 1982	1986	88	C7 Radios per capita	1402.39	.36	.0001
			C9 Television sets per capita	6537.90	.05	.0070
f) 1982	1986	LDCs	C18 Welfare spending per capita	162.69	.44	.0001
			C1 Per capita GNP	(1.64)	.07	.0027
			C34 Military budget/GNP	(-46.13)	.05	.0068
g) 1982	1982-86	88	C1 Per capita GNP	-1.29	.30	.0001
h) 1982	1982-86	LDCs	C33 % Population in army	-101.83	.24	.0001
			C1 Per capita GNP	-1.09	.09	.0050
			C31 % Years at war	-3.15	.07	.0084
			C18 Welfare spending per capita	.40	.06	.0109
i) 1982-86	1982-1986	88	C16 Education spending per capita	-.96	.35	.0001
j) 1982-86	1982-1986	LDCs	C1 Per capita GNP	-1.80	.32	.0001
			C46 % Troops abroad	-.34	.08	.0045

Note: C variables explaining less than 5% of the variance omitted.
Parentheses refer to variables later removed from the regression.
"% Years" refers to the percentage of years since 1960.

Table 6.25
Regressions on Percentage of Deaths from Industrial Accidents (B16)

	Year of C Variables	Year of B Variable	Sample Size	Name of C Variable	Parameter Estimate	% Variance (Partial)	Probability (F Value)
a)	1982	1982	88	C10 Foreign investment/GDP	.00	.10	.0028
				C55 Cancer deathrate	.00	.08	.0049
				C43 % Arms imports from West	.00	.05	.0194
b)	1982	1982	LDCs	C8 Telephones per capita	.00	.15	.0010
				C55 Cancer deathrate	.00	.07	.0202
c)	1986	1986	88	C21 % Voter turnout	.00	.12	.0011
				C10 Foreign investment/GDP	.00	.05	.0257
d)	1986	1986	LDCs	C21 % Voter turnout	.00	.18	.0004
				C25 Coups/years independent	-.21	.05	.0430
e)	1982	1986	88	C21 % Voter turnout	.00	.08	.0071
f)	1982	1986	LDCs	C55 Cancer deathrate	.00	.12	.0043
				C42 Arms exporter	.01	.06	.0290
g)	1982	1982-86	88	C23 % Seats held by majority	(-.03)	.05	.0351
				C6 Newspaper readers per capita	.01	.05	.0242
				C33 % Population in army	-1.89	.05	.0237
h)	1982	1982-86	LDCs	C13 Trade import concentration	.00	.06	.0444
				C29 % Years at civil war	.09	.06	.0451
				C35 Arms imports/GNP	-.38	.05	.0452
i)	1982-86	1982-1986	88	C23 % Seats held by majority	-.10	.11	.0017
j)	1982-86	1982-1986	LDCs	C15 Income inequality	-.00	.17	.0006
				C55 Cancer deathrate	.01	.09	.0076
				C22 Parties in parliament	-.00	.06	.0193

Note: C variables explaining less than 5% of the variance omitted.
Parentheses refer to variables later removed from the regression.
"% Years" refers to the percentage of years since 1960.

Table 6.26

Regressions on the Right of Unions to Federate (B21)

Year of C Variables	Year of B Variable	Sample Size	Name of C Variable	Parameter Estimate	% Variance (Partial)	Probability (F Value)
a) 1982	1982	88	C23 % Seats held by majority	-1.46	.29	.0001
			C54 % Leftwingers in parliament	-.34	.10	.0003
			C35 Arms imports/GNP	-4.78	.07	.0004
			C44 US civilian aid/GNP	1.36	.06	.0024
b) 1982	1982	LDCs	C54 % Leftwingers in parliament	-.67	.29	.0001
			C1 Per capita GNP	-.16	.09	.0041
			C28 Government repression	-.18	.08	.0035
c) 1986	1986	88	C23 % Seats held by majority	(-.42)	.27	.0001
			C21 % Voter turnout	-.00	.08	.0017
			C40 Terrorist incidents	.40	.05	.0081
			C19 % Direct taxes collected	.49	.06	.0027
			C35 Arms imports/GNP	-2.19	.05	.0165
d) 1986	1986	LDCs	C54 % Leftwingers in parliament	-.62	.23	.0001
			C22 Parties in parliament	.02	.08	.0081
			C33 % Population in army	-11.57	.06	.0162
			C40 Terrorist incidents	.50	.07	.0093
			C19 % Direct taxes collected	.83	.05	.0165
e) 1982	1986	88	C23 % Seats held by majority	-1.22	.26	.0001
			C54 % Leftwingers in parliament	-.71	.12	.0001
			C28 Government repression	-.14	.06	.0047
f) 1982	1986	LDCs	C54 % Leftwingers in parliament	-.86	.29	.0001
			C28 Government repression	-.20	.06	.0165
			C3 % Agriculture workers	.75	.06	.0149
g) 1982	1982-86	88	C19 % Direct taxes collected	.55	.07	.0145
h) 1982	1982-86	LDCs	C19 % Direct taxes collected	.50	.07	.0254
			C57 Suicide deathrate	.00	.08	.0158
i) 1982-86	1982-1986	88	C30 Domestic violence deathrate	-862.48	.08	.0064
			C21 % Voter turnout	.01	.06	.0149
			C24 Taxes/GNP	61.47	.05	.0203
j) 1982-86	1982-1986	LDCs	C21 % Voter turnout	.01	.09	.0149
			C3 % Agriculture workers	-2.10	.08	.0148
			C30 Domestic violence deathrate	-992.45	.08	.0121
			C19 % Direct taxes collected	-.79	.08	.0068
			C10 Foreign investment/GDP	-.00	.08	.0056

Note: C variables explaining less than 5% of the variance omitted.
Parentheses refer to variables later removed from the regression.

Table 6.27
Regressions on Family Allowance Benefits (B26)

Year of C Variables	Year of B Variable	Sample Size	Name of C Variable	Parameter Estimate	% Variance (Partial)	Probability (F Value)
a) 1982	1982	88	C9 Television sets per capita	5.30	.52	.0001
			C56 Heart disease deathrate	.00	.08	.0001
b) 1982	1982	LDCs	C56 Heart disease deathrate	.00	.31	.0001
			C18 Welfare spending per capita	.24	.14	.0002
			C49 Former British colony	-1.01	.08	.0125
c) 1986	1986	88	C18 Welfare spending per capita	.23	.54	.0001
			C28 Government repression	(-.21)	.07	.0001
d) 1986	1986	LDCs	C18 Welfare spending per capita	.15	.30	.0001
			C56 Heart disease deathrate	.00	.10	.0015
			C45 US military aid/GNP	-1.06	.06	.0074
e) 1982	1986	88	C9 Television sets per capita	2.63	.51	.0001
			C56 Heart disease deathrate	.00	.08	.0001
f) 1982	1986	LDCs	C56 Heart disease deathrate	.00	.29	.0001
			C18 Welfare spending per capita	.21	.14	.0002
g) 1982	1982-86	88	C20 Inflation rate	.18	.12	.0008
h) 1982	1982-86	LDCs	C20 Inflation rate	.17	.16	.0008
i) 1982-86	1982-1986	88	C5 % Urban population	-.01	.05	.0360
j) 1982-86	1982-1986	LDCs	C5 % Urban population	-.01	.08	.0216

Note: C variables explaining less than 5% of the variance omitted.
Parentheses refer to variables later removed from the regression.

Table 6.28
Regressions on Percentage of Children Immunized (B34)

	Year of C Variables	Year of B Variable	Sample Size	Name of C Variable	Parameter Estimate	% Variance (Partial)	Probability (F Value)
a)	1982	1982	88	C6 Newspaper readers per capita	7.91	.40	.0001
				C54 % Leftwingers in parliament	15.53	.10	.0001
b)	1982	1982	LDCs	C17 Health spending per capita	12.37	.46	.0001
				C55 Cancer deathrate	.01	.08	.0013
				C6 Newspaper readers per capita	9.48	.06	.0008
c)	1986	1986	88	C4 KWH consumption per capita	(2.01)	.48	.0001
				C10 Foreign investment/GDP	.05	.07	.0007
d)	1986	1986	LDCs	C4 KWH consumption per capita	(6.64)	.43	.0001
				C10 Foreign investment/GDP	.10	.07	.0014
e)	1982	1986	88	C6 Newspaper readers per capita	6.64	.43	.0001
				C25 Coups/years independent	-52.48	.09	.0001
				C16 Education spending per capita	9.52	.06	.0035
f)	1982	1986	LDCs	C17 Health spending per capita	.07	.48	.0001
				C2 GNP per capita growth rate	(.37)	.08	.0010
g)	1982	1982-86	88	C35 Arms imports/GNP	324.30	.10	.0024
				C43 % Arms imports from West	1.83	.09	.0026
				C15 Income inequality	.03	.05	.0184
h)	1982	1982-86	LDCs	C35 Arms imports/GNP	290.07	.10	.0089
				C43 % Arms imports from West	1.73	.12	.0025
				C15 Income inequality	.06	.05	.0328
i)	1982-86	1982-1986	88	C33 % Population in army	(115.72)	.13	.0006
				C28 Government repression	6.05	.08	.0058
				C43 % Arms imports from West	-1.75	.08	.0035
j)	1982-86	1982-1986	LDCs	C33 % Population in army	(192.48)	.15	.0014
				C43 % Arms imports from West	-1.77	.10	.0049
				C28 Government repression	10.45	.09	.0057
				C30 Domestic violence deathrate	-49571.43	.05	.0215

Note: C variables explaining less than 5% of the variance omitted.
      Parentheses refer to variables later removed from the regression.

Table 6.29
Regressions on Percentage of Housing with Safe Drinking Water (B40)

	Year of C Variables	Year of B Variable	Sample Size	Name of C Variable	Parameter Estimate	% Variance (Partial)	Probability (F Value)
a)	1982	1982	88	C4 KWH consumption per capita	8.97	.74	.0001
b)	1982	1982	LDCs	C4 KWH consumption per capita	11.06	.63	.0001
c)	1986	1986	88	C4 KWH consumption per capita	11.89	.73	.0001
d)	1986	1986	LDCs	C4 KWH consumption per capita C53 Ethnolinguistic heterogeneity	13.48 (-.06)	.65 .05	.0001 .0015
e)	1982	1986	88	C4 KWH consumption per capita C53 Ethnolinguistic heterogeneity	(2.35) -.19	.69 .05	.0001 .0001
f)	1982	1986	LDCs	C4 KWH consumption per capita C53 Ethnolinguistic heterogeneity	2.84 -.26	.60 .07	.0001 .0003
g)	1982	1982-86	88	C19 % Direct taxes collected	-13.30	.10	.0027
h)	1982	1982-86	LDCs	C19 % Direct taxes collected	-15.00	.12	.0047
i)	1982-86	1982-1986	88	C2 GNP per capita growth rate	.06	.05	.0351
j)	1982-86	1982-1986	LDCs	C6 Newspaper readers per capita C2 GNP per capita growth rate	1.57 .06	.06 .05	.0399 .0577

Note: C variables explaining less than 5% of the variance omitted.
    Parentheses refer to variables later removed from the regression.

Table 6.30
Regressions on Life Expectancy (B54)

	Year of C Variables	Year of B Variable	Sample Size	Name of C Variable	Parameter Estimate	% Variance (Partial)	Probability (F Value)
a)	1982	1982	88	C6 Newspaper readers per capita	519.78	.76	.0001
b)	1982	1982	LDCs	C6 Newspaper readers per capita	3.46	.70	.0001
				C53 Ethnolinguistic heterogeneity	-.07	.06	.0001
c)	1986	1986	88	C6 Newspaper readers per capita	2.62	.76	.0001
d)	1986	1986	LDCs	C6 Newspaper readers per capita	3.65	.70	.0001
				C53 Ethnolinguistic heterogeneity	-.05	.07	.0001
e)	1982	1986	88	C6 Newspaper readers per capita	2.76	.76	.0001
				C53 Ethnolinguistic heterogeneity	-.05	.05	.0001
f)	1982	1986	LDCs	C6 Newspaper readers per capita	3.83	.71	.0001
				C53 Ethnolinguistic heterogeneity	-.09	.08	.0001
g)	1982	1982-86	88	C54 % Leftwingers in parliament	-3.35	.15	.0002
				C32 War deathrate	2360.43	.05	.0182
				C45 US military aid/GNP	-.46	.06	.0103
				C52 % Moslem	.36	.06	.0072
h)	1982	1982-86	LDCs	C54 % Leftwingers in parliament	-4.00	.19	.0003
				C52 % Moslem	.29	.07	.0189
				C30 Domestic violence deathrate	-742.19	.06	.0177
				C53 Ethnolinguistic heterogeneity	-.03	.05	.0276
				C46 % Troops abroad	-.30	.05	.0248
				C10 Foreign investment/GDP	.01	.05	.0136
i)	1982-86	1982-1986	88	C32 War deathrate	-8794.46	.11	.0020
				C33 % Population in army	-199.80	.10	.0013
j)	1982-86	1982-1986	LDCs	C22 Parties in parliament	-9710.70	.11	.0059
				C33 % Population in army	-228.40	.13	.0018
				C28 Government repression	1.02	.05	.0339
				C4 KWH consumption per capita	1.02	.06	.0170
				C25 Coups/years independent	-25.69	.06	.0189
				C46 % Troops abroad	(-.26)	.05	.0137

Note: C variables explaining less than 5% of the variance omitted.
Parentheses refer to variables later removed from the regression.

Table 6.31
Regressions on Percentage Enrolled in Secondary Education (B59)

	Year of C Variables	Year of B Variable	Sample Size	Name of C Variable	Parameter Estimate	% Variance (Partial)	Probability (F Value)
a)	1982	1982	88	C4 KWH consumption per capita	3.74	.67	.0001
				C6 Newspaper readers per capita	8.85	.06	.0001
b)	1982	1982	LDCs	C6 Newspaper readers per capita	9.63	.55	.0001
				C9 Television sets per capita	74.97	.07	.0007
c)	1986	1986	88	C4 KWH consumption per capita	8.49	.69	.0001
d)	1986	1986	LDCs	C4 KWH consumption per capita	6.71	.57	.0001
				C7 Radios per capita	41.17	.08	.0003
e)	1982	1986	88	C4 KWH consumption per capita	7.07	.70	.0001
f)	1982	1986	LDCs	C4 KWH consumption per capita	5.68	.58	.0001
				C33 % Population in army	657.56	.07	.0011
				C6 Newspaper readers per capita	9.38	.07	.0003
				C13 Trade import concentration	-.03	.05	.0003
g)	1982	1982-86	88	C43 % Arms imports from West	.77	.08	.0083
				C34 Military budget/GNP	2.17	.06	.0142
				C51 % Roman Catholic	.62	.06	.0136
h)	1982	1982-86	LDCs	C43 % Arms imports from West	.80	.10	.0077
				C34 Military budget/GNP	2.07	.08	.0175
				C13 Trade import concentration	.01	.07	.0181
i)	1982-86	1982-1986	88	C43 % Arms imports from West	-.65	.09	.0051
j)	1982-86	1982-1986	LDCs	C43 % Arms imports from West	-.66	.12	.0050
				C4 KWH consumption per capita	.99	.07	.0259

Note: C variables explaining less than 5% of the variance omitted.

Appendix C

Table 6.32
Regressions on Percentage of Registered Public Library Users (B74)

Year of C Variables	Year of B Variable	Sample Size	Name of C Variable	Parameter Estimate	% Variance (Partial)	Probability (F Value)
a) 1982	1982	88	C8 Telephones per capita	.36	.36	.0001
			C54 % Leftwingers in parliament	1.38	.09	.0004
b) 1982	1982	LDCs	C9 Television sets per capita	11.48	.39	.0001
			C54 % Leftwingers in parliament	1.36	.09	.0014
			C44 US civilian aid/GNP	7.27	.06	.0035
c) 1986	1986	88	C6 Newspaper readers per capita	.41	.12	.0012
			C5 % Urban population	-.02	.07	.0094
d) 1986	1986	LDCs	C6 Newspaper readers per capita	.44	.22	.0001
			C56 Heart disease deathrate	.00	.09	.0052
e) 1982	1986	88	C10 Foreign investment/GDP	.35	.05	.0323
f) 1982	1986	LDCs	C15 Income inequality	-.36	.09	.0128
g) 1982	1982-86	88	C53 Ethnolinguistic heterogeneity	.92	.06	.0241
h) 1982	1982-86	LDCs	C3 % Agriculture workers	(119.50)	.06	.0546
i) 1982-86	1982-1986	88	C29 % Years with civil war	-386.37	.19	.0001
			C21 % Voter turnout	-1.75	.06	.0129
j) 1982-86	1982-1986	LDCs	C29 % Years with civil war	-321.44	.19	.0002
			C9 Television sets per. capita	-1305.71	.08	.0081
			C26 Military rule	-90.75	.05	.0269

Note: C variables explaining less than 5% of the variance omitted.
      Parentheses refer to variables later removed from the regression.

Table 6.33
Regressions on Artistic Freedom (B89)

Year of C Variables	Year of B Variable	Sample Size	Name of C Variable	Parameter Estimate	% Variance (Partial)	Probability (F Value)
a) 1982	1982	88	C23 % Seats held by majority	-2.63	.27	.0001
			C54 % Leftwingers in parliament	-1.24	.13	.0001
			C4 KWH consumption per capita	-.33	.06	.0028
b) 1982	1982	LDCs	C54 % Leftwingers in parliament	-1.31	.33	.0001
			C22 Parties in parliament	-.07	.06	.0171
c) 1986	1986	88	C23 % Seats held by majority	-2.44	.28	.0001
			C34 Military budget/GNP	-.12	.08	.0012
d) 1986	1986	LDCs	C34 Military budget/GNP	-.28	.23	.0001
			C54 % Leftwingers in parliament	-1.40	.13	.0012
			C20 Inflation rate	.31	.07	.0065
e) 1982	1986	88	C23 % Seats held by majority	-2.20	.27	.0001
			C34 Military budget/GNP	-.30	.09	.0009
			C54 % Leftwingers in parliament	-1.00	.07	.0020
f) 1982	1986	LDCs	C54 % Leftwingers in parliament	-.89	.25	.0001
			C34 Military budget/GNP	-.30	.14	.0003
g) 1982	1982-86	88	C49 Former British colony	-.34	.15	.0002
			C25 Coups/years independent	-.76	.05	.0169
h) 1982	1982-86	LDCs	C49 Former British colony	-.31	.17	.0006
			C15 Income inequality	(.00)	.07	.0209
			C22 Parties in parliament	-.06	.07	.0122
			C57 Suicide deathrate	-.00	.05	.0286
			C26 Military rule	-.18	.05	.0169
i) 1982-86	1982-1986	88	C14 Food import dependency	-.00	.09	.0042
			C45 US military aid/GNP	-3.10	.07	.0117
j) 1982-86	1982-1986	LDCs	C45 US military aid/GNP	-3.94	.09	.0139
			C25 Coups/years independent	2.81	.07	.0381

Note: C variables explaining less than 5% of the variance omitted.
Parentheses refer to variables later removed from the regression.

Appendix C

Table 6.34
Regressions on Foreign Aid Sent Abroad/GNP (B91)

Year of C Variables	Year of B Variable	Sample Size	Name of C Variable	Parameter Estimate	% Variance (Partial)	Probability (F Value)
a) 1982	1982	88	C1 Per capita GNP	2.23	.56	.0001
			C6 Newspaper readers per capita	(-.18)	.07	.0001
b) 1982	1982	LDCs	C1 Per capita GNP	1.85	.28	.0001
			C6 Newspaper readers per capita	-.36	.19	.0001
			C35 Arms imports/GNP	7.05	.06	.0054
			C46 % Troops abroad	-.18	.06	.0027
c) 1986	1986	88	C17 Health spending per capita	.26	.48	.0001
d) 1986	1986	LDCs	C16 Education spending per capita	.39	.16	.0009
			C52 % Moslem	.11	.05	.0406
			C3 % Agriculture workers	3.40	.06	.0174
e) 1982	1986	88	C1 Per capita GNP	48.61	.20	.0001
			C6 Newspaper readers per capita	-28.69	.15	.0001
f) 1982	1986	LDCs	C14 Food import dependency	.06	.19	.0003
			C1 Per capita GNP	46.83	.05	.0354
			C6 Newspaper readers per capita	-18.15	.14	.0003
			C12 Trade export concentration	-.14	.05	.0226
g) 1982	1982-86	88	C35 Arms imports/GNP	-366.64	.27	.0001
h) 1982	1982-86	LDCs	C35 Arms imports/GNP	-192.52	.26	.0001
			C1 Per capita GNP	-20.25	.07	.0128
			C7 Radios per capita	33.79	.12	.0005
			C33 % Population in army	848.12	.07	.0039
i) 1982-86	1982-1986	88	C35 Arms imports/GNP	-179.48	.28	.0001
			C32 War deathrate	26291.77	.08	.0019
j) 1982-86	1982-1986	LDCs	C35 Arms imports/GNP	-211.89	.28	.0001
			C32 War deathrate	(15974.58)	.09	.0035
			C4 KWH consumption per capita	-6.55	.06	.0103
			C9 Television sets per capita	213.54	.06	.0077

Note: C variables explaining less than 5% of the variance omitted.
Parentheses refer to variables later removed from the regression.

Table 6.35
Regressions on Percentage Suffering Economic Discrimination (B5)

Year of C Variables	Year of B Variable	Sample Size	Name of C Variable	Parameter Estimate	% Variance (Partial)	Probability (F Value)
a) 1982	1982	88	C56 Heart disease deathrate	.00	.13	.0007
			C44 US civilian aid/GNP	1.50	.05	.0231
			C52 % Moslem	.07	.05	.0199
b) 1982	1982	LDCs	C23 % Seats held by majority	-3.02	.16	.0001
			C44 US civilian aid/GNP	3.44	.07	.0220
c) 1986	1986	88	C38 Minority economic grievances	1.06	.32	.0001
			C53 Ethnolinguistic heterogeneity	.02	.11	.0001
			C33 % Population in armed forces	62.09	.06	.0033
d) 1986	1986	LDCs	C37 Minority political grievances	.33	.33	.0001
			C53 Ethnolinguistic heterogeneity	.02	.12	.0005
			C36 Arms imports/military budget	.99	.05	.0123
e) 1982	1986	88	C32 War deathrate	43205.30	.19	.0001
			C53 Ethnolinguistic heterogeneity	.21	.19	.0001
f) 1982	1986	LDCs	C32 War deathrate	38422.95	.19	.0002
			C53 Ethnolinguistic heterogeneity	.27	.18	.0001
g) 1982	1982-86	88	C52 % Moslem	5.02	.12	.0012
			C24 Taxes/GNP	-2832.57	.08	.0062
			C18 Welfare spending per capita	1.06	.07	.0056
h) 1982	1982-86	LDCs	C52 % Moslem	2.34	.16	.0009
			C24 Taxes/GNP	-3862.93	.12	.0021
			C32 War deathrate	47281.50	.09	.0018
			C44 US civilian aid/GNP	-93.06	.08	.0071
i) 1982-86	1982-1986	88	C32 War deathrate	-58272.11	.16	.0001
			C19 % Direct taxes collected	-47.57	.11	.0008
			C43 % Arms imports from West	2.18	.07	.0030
			C21 % Voter turnout	.72	.06	.0052
j) 1982-86	1982-1986	LDCs	C32 War deathrate	-63650.19	.17	.0005
			C54 % Leftwingers in parliament	42.31	.07	.0191

Note: C variables explaining less than 5% of the variance omitted.

Table 6.36
Regressions on Percentage of Females in Elementary Schools (B58)

Year of C Variables	Year of B Variable	Sample Size	Name of C Variable	Parameter Estimate	% Variance (Partial)	Probability (F Value)
a) 1982	1982	88	C6 Newspaper readers per capita	7.28	.39	.0001
			C27 % Years with military rule	(-3.34)	.06	.0046
b) 1982	1982	LDCs	C6 Newspaper readers per capita	7.79	.34	.0001
			C27 % Years with military rule	(-2.35)	.07	.0064
			C50 % Protestant	4.51	.06	.0108
c) 1986	1986	88	C3 % Agriculture workers	-11.49	.26	.0001
			C52 % Moslem	-2.39	.11	.0002
d) 1986	1986	LDCs	C6 Newspaper readers per capita	5.92	.19	.0003
			C52 % Moslem	-2.22	.09	.0053
			C19 % Direct taxes collected	26.84	.07	.0133
			C45 US military aid/GNP	-35.26	.05	.0262
e) 1982	1986	88	C6 Newspaper readers per capita	-3.53	.28	.0001
			C52 % Moslem	-3.06	.07	.0026
f) 1982	1986	LDCs	C6 Newspaper readers per capita	4.59	.21	.0001
			C52 % Moslem	-2.93	.08	.0090
			C10 Foreign investment/GDP	.07	.07	.0127
g) 1982	1982-86	88	C43 % Arms imports from West	(1.50)	.05	.0335
			C12 Trade export concentration	-.01	.05	.0252
h) 1982	1982-86	LDCs	C12 Trade export concentration	-.01	.06	.0434
			C32 War deathrate	-8010.33	.05	.0505
i) 1982-86	1982-1986	88	C10 Foreign investment/GDP	-.02	.06	.0252
j) 1982-86	1982-1986	LDCs	C30 Domestic violence deathrate	-9120.19	.05	.0630

Note: C variables explaining less than 5% of the variance omitted.
Parentheses refer to variables later removed from the regression.
"% Years" refers to the percentage of years since 1960.

REFERENCES

Adelman, Irma, and Morris, Cynthia Taft (1967). *Society, Politics, and Economic Development: A Quantitative Approach.* Baltimore: Johns Hopkins University Press.

Alston, Philip (1982). "International Trade as an Investment of Positive Human Rights Policy." *Human Rights Quarterly,* 4(May):155–183.

Amnesty International (1962–). *Report.* London: Amnesty International, annual.

Anderberg, M. R. (1973). *Cluster Analysis for Applications.* New York: Academic Press.

Arat, Zehra F. (1991). *Democracy and Human Rights in Developing Countries.* Denver: Riener.

Arendt, Hannah (1951). *The Origins of Totalitarianism.* New York: Harcourt, Brace.

Awanohara, Susumu, Vatikiotis, Michael, and Islam, Shada (1993). "Vienna Showdown." *Far Eastern Economic Review,* 156(June 17):16–17, 20.

Banks, Arthur S. (1971). *Cross-Policy Time-Series Data.* Cambridge, MA: MIT Press.

———. (1972). "Correlates of Democratic Performance." *Comparative Politics,* 4(January):217–230.

———. (1975–). *Political Handbook of the World.* New York: McGraw-Hill.

———. (1979). *Cross-National Time Series Data Archive.* Binghamton, NY: Center for Social Analysis, State University of New York.

Banks, Arthur S., and Textor, Robert B. (1963). *A Cross-Policy Survey.* Cambridge, MA: MIT Press.

Banks, David L. (1985). "Patterns of Oppression: A Statistical Analysis of Human Rights." *American Statistical Association, Proceedings of the Social Statistics Section,* 62:154–162.

———. (1986). "The Analysis of Human Rights Data Over Time." *Human Rights Quarterly,* 8(December):654–680.

———. (1992). "New Patterns of Oppression: An Updated Analysis of Human Rights Data." In *Human Rights and Statistics: Getting the Record Straight,* edited by Thomas B. Jabine and Richard P. Claude, chapter 14. Philadelphia: University of Pennsylvania Press.

Barsh, Russel L. (1993). "Measuring Human Rights: Problems of Methodology and Purpose." *Human Rights Quarterly*, 15(February):87–121.

Bentham, Jeremy (1780). *Introduction to the Principles of Morals and Legislation*. Oxford: Clarendon, 1907.

Bigongiari, Dino, ed. (1953). *The Political Ideas of St. Thomas Aquinas*. New York: Hafner.

Blitz, Mark (1982). "Human Rights Policy and the Doctrine of Natural Rights." In *Human Rights and American Foreign Policy*, edited by Fred E. Baumann, pp. 71–85. Gambier, OH: Public Affairs Conference Center, Kenyon College.

Blondel, Jean (1969). *An Introduction to Comparative Government*. New York: Praeger.

Boli-Bennett, John (1981). "Human Rights or State Expansion? Cross-National Definitions of Constitutional Rights, 1870–1970." In *Global Human Rights: Public Policies, Comparative Measures, and NGO Strategies*, edited by Ved P. Nanda, James R. Scarritt, and George W. Shepherd, Jr., chapter 11. Boulder, CO: Westview.

Bollen, Kenneth A. (1979). "Political Democracy and the Timing of Development." *American Sociological Review*, 44(August):572–587.

———. (1980). "Issues in the Comparative Measurement of Political Democracy." *American Sociological Review*, 45(June):370–390.

———. (1983). "World System Position, Dependency, and Democracy: The Cross-National Evidence." *American Sociological Review*, 48(August):468–479.

———. (1986). "Political Rights and Political Liberties in Nations: An Evaluation of Human Rights Measures, 1950 to 1984." *Human Rights Quarterly*, 8(December): 567–591.

Bollen, Kenneth A., and Grandjean, Burke D. (1981). "The Dimension(s) of Democracy: Further Issues in the Measurement and Effects of Political Democracy." *American Sociological Review*, 46(October):651–659.

Bollen, Kenneth A., and Jackman, Robert W. (1985). "Political Democracy and the Size Distribution of Income." *American Sociological Review*, 50(August):438–457.

———. (1989). "Democracy, Stability, and Dichotomies." *American Sociological Review*, 54(August):612–620.

Boswell, Terry, and Dixon, William J. (1990). "Dependency and Rebellion: A Cross-National Analysis." *American Sociological Review*, 55(August):540–559.

Burke, Edmund (1789/1790). *Reflections on the Revolution in France*. Indianapolis: Hackett, 1987.

Cain, Michael, Claude, Richard P., and Jabine, Thomas B. (1992). "A Guide to Human Rights Data Sources." In *Human Rights and Statistics: Getting the Record Straight*, edited by Thomas B. Jabine and Richard P. Claude, chapter 15. Philadelphia: University of Pennsylvania Press.

Carleton, David, & Stohl, Michael (1985). "The Foreign Policy of Human Rights: Rhetoric and Reality from Jimmy Carter to Ronald Reagan." *Human Rights Quarterly*, 7(May):205–229.

Carmichael, Stokely, and Hamilton, Charles V. (1967). *Black Power: The Politics of Liberation in America*. New York: Random House.

Chan, Steve (1984). "Mirror, Mirror on the Wall . . . : Are the Freer Countries More Pacific?" *Journal of Conflict Resolution*, 28(December):617–648.

Charny, Israel W. (1982). *How Can We Commit the Unthinkable? Genocide, the Human Cancer*. Boulder, CO: Westview.

China, Republic of (1945–). *Statistical Yearbook of the Republic of China*. Taipei: Republic of China, annual.

Chomsky, Noam (1991). *Deterring Democracy*. New York: Hill & Wang.

Chomsky, Noam, and Herman, Edward S. (1979). *Third World Fascism and the Washington Connection*. Boston: South End Press.

Cingranelli, David L., ed. (1988). *Human Rights: Theory and Measurement*. New York: St. Martin's Press.

Cingranelli, David L., and Pasquarello, Thomas E. (1985). "Human Rights Practices and the Distribution of U.S. Foreign Aid to Latin American Countries." *American Journal of Political Science*, 29(August):539–563.

Cingranelli, David L., and Wright, Kevin N. (1988). "Correlates of Due Process." In *Human Rights: Theory and Measurement*, edited by David L. Cingranelli, chapter 9. New York: St. Martin's Press.

Claude, Richard P. (1976). "The Classical Model of Human Rights Development." In *Comparative Human Rights*, edited by Richard P. Claude, chapter 1. Baltimore: Johns Hopkins University Press.

Cohen, Roberta (1979). "Human Rights Decision-Making in the Executive Branch: Some Proposals for a Coordinated Strategy." In *Human Rights and American Foreign Policy*, edited by Donald P. Kommers and Gilburt D. Loescher, chapter 10. Notre Dame, IN: University of Notre Dame Press.

Cohn, Norman (1967). *Warrant for Genocide: The Myth of Jewish World-Conspiracy and the Protocols of the Elders of Zion*. New York: Harper & Row.

———. (1970). *The Pursuit of the Millennium: Revolutionary Millenarians and Mystical Anarchists of the Middle Ages*. New York: Oxford University Press.

———. (1977). *Europe's Inner Demons: An Enquiry Inspired by the Great Witch-Hunt*. New York: Meridian.

Conway, Henderson (1982). "Military Regimes and Rights in Developing Countries." *Human Rights Quarterly*, 4(1):110–123.

Coppedge, Michael, and Reinecke, Wolfgang (1988). "A Scale of Polyarchy." In *Freedom in the World: Political Rights and Civil Liberties, 1987–1988*, edited by Raymond D. Gastil, pp. 101–125. Lanham, MD: Freedom House.

Cranston, Maurice (1983). "Are There Any Human Rights?" *Daedalus*, 112(Fall):1–17.

Cutright, Phillips (1963). "National Political Development: Its Measurement and Social Correlates." *American Sociological Review*, 28(April):253–264.

———. (1965). "Political Structure, Economic Development, and National Social Security Programs." *American Journal of Sociology*, 70(March):537–550.

———. (1967a). "Inequality: A Cross-National Analysis." *American Sociological Review*, 32(August):562–578.

———. (1967b). "Income Redistribution: A Cross-National Analysis." *Social Forces*, 46(December):180–190.

Cutright, Phillips, and Wiley, James A. (1969). "Modernization and Political Representation, 1927–1966." *Studies in Comparative International Development*, 5(2):23–44.

Dahl, Robert A. (1971). *Polyarchy: Participation and Opposition*. New Haven, CT: Yale University Press.

Denison, Edward F. (1974). *Accounting for United States Economic Growth*. Washington, DC: Brookings.

Derian, Patricia (1979). "Human Rights in American Foreign Policy." *Notre Dame Lawyer*, 55(December):264–280.

Dixon, William J. (1984). "Trade Concentration, Economic Growth, and the Provision of Basic Human Needs." *Social Science Quarterly*, 65(September):761–774.

Donnelly, Jack (1989). *Universal Human Rights in Theory and Practice*. Ithaca, NY: Cornell University Press.

Donnelly, Jack, and Howard, Rhoda E. (1988). "Assessing National Human Rights Performance: A Theoretical Framework." *Human Rights Quarterly*, 10(May):214–248.

Duff, Ernest A., and McCamant, John F. (1976). *Violence and Repression in Latin America*. New York: Free Press.

Durr, Clifford (1981). *Jesus as a Free Speech Victim: Trial by Terror 2000 Years Ago*. New York: Basic Pamphlets.

Duvall, Raymond D., and Stohl, Michael (1988). "Governance by Terror." In *The Politics of Terrorism*, 3rd ed., edited by Michael Stohl, chapter 7. New York: Dekker.

Eisler, Riane T. (1987). *The Chalice and the Blade: Our History, Our Future*. San Francisco: Harper & Row.

Etzioni, Amitai (1991). *A Responsive Society: Collected Essays on Building Deliberate Social Change*. San Francisco: Jossey-Bass.

———. (1993). *The Spirit of Community: Rights, Responsibilities, and the Communitarian Agenda*. New York: Crown Publishers.

Euromonitor (1962–). *European Marketing Data and Statistics*. Detroit: Gale, annual.

———. (1975/1976–). *International Marketing Data and Statistics*. Detroit: Gale, annual.

Europa Publications (1926–). *The Europa World Year Book*. London: Europa Publications, annual.

Fairbanks, Charles H., Jr. (1982). "The British Campaign Against the Slave Trade: An Example of Successful Human Rights Policy." In *Human Rights and American Foreign Policy*, edited by Fred E. Baumann, pp. 87–135. Gambier, OH: Public Affairs Conference Center, Kenyon College.

Farer, Tom J. (1983). "Human Rights and Human Welfare in Latin America." *Daedalus*, 112(Fall):139–170.

Feierabend, Ivo K., and Feierabend, Rosalind L. (1971a). "Aggressive Behavior Within Polities, 1948–62: A Cross-National Study." In *Macro-Quantitative Analysis: Conflict, Development, and Democratization*, edited by John V. Gillespie and Betty A. Nesvold, chapter 6. Beverly Hills, CA: Sage.

———. (1971b). "The Relationship of Systemic Frustration, Political Coercion, International Tension and Political Instability: A Cross-National Analysis." In *Macro-Quantitative Analysis: Conflict, Development, and Democratization*, edited by John V. Gillespie and Betty A. Nesvold, chapter 19. Beverly Hills, CA: Sage.

Feierabend, Ivo K., Feierabend, Rosalind L., and Bororiak, Darlene L. (1967). "Empirical Typologies of Political Systems: Aggression Prototypes." Paper prepared for presentation at the biennial Congress of the International Political Science Association, Brussels, September.

Feierabend, Ivo K., Feierabend, Rosalind, L., and Nesvold, Betty A. (1969a). "Social Change and Political Violence: Cross-National Patterns." In *Violence in America: American, Historical and Comparative Perspectives*, edited by Hugh Davis Graham and Ted Robert Gurr, chapter 18. New York: Signet.

Feierabend, Rosalind L., Feierabend, Ivo K., and Nesvold, Betty A., with Violet M. Burkhardt and Rose M. Kelly (1969b). "Intergroup Conflict: A Cross-National Analysis." Paper prepared for presentation to the annual convention of the American Political Science Association, New York, September.

Fein, Helen (1993). *Genocide: A Sociological Perspective.* Newbury Park, CA: Sage.

Fitzgibbon, Russell H. (1956). "A Statistical Evaluation of Latin American Democracy." *Western Political Quarterly,* 9(September):607–619.

Fitzgibbon, Russell H., and Johnson, Kenneth F. (1961). "Measurement of Latin American Political Change." *American Political Science Review,* 55(September):515–526.

Flanigan, William, and Fogelman, Edwin (1971a). "Patterns of Democratic Development: A Quantitative Analysis." In *Macro-Quantitative Analysis: Conflict, Development, and Democratization,* edited by John V. Gillespie and Betty A. Nesvold, chapter 20. Beverly Hills, CA: Sage.

———. (1971b). "Patterns of Democratic Development: An Historical Comparative Analysis." In *Macro-Quantitative Analysis: Conflict, Development, and Democratization,* edited by John V. Gillespie and Betty A. Nesvold, chapter 21. Beverly Hills, CA: Sage.

Food and Agriculture Organization of the United Nations (FAO) (1947–). *Production Yearbook.* Rome: FAO, annual.

Forsythe, David P. (1991). *The Internationalization of Human Rights.* Lexington, MA: Lexington Books.

Forsythe, David P., and Wiseberg, Laurie (1979). "Human Rights Protection: A Research Agenda." *Human Rights Quarterly,* 1(4):1–25.

Frakt, Phyllis M. (1977). "Democracy, Political Activity, Economic Development, and Governmental Responsiveness: The Case of Labor Policy." *Comparative Political Studies,* 10(July):177–212.

Frank, Andre Gunder (1967). *Capitalism and Development in Latin America: Historical Studies of Chile and Brazil.* New York: Monthly Review Press.

Freud, Sigmund (1930). *Civilization and Its Discontents.* London: Hogarth.

Friedman, Milton (1988). "A Statistical Note on the Gastil Survey of Freedom." In *Freedom in the World,* edited by Raymond D. Gastil, pp. 183–187. Lanham, MD: Freedom House.

Fromm, Erich (1941). *Escape from Freedom.* New York: Avon, 1965.

Ganji, Manouchehr (1975). *The Realization of Economic, Social and Cultural Rights: Problems, Policies, Progress.* New York: United Nations.

Gastil, Raymond D. (1973). "Comparative Survey of Freedom." *Freedom at Issue,* 17:4.

———. (1978–). *Freedom in the World: Political Rights & Civil Liberties.* New York: Freedom House, annual.

Goldstein, Robert J. (1986). "The Limitations of Using Quantitative Data in Studying Human Rights Abuses." *Human Rights Quarterly,* 8(November):607–627.

Gould, Steven Jay (1980). "Jensen's Last Stand." *New York Review of Books,* 27(May 1):38–44.

Greenberg, Edward S. (1982). "In Order to Save It, We Had to Destroy It: Reflections on the United States and International Human Rights." In *Human Rights and American Foreign Policy,* edited by Fred E. Baumann, pp. 39–69. Gambier, OH: Public Affairs Conference Center, Kenyon College.

Grotius, Hugo (1625). *De iure belli ac pacis*. Oxford: Clarendon, 1925.

Gupta, Dipak K., Jongman, Albert J., and Schmid, Alex P. (1994). "Creating a Composite Index for Assessing Country Performance in the Field of Human Rights: Proposal for a New Methodology." *Human Rights Quarterly*, 15(1):131–162.

Gurr, Ted Robert (1966). *New Error-Compensated Measures for Comparing Nations: Some Correlates of Civil Violence*. Princeton, NJ: Center of International Studies, Princeton University.

———. (1970). *Why Men Rebel*. Princeton, NJ: Princeton University Press.

———. (1986). "The Political Origins of State Violence and Terror: A Theoretical Analysis." In *Government Violence and Repression: An Agenda for Research*, edited by Michael Stohl and George A. Lopez, chapter 3. Westport, CT: Greenwood Press.

———. (1988). "War, Revolution, and the Growth of the Coercive State." *Comparative Political Studies*, 21(April):45–65.

———. (1993). *Minorities at Risk: A Global View of Ethnopolitical Conflicts*. Washington, DC: U.S. Institute of Peace.

Gurr, Ted Robert, and Gurr, Erika B. K. (1983). "Group Discrimination and Potential Separatism in 1960 and 1975." In *World Handbook of Political and Social Indicators*, volume 1, 3rd ed., edited by Charles L. Taylor and David Jodice, pp. 50–57, 66–75. New Haven, CT: Yale University Press.

Guttman, Louis (1944). "A Basis for Scaling Qualitative Data." *American Sociological Review*, 9(February):139–150.

Haas, Michael (1965). "Societal Approaches to the Study of War." *Journal of Peace Research*, 2(4):307–323.

———. (1968). "Social Change and National Aggressiveness, 1900–1960." In *Quantitative International Politics: Insights and Evidence*, edited by J. David Singer, pp. 215–244. New York: Free Press.

———. (1974). *International Conflict*. Indianapolis: Bobbs-Merrill.

———. (1986). "Dimensions of Human Rights: A Multivariate Analysis." Paper presented at the annual convention of the Southwestern Social Science Association, Houston, March.

———. (1989). "Correlates of Human Rights: A Multivariate Analysis." Paper presented at the annual convention of the International Studies Association, London, March.

———. (1991). *Genocide by Proxy: Cambodian Pawn on a Superpower Chessboard*. Westport, CT: Praeger.

Harff, Barbara (1986). "Genocide as State Terrorism." In *Government Violence and Repression: An Agenda for Research*, edited by Michael Stohl and George A. Lopez, chapter 6. Westport, CT: Greenwood Press.

Harff, Barbara, and Gurr, Ted Robert (1988). "Toward an Empirical Theory of Genocides and Politicides: Identification and Measurement of Cases Since 1945." *International Studies Quarterly*, 32(September):359–371.

Harman, Harry H. (1976). *Modern Factor Analysis*, 3rd ed. Chicago: University of Chicago Press.

Hewitt, Christopher (1977). "The Effect of Political Democracy and Social Democracy on Equality in Industrial Societies." *American Sociological Review*, 42(June): 450–464.

Hibbs, Douglas A., Jr. (1973). *Mass Political Violence: A Cross-National Causal Analysis*. New York: Wiley.

Hicks, Alexander (1988). "Social Democracy, Corporatism and Economic Growth." *Journal of Politics*, 50(August):677–704.

Hicks, Norman L. (1979). "Growth vs. Basic Needs: Is There a Trade-Off?" *World Development*, 7(November/December):985–994.

Hobbes, Thomas (1651). *The Leviathan*. Cambridge: Cambridge University Press, 1991.

Hocking, R. R. (1976). "The Analysis and Selection of Variables in Linear Regression." *Biometrics*, 32(March):1–50.

Hoffmann, Stanley (1983). "Reaching for the Most Difficult: Human Rights as a Foreign Policy Goal." *Daedalus*, 112(Fall):19–49.

Holleman, Warren Lee (1987). *The Human Rights Movement*. New York: Praeger.

Horowitz, Irving Louis, ed. (1967). *The Rise and Fall of Project Camelot: Studies in the Relationship Between Social Science and Practical Politics*. Cambridge, MA: MIT Press.

———. (1976). *Genocide: State Power and Mass Murder*. New Brunswick, NJ: Transaction. (The third edition in 1980 was retitled *Taking Lives*.)

Howard, Rhoda E. (1990). "Monitoring Human Rights; Problems of Consistency." *Ethics & International Affairs*, 4:33–51.

Howard, Rhoda E., and Donnelly, Jack. (1986a). "Human Dignity, Human Rights, and Political Regimes." *American Political Science Review*, 80(September):801–818.

———. (1986b). "Introduction." In *International Handbook of Human Rights*, edited by Jack Donnelly and Rhoda E. Howard, chapter 1. Westport, CT: Greenwood Press.

Humana, Charles (1984). *World Human Rights Guide*, 1st ed. New York: Pica Press.

———. (1987). *World Human Rights Guide*, 2nd ed. New York: Pan Books.

———. (1992). *World Human Rights Guide*, 3rd ed. New York: Oxford University Press.

Huntington, Samuel P. (1968). *Political Order in Changing Societies*. New Haven, CT: Yale University Press.

———. (1981). *American Politics: The Politics of Disharmony*. Cambridge, MA: Harvard University Press.

Innes, Judith E. (1992). "Human Rights Reporting as a Policy Tool: An Examination of the State Department *Country Reports*." In *Human Rights and Statistics: Getting the Record Straight*, edited by Thomas B. Jabine and Richard P. Claude, chapter 9. Philadelphia: University of Pennsylvania Press.

International Labour Organization (1935/1936–). *Year Book of Labour Statistics*. Geneva: International Labour Office, annual.

International Monetary Fund (IMF) (1977–). *Government Finance Statistics Yearbook*. Washington, DC: IMF, annual.

Jackman, Robert W. (1975). *Politics and Social Equality: A Comparative Analysis*. New York: Wiley.

———. (1987). "The Politics of Economic Growth in the Industrial Democracies, 1974–80: Leftist Strength or North Sea Oil?" *Journal of Politics*, 49(February):246–256.

———. (1989). "The Politics of Economic Growth, Once Again." *Journal of Politics*, 51(August):646–661.

Johnson, Kenneth F. (1976). "Measuring the Scholarly Image of Latin American Democracy, 1945–1970." *Statistical Abstract of Latin America*, 17:347–365.

———. (1982). "The 1980 Image-Index of Latin American Political Democracy." *Latin American Research Review*, 17:193–201.

Johnson, M. Glen (1988). "Human Rights in Divergent Conceptual Settings: How Do Ideas Influence Policy Choices?" In *Human Rights: Theory and Measurement*, edited by David L. Cingranelli, chapter 2. New York: St. Martin's Press.

Kant, Immanuel (1795). *Perpetual Peace: A Philosophic Essay*. New York: Columbia University Press, 1939.

Keesing's Contemporary Archive (1931–). Harlow, England: Longman Group, monthly.

Kerr, Clark, Dunlop, John T., Harbison, Frederick H., and Myers, Charles A. (1964). *Industrialism and the Industrial State*. New York: Oxford University Press.

Kirkpatrick, Jeane J. (1979). "Dictatorships and Double Standards." *Commentary*, 68(November):34–45.

———. (1981). "Human Rights and American Foreign Policy: A Symposium." *Commentary*, 70(November):42–45.

———. (1982). "Human Rights and Foreign Policy." In *Human Rights and American Foreign Policy*, edited by Fred E. Baumann, pp. 1–11. Gambier, OH: Public Affairs Conference Center, Kenyon College.

Kolakowski, Leszek (1983). "Marxism and Human Rights." *Daedalus*, 112(Fall):81–92.

Kommers, Donald (1970). "Cross National Comparisons of Constitutional Courts: Toward a Theory of Judicial Review." Paper prepared for presentation at the annual convention of the American Political Science Association, Los Angeles, September.

Kornhauser, William (1959). *The Politics of Mass Society*. Glencoe, IL: Free Press.

Kuhn, Thomas S. (1962). *The Structure of Scientific Revolutions*. Chicago: University of Chicago Press.

Kuper, Leo (1981). *Genocide: Its Political Use in the Twentieth Century*. New Haven, CT: Yale University Press.

Lange, Peter, and Garrett, Geoffrey (1985). "The Politics of Growth: Strategic Interaction and Economic Performance in the Advanced Industrial Countries, 1974–1980." *Journal of Politics*, 47(August):792–827.

———. (1987). "The Politics of Growth Reconsidered." *Journal of Politics*, 49(February):257–274.

Lee Hsien Long (1987). *When the Press Misinforms*. Singapore: Information Division, Ministry of Commerce and Industry.

Lenin, Vladimir I. (1917). *Imperialism: The Highest Stage of Capitalism*. Peking: People's Publishing House, 1964.

Lenski, Gerhard (1966). *Power and Privilege: A Theory of Social Stratification*. New York: McGraw-Hill.

Lerner, Daniel (1958). *The Passing of Traditional Society: Modernizing the Middle East*. New York: Free Press.

Lifton, Robert J. (1986). *The Nazi Doctors: Medical Killing and the Psychology of Genocide*. New York: Basic Books.

Lindblom, Charles E. (1977). *Politics and Markets: The World's Political Economic Systems*. New York: Basic Books.

Lipset, Seymour M. (1959). "Some Social Requisites of Democracy: Economic Development and Political Legitimacy." *American Political Science Review*, 53(March):69–105.

————. (1994). "The Social Requisites of Democracy Revisited." *American Sociological Review*, 59(February):1–22.

Lizhi, Fang (1990). "The Chinese Amnesia." *New York Review of Books*, 37(October 27):30–31.

Locke, John (1688). *Second Treatise of Government*. Cambridge: Cambridge University Press, 1967.

London, Bruce, and Robinson, Thomas D. (1989). "The Effect of International Dependence on Income Inequality and Political Violence." *American Sociological Review*, 54(April):305–307.

Lopez, George A., and Stohl, Michael (1992). "Problems of Concept and Measurement in the Study of Human Rights." In *Human Rights and Statistics: Getting the Record Straight*, edited by Thomas B. Jabine and Richard P. Claude, chapter 8. Philadelphia: University of Pennsylvania Press.

Lowenstein, Ralph L. (1967). *Measuring World Press Freedom as a Political Indicator*. Ph.D. dissertation. Columbia: University of Missouri.

Mackie, Thomas T., and Rose, Richard (1974). *The International Almanac of Electoral History*. London: Macmillan.

Maoz, Zeev, and Abdolali, Nasrin (1989). "Regime Types and International Conflict, 1811–1976." *Journal of Conflict Resolution*, 33(March):3–35.

Maoz, Zeev, and Russett, Bruce (1993). "Normative and Structural Causes of Democratic Peace, 1946–1986." *American Political Science Review*, 87(September):624–638.

Marcuse, Herbert (1955). *Eros and Civilization: A Philosophical Inquiry into Freud*. Boston: Beacon.

Markus, Gregory B., and Nesvold, Betty A. (1972). "Governmental Coerciveness and Political Instability: An Exploratory Study of Cross-National Patterns." *Comparative Political Studies*, 5(July):231–244.

Marshall, Thomas H. (1964). *Class, Citizenship, and Social Development*. Garden City, NY: Doubleday.

Marx, Karl (1844). *A World Without Jews*. New York: Philosophical Library.

Marx, Karl, and Friedrich Engels (1848). *Manifesto of the Communist Party*. Reprinted in *The Marx-Engels Reader*, edited by Robert C. Tucker, pp. 331–362. New York: Norton, 1972.

Mazian, Florence (1990). *Why Genocide? The Armenian and Jewish Experiences in Perspective*. Ames: Iowa State University Press.

McCamant, John F. (1981). "A Critique of Present Measures of 'Human Rights Development' and an Alternative." In *Global Human Rights: Public Policies, Comparative Measures, and NGO Strategies*, edited by Ved P. Nanda, James R. Scarritt, and George W. Shepherd, Jr., chapter 9. Boulder, CO: Westview.

McCrone, Donald J., and Cnudde, Charles F. (1967). "Toward a Communications Theory of Democratic Political Development." *American Political Science Review*, 61(March):72–79.

McNitt, Andrew D. (1988). "Some Thoughts on the Systemic Measurement of the Abuse of Human Rights." In *Human Rights: Theory and Measurement*, edited by David L. Cingranelli, chapter 5. New York: St. Martin's Press.

Michels, Roberto (1915). *Political Parties*. New York: Collier.

Milliband, Ralph (1969). *The State in Capitalist Society*. London: Weidenfeld & Nicolson.

Mills, C. Wright (1956). *The Power Elite*. New York: Oxford University Press.

Mitchell, Christopher, Stohl, Michael, Carleton, David, and Lopez, George A. (1986). "State Terrorism: Issues of Concept and Measurement." In *Government Violence and Repression: An Agenda for Research*, edited by Michael Stohl and George A. Lopez, chapter 1. Westport, CT: Greenwood Press.

Mitchell, Neil, J., and McCormick, James M. (1988). "Economic and Political Explanations of Human Rights Violations." *World Politics*, 40(July):476–498.

Moaddel, Mansoor (1994). "Political Conflict in the World Economy: A Cross-National Analysis of Modernization and World-System Theories." *American Sociological Review*, 59(April):276–303.

Moon, Bruce E., and Dixon, William J. (1985a). "Military Effects on the Provision of Basic Needs." Paper presented at the annual convention of the International Studies Association, Washington, April.

————. (1985b). "Politics, the State, and Basic Human Needs: A Cross-National Study." *American Journal of Political Science*, 29 (November):661–694.

Morgan, T. Clifton, and Campbell, Sally Howard (1991). "Domestic Structure, Decisional Constraints, and War." *Journal of Conflict Resolution*, 35(June): 187–211.

Morris, Morris D. (1979). *Measuring Conditions of the World's Poor: The Physical Quality of Life Index*. New York: Pergamon.

Mosca, Gaetano (1896). *The Ruling Class*. New York: McGraw-Hill, 1939.

Muller, Edward N. (1988). "Democracy, Economic Development, and Income Inequality." *American Sociological Review*, 53(February):50–68.

Muller, Edward N., and Seligson, Mitchell A. (1987). "Inequality and Insurgency." *American Political Science Review*, 81(June):425–449.

Muskie, Edmund S. (1980). "The Foreign Policy of Human Rights." *Department of State Bulletin*, 80(December):7–9.

Myrdal, Gunnar (1957). *Economic Theory and Under-Developed Regions*. London: Duckworth.

Nanda, Ved P. (1981). "Human Rights and U.S. Foreign Policy under Carter: Continuity and Change." In *Global Human Rights: Public Policies, Comparative Measures, and NGO Strategies*, edited by Ved P. Nanda, James R. Scarritt, and George W. Shepherd, Jr., chapter 1. Boulder, CO: Westview.

Nesvold, Betty A. (1969). "Scalogram Analysis of Political Violence." *Comparative Political Studies*, 2(July):172–194.

Neubauer, Deane E. (1967). "Some Conditions of Democracy." *American Political Science Review*, 61(December):1002–1009.

Nixon, Raymond B. (1960). "Factors Related to Freedom in National Press Systems." *Journalism Quarterly*, 37(Winter):13–28.

————. (1965). "Freedom in the World's Press: A Fresh Appraisal with New Data." *Journalism Quarterly*, 42(Winter):3–5, 118–119.

Nowak, Manfred, and Swinehart, Theresa, eds. (1989). *Human Rights in Developing Countries: 1989 Yearbook*. Arlington, VA: Engel.

Organski, A.F.K. (1965). *The Stages of Political Development*. New York: Knopf.

Owen, Edgar (1987). *The Future of Freedom in the Developing World*. New York: Pergamon.

Pareto, Vilfredo (1916). *The Mind and Society*. New York: Harcourt, Brace, 1935.

Park, Han S. (1987). "Correlates of Human Rights." *Human Rights Quarterly*, 9(August):405–413.

Pasquarello, Thomas E. (1988). "Human Rights and U.S. Bilateral Aid Allocations to Africa." In *Human Rights: Theory and Measurement*, edited by David L. Cingranelli, chapter 14. New York: St. Martin's Press.

Paukert, Felix (1973). "Income Distribution at Different Levels of Development." *International Labour Review*, 108(August-September):97–125.

Poe, Steven C. (1991). "Human Rights and the Allocation of U.S. Military Assistance." *Journal of Peace Research*, 28(2):205–216.

Poe, Steven C., and Sirirangsi, Rangsima (1992). "Human Rights and U.S. Economic Aid to Africa." *International Interactions*, 18(4):309–322.

Population Crisis Committee (1987). *The International Human Suffering Index*. Washington, DC: Population Crisis Committee.

———. (1992). *The International Human Suffering Index*. Washington, DC: Population Crisis Committee.

Poulantzas, Nicos (1972). *Political Power and Social Classes*. Atlantic Highland, NJ: Humanities Press, 1976.

Pritchard, Kathleen (1988). "Comparative Human Rights: Promise and Practice." In *Human Rights: Theory and Measurement*, edited by David L. Cingranelli, chapter 8. New York: St. Martin's Press.

———. (1989). "Human Rights and Development." In *Human Rights and Development: International Views*, edited by David P. Forsythe, chapter 19. New York: St. Martin's Press.

Riggs, Fred W. (1984). "Development." In *Social Science Concepts: A Systematic Analysis*, edited by Giovanni Sartori, pp. 125–203. Beverly Hills, CA: Sage.

Rimlinger, Gaston V. (1983). "Capitalism and Human Rights." *Daedalus*, 112(Fall):51–79.

Rokkan, Stein, and Meyriat, Jean (1969). *International Guide to Electoral Statistics*. Paris: Mouton.

Romulo, Roberto R. (1993). "We Must Try Harder." *Far Eastern Economic Review*, 156(August 12):24.

Rosh, Robert M. (1988). "Militarization, Human Rights and Basic Needs in the Third World." *Human Rights: Theory and Measurement*, edited by David L. Cingranelli, chapter 11. New York: St. Martin's Press.

Rubenstein, Richard (1983). *The Age of Triage*. Boston: Beacon.

Rubison, Richard (1976). "The World-Economy and the Distribution of Income Within States: A Cross-National Study." *American Sociological Review*, 41(August): 639–659.

Rubison, Richard, and Quinlan, Dan (1977). "Democracy and Social Equality: A Reanalysis." *American Sociological Review*, 42(August):611–623.

Rummel, R. J. (1972). *The Dimensions of Nations*. Beverly Hills, CA: Sage.

———. (1983). "Libertarianism and International Violence." *Journal of Conflict Resolution*, 27(March):27–71.

Russett, Bruce N., Alker, Hayward R., Jr., Deutsch, Karl W., and Lasswell, Harold D. (1964). *World Handbook of Political and Social Indicators*, 1st ed. New Haven, CT: Yale University Press.

Rustow, Dankwart A. (1967). *World of Nations: Problems of Political Modernization*. Washington, DC: Brookings.

Samuelson, Douglas A., and Spirer, Herbert F. (1992). "Use of Incomplete and Distorted Data in Inference About Human Rights Violations." In *Human Rights and Sta-*

tistics: Getting the Record Straight, edited by Thomas B. Jabine and Richard P. Claude, chapter 3. Philadelphia: University of Pennsylvania Press.

Schoultz, Lars (1981a). "U.S. Foreign Policy and Human Rights Violations in Latin America: A Comparative Analysis of Foreign Aid Distributions." *Comparative Politics*, 13(January):149–170.

———. (1981b). "U.S. Policy Toward Human Rights in Latin America: A Comparative Analysis of Two Administrations." In *Global Human Rights: Public Policies, Comparative Measures, and NGO Strategies*, edited by Ved P. Nanda, James R. Scarritt, and George W. Shepherd, Jr., chapter 6. Boulder, CO: Westview.

Schutz, R. R. (1951). "On the Measurement of Income Inequality." *American Economic Review*, 41(March):107–122.

Seymour, Charles, and Frary, Donald P. (1918). *How the World Votes: The Story of Democratic Development in Elections*. Springfield, MA: Nichols.

Shapiro, S. S., and Wilk, M. B. (1965). "An Analysis of Variance Test for Normality (Complete Samples)." *Biometrika*, 52(3–4):591–611.

Shue, Henry (1980). *Basic Rights: Subsistence, Affluence, and U.S. Foreign Policy*. Princeton, NJ: Princeton University Press.

Sivard, Ruth Leger (1975–). *World Military and Social Expenditures*. Washington, DC: World Priorities, annual.

Smith, Adam (1776). *An Inquiry into the Nature and Causes of the Wealth of Nations*. New York: Modern Library, 1937.

Smith, Arthur K., Jr. (1969). "Socio-Economic Development and Political Democracy: A Causal Analysis." *American Journal of Political Science*, 13(February):95–125.

Spalding, Nancy (1988). "Democracy and Human Rights in the Third World." In *Human Rights: Theory and Measurement*, edited by David L. Cingranelli, chapter 10. New York: St. Martin's Press.

Stack, Steven (1978). "Internal Political Organization and the World Economy of Income Inequality." *American Sociological Review*, 43(April):271–272.

Statistical Analysis System (SAS) Institute (1982). *User's Guide: Statistics*. Cary, NC: SAS Institute.

Staub, Ervin (1989). *The Roots of Evil: The Psychological and Cultural Origins of Genocide and Other Forms of Group Violence*. Cambridge: Cambridge University Press.

Stohl, Michael (1986). "The Superpowers and International Terrorism." In *Government Violence and Repression: An Agenda for Research*, edited by Michael Stohl and George A. Lopez, chapter 8. Westport, CT: Greenwood Press.

Stohl, Michael, Carleton, David, and Johnson, Steven E. (1984). "Human Rights and U.S. Foreign Assistance from Nixon to Carter." *Journal of Peace Research*, 21(3):215–226.

Stohl, Michael, Carleton, David, Lopez, George A., and Samuels, Stephen (1986). "State Violations of Human Rights: Issues and Problems of Measurement." *Human Rights Quarterly*, 8(November):592–606.

Strouse, James C., and Claude, Richard P., eds. (1976). *Comparative Human Rights*. Baltimore, MD: Johns Hopkins University Press.

Szabo, Imre (1982). "Historical Foundations of Human Rights and Subsequent Developments." In *The International Dimensions of Human Rights*, volume 1, edited by Karal Vasak and Philip Alston, pp. 11–42. Westport, CT: Greenwood Press.

Taylor, Charles Lewis, and Hudson, Michael C. (1972). *World Handbook of Political and Social Indicators*, 2nd ed. New Haven, CT: Yale University Press.

Taylor, Charles Lewis, and Jodice, David A. (1983). *World Handbook of Political and Social Indicators*, 2 vols., 3rd ed. New Haven, CT: Yale University Press.

Tilly, Charles (1978). *From Mobilization to Revolution*. Reading, MA: Addison-Wesley.

Timberlake, Michael, and Williams, Kirk R. (1984). "Dependence, Political Exclusion, and Government Repression: Some Cross-National Evidence." *American Sociological Review*, 49(February):141–146.

Tolley, Howard, Jr. (1987). *The U.N. Commission on Human Rights*. Boulder, CO: Westview.

Tracy, Tom J. (1983). "Human Rights and Human Welfare in Latin America." *Daedalus*, 112(Fall):171–196.

Travis, Rick (1989). "Economic Involvement and Democratic Practices: Assessing Their Impact on U.S. Foreign Aid Allocations." Paper presented at the annual convention of the International Studies Association, London, March.

Tuck, Richard (1979). *Natural Rights Theories*. Cambridge: Cambridge University Press.

Union of Soviet Socialist Republics (USSR) (1964). *Atlas Narodov Mira*. Moscow: N. N. Miklukho-Maklaya Institute of Ethnography, Academy of Sciences, Department of Geodesy and Cartography, State Geological Committee.

United Nations Center for Human Rights and United Nations Institute for Training and Research (1991). *Manual on Human Rights Reporting Under Six Major International Human Rights Instruments*. New York: United Nations.

United Nations Conference on Trade and Development (UNCTAD) (1990). *Handbook of International Trade and Development Statistics*. Geneva: United Nations.

United Nations Development Program (UNDP) (1990–). *Human Development Report*. New York: Oxford University Press, annual.

United Nations Educational, Scientific, and Cultural Organization (UNESCO) (1963–). *Statistical Yearbook*. Paris: UNESCO, annual.

United Nations Statistical Office (1948a–). *Demographic Yearbook*. New York: United Nations, annual.

———. (1948b–). *Statistical Yearbook*. New York: United Nations, annual.

———. (1963–). *Compendium of Social Statistics and Indicators*. New York: United Nations, irregularly issued.

———. (1966–). *Directions of Trade Statistics Yearbook*. New York: United Nations, annual.

———. (1967–). *Industrial Statistics Yearbook*. New York: United Nations, annual.

United States Department of Commerce, International Trade Administration (1981). "Guide to Commercial Holidays in 1982." *Business America*, 4(December 14): 8–15.

———. (1986). "Guide to Commercial Holidays in 1986." *Business America*, 9(January 6):25–32.

United States Department of Health and Human Services (1958–). *Social Security Programs Throughout the World*. Washington, DC: Social Security Administration Research Report series, biennial.

United States Department of State (1945–). *U.S. Overseas Loans & Grants*. Washington, DC: Agency for International Development.

———. (1977–). *Country Reports on Human Rights Practices*. Washington, DC: Reports submitted to the Committee on Foreign Relations, Senate, and Committee on Foreign Affairs, House of Representatives, annual.

———. (1981–). *World Fact Book*. Washington, DC: Central Intelligence Agency, annual.

———. (1983–). *Patterns of Global Terrorism*. Washington, DC: Office of the Coordinator for Counterterrorism, annual.

Vance, Cyrus R. (1977). "Law Day Address on Human Rights Policy." Reprinted in *Human Rights and American Foreign Policy*, edited by Donald P. Kommers and Gilburt D. Loescher, pp. 309–315. Notre Dame, IN: University of Notre Dame Press, 1979.

Van Den Berghe, Pierre L. (1981). *The Ethnic Phenomenon*. New York: Elsevier.

Vatikiotis, Michael, and Delfs, Robert (1993). "Cultural Divide." *Far Eastern Economic Review*, 156(June 17):20, 22.

Vincent, Jack (1987). "Freedom and International Conflict: Another Look." *International Studies Quarterly*, 3(March):103–112.

Vincent, R. J. (1986). *Human Rights and International Relations*. Cambridge: Cambridge University Press.

von Mises, Ludwig (1981). *Socialism: An Economic and Sociological Analysis*. Indianapolis: Liberty Classics.

Vorhies, Frank, and Glahe, Fred (1988). "Liberty and Social Progress: A Geographical Examination." In *Freedom in the World*, edited by Raymond D. Gastil, pp. 189–201. Lanham, MD: Freedom House.

Waldron, Jeremy (1987). *Nonsense upon Stilts: Bentham, Burke, and Marx on the Rights of Man*. New York: Methuen.

Walton, John, and Ragin, Charles (1990). "Global and National Sources of Political Protest: Third World Responses to the Debt Crisis." *American Sociological Review*, 55(December):876–890.

Weber, Max (1913). *The Theory of Social and Economic Organization*. Glencoe, IL: Free Press.

———. (1918). *Economy and Society: An Outline of Interpretive Sociology*. Berkeley: University of California Press, 1979.

Weede, Erich (1980). "Beyond Misspecification in Sociological Analyses of Income Inequality." *American Sociological Review*, 45(June):497–501.

———. (1984). "Democracy and War Involvement." *Journal of Conflict Resolution*, 28(December):649–664.

Weinstein, Warren (1983). "Human Rights in Africa: Dilemmas and Options." *Daedalus*, 112(Fall):171–196.

Weisberg, Laurie S., and Scoble, Harry M. (1981). "Problems of Comparative Research on Human Rights." In *Global Human Rights: Public Policies, Comparative Measures, and NGO Strategies*, edited by Ved P. Nanda, James R. Scarritt, and George W. Shepherd, Jr., chapter 10. Boulder, CO: Westview.

Wolpin, Miles (1986). "State Terrorism and Repression in the Third World: Parameters and Prospects." In *Government Violence and Repression: An Agenda for Research*, edited by Michael Stohl and George A. Lopez, chapter 5. Westport, CT: Greenwood Press.

World Bank (1968–). *Social Indicators of Development.* Baltimore: Johns Hopkins Press, annual.

———. (1976–). *World Tables.* Washington, DC: World Bank, annual.

———. (1978–). *World Development Report.* New York: Oxford University Press, annual.

World Health Organization (WHO) (1939–). *Statistical Annual.* Geneva: WHO, annual.

World Resources Institute (1988/1989). *World Resources, 1988–89: A Report.* New York: Basic Books.

Ziegler, Harmon (1988). "The Interrelationships of Freedom, Equality, and Development." In *Freedom in the World*, edited by Raymond D. Gastil, pp. 203–228. Lanham, MD: Freedom House.

Zvobgo, Eddison J. M. (1979). "A Third World View." In *Human Rights and American Foreign Policy*, edited by Donald P. Kommers and Gilburt D. Loescher, chapter 5. Notre Dame, IN: University of Notre Dame Press.

INDEX

About the Author

MICHAEL HAAS is Professor of Political Science at the University of Hawaiʻi at Manoa. The author of many books, the following have been published by Praeger: *The Pacific Way* (1989), *Korean Unification* (1989), *The Asian Way to Peace* (1989), *Cambodia, Pol Pot, and the United States* (1991), *Genocide by Proxy* (1991), *Polity and Society* (1992), and *Institutional Racism: The Case of Hawaiʻi* (1992).

ISBN 0-275-94352-6

EAN

90000>

9 780275 943523

HARDCOVER BAR CODE